ESSAYS IN THE LAW

ESSAYS IN THE LAW

BY

THE RIGHT HON.

SIR FREDERICK POLLOCK, BART.

LL.D., D.C.L., K.C.

ARCHON BOOKS
1969

SBN: 208 00807 1
LIBRARY OF CONGRESS CATALOG CARD NUMBER: 77-92149
PRINTED IN THE UNITED STATES OF AMERICA

TO

MY FRIEND AND FELLOW-WORKER

PAUL VINOGRADOFF

PREFACE

THESE papers, written at various times in the last thirty years or so, are now collected at the instance of certain learned friends. As the title denotes, the treatment is from a lawyer's point of view throughout, but the subject-matter is strictly professional in only two or three cases, and may be not less interesting on the whole to historical than to legal students.

Supplemental matter is in the main confined to the notes, and the text left to speak as at the date of first publication. Lapse of time is, however, now and then smoothed over by the change of a few words, and in the account of *Arabiniana*, that strange little book which fulfils all the conditions of a law report quotable in court, though it is of no conceivable use for that purpose, the biographical details are amended from later information.

References to the places of original publication (a thing I have often missed in other men's works) are given throughout for the convenience of cataloguers and bibliographers, whose deserving labours are not yet sufficiently recognised and assisted in the world of letters.

LINCOLN'S INN, *April* 1922.

CONTENTS

I. The History of Comparative Jurisprudence— PAGE

The subject and name modern 1
Methods of comparison 4
Evolution in political and natural science . . . 10
Early forms of comparative legal study . . . 12
Common and Canon Law in England: St. German . 16
Leibniz, Montesquieu, Vico 18
Modern development 25

II. The History of the Law of Nature—

i. Origins: Aristotle: Stoics 31
Roman *ius gentium* and *ius naturale* . . . 34
The Middle Ages 38
Natural, divine, and positive law 42
Imperial and Papal controversialists . . . 45
The Reformation controversies 49
England: Fortescue: Chancery: Law Merchant . 53
"Reason" in the Common Law 57
Hobbes: Later transformation 59
ii. Modern Law of Nations: Grotius . . . 62
Lord Stowell 66
Natural justice in the Common Law . . . 68
British possessions abroad 73
"Justice, equity, and good conscience" . . . 75
Singular case of Penang 76

III. Locke's Theory of the State—

Apologia for the Convention Parliament . . . 80
Locke's criticism of Filmer, why not expressly of Hobbes 81
Influence of English legal doctrine 85
Locke on the state of nature 87

III. LOCKE'S THEORY OF THE STATE (*continued*)— PAGE

Locke on natural right of property 90
Locke on political allegiance 92
Locke on legislative authority 95
Locke on the executive 97
Locke on parliamentary representation . . . 99
Later influence of Locke 101
Appendix: The Social Contract in Hobbes and Locke 102

IV. GOVERNMENT BY COMMITTEES IN ENGLAND—

The place of committees in English affairs . . 110
The word 112
Varieties in composition and functions . . . 113
Committees of the King's Council 117
The Judicial Committee 119
Administrative committees 121
Modern nominal Boards 123
The Cabinet 124
The Imperial Defence Committee 126
Parliament: "Committee of the whole" . . . 130
Committees in Civil War time 131
Government of the Inns of Court 134
Council of Law Reporting 137

V. GIFTS OF CHATTELS WITHOUT DELIVERY—

The question proposed 141
Principle and authority 143
Gift at election 144
Archaic doctrine 145
Where custody with donee or third person . . 146

VI. HAS THE COMMON LAW RECEIVED THE FICTION THEORY OF CORPORATIONS?—

"Artificial Person" in English law 153
Modern dicta 155
Statutory limitations 158
Blackstone 160
The *Sutton's Hospital* case 163
Sir John Davies 171
Summary of seventeenth-century doctrine . . . 174
The *Year Books* 175

VII. The Transformation of Equity—

	PAGE
General notion and purpose of Equity	180
Dispensing power	182
Compromise in early law	185
Equitable jurisdiction of justices in eyre	187
Witchcraft in the Chancery	190
St. German on Equity	192
Chancery and the Pilgrim Fathers	194
Chancery Division not a court of conscience	195
Appendix: A Note on *Shylock* v. *Antonio*	196

VIII. Archaism in Modern Law—

Ceremonial survivals	200
Formalism without executive power	203
Archaic proofs and pleading	204
Solemnity of charters	208
The grand jury	210
Unanimity of petty jury	215
Sale of goods: archaism restored by Statute of Frauds	218
Germanic seisin and Roman *dominium*	220

IX. Judicial Records—

"Reference to the record"	222
Henry of Bratton and later pleaders	223
What is a court of record?	229
Relation of records to reports	231
Procedure and substantive law	235
Study of mediæval law at Universities	237
Semi-judicial records	239
Useful books	239

X. English Law Reporting—

The *Law Reports* not official	242
Constitution and method	247
The reporter's work	251
Preparation and publication	255

XI. Lay Fallacies in the Law—

The law not an ethical code	259
Misunderstanding of Cicero	260

XI. Lay Fallacies in the Law (*continued*)—

PAGE

And of Horace 263
Non-ethical positive rules 267
Moral influence of legal standards 268
Professional discipline 270
European law in the East 271
Law as a work of art 273
Judicial function not inquisitorial 275
Administrative jurisdiction 276
Jarndyce v. *Jarndyce* 277

XII. Reformation and Modern Doctrine of Divorce—

Ambiguities 279
The *Reformatio Legum* 280
Elizabethan practice 281
Mr. Kitchin's book 282
Marriage not an ordinary contract 283
The Roman Republican custom 284
The report of the Royal Commission 285
Rome and the German Civil Code 286

XIII. *Arabiniana*—

Serjeant Arabin 287
His justice 289
Extracts from his dicta 291
A. reprinted at Philadelphia 298
Sydney Smith commends *A.* 299
Correct in form as a book of reports 300

INDEX 301

I

THE HISTORY OF COMPARATIVE JURISPRUDENCE[1]

The name of comparative jurisprudence is modern; our current use of the term, with the full meaning which it now bears, is barely a generation old. It seems that about, or possibly before, 1830, some one applied the name of general or comparative jurisprudence to the process of ascertaining the "principles common to maturer systems" of law, "or the various analogies obtaining between them"; the result of which process, it seems to have been supposed, would be a system of universal principles of positive law.[2] We are not now concerned to enquire what useful results we should derive from the proposed operation; I do not think any one would now maintain that a philosophy of law was likely to be among them. Whatever may be the value of the process or method thus indicated, it is not what we now call comparative

[1] A farewell lecture delivered in the University of Oxford on January 24, 1903, with a few later corrections and additions.

[2] Austin's fragment *On the Uses of the Study of Jurisprudence*, written in 1834 (A. on Jurisp., ed. 1869, ii. 1107). I have not been able to discover what writer is alluded to.

jurisprudence or *droit comparé*. In the succeeding generation a learned and brilliant reviewer of the first edition of Maine's *Ancient Law*, whom I am permitted to identify as Mountague Bernard, wrote thus: "The fields of study immediately adjacent to Law are History and Ethics, each of which, indeed, may be so extended as to include a great portion of it; while law itself embraces a vast region, the domain of comparative jurisprudence, of which English Law forms a small province."[1] No further light is thrown by the context on the precise meaning to be attached to the term. The learned writer, however, fully recognised that existing legal institutions cannot be understood without some knowledge of their history, and therefore he cannot be supposed to have regarded comparative jurisprudence as a thing standing apart from historical study and discrimination. Still, its object seems to have been conceived as practice rather than knowledge, the collection of materials for useful amendment or assimilation of existing laws rather than any scientific or philosophical construction. In technical terms, comparative jurisprudence was regarded wholly or mainly as a handmaid to the theory of legislation.

About ten years later we find Sir Henry Maine himself speaking of comparative jurisprudence, in his opening lecture on Village Communities, as not having for its object to throw light upon the history of law. "What it does is to take the legal systems of two distinct societies under some one head of law

[1] *Quart. Rev.* cx. 115 (July 1861).

—as, for example, some one kind of Contract, or the department of Husband and Wife—and to compare these chapters of the systems under consideration. It takes the heads of law which it is examining at any point of their historical development, and does not affect to discuss their history, to which it is indifferent." Maine goes on to state, as a proposition "universally admitted by competent jurists, that, if not the only function, the chief function of comparative jurisprudence is to facilitate legislation and the practical improvement of law." The use of it is that "by the examination and comparison of laws" and methods of legal reasoning "the most valuable materials are obtained for legal improvement." He adds that the enquiry to be pursued in the following lecture—namely, the examination of the tenure of land, with its legal and economic incidents, in certain parts of India, in comparison with the history of corresponding institutions in Europe—"can only be said to belong to comparative jurisprudence, if the word 'comparative' be used as it is used in such expressions as 'comparative philology' and 'comparative mythology.'" It seems to us, at this day, difficult to understand why any one should have taken exception to such use; and in fact the analogy of comparative jurisprudence to comparative philology was clearly stated as early as 1857 by Emerico Amari, of whom I shall speak later. Maine, however, continues, in a rather apologetic tone: "I think I may venture to affirm that the comparative method, which has already been fruitful of such wonderful results, is not distinguishable in some of its applications from the historical method." It is curious to see how far the master still was, ten years after the publication of *Ancient Law*, from realising the importance of his own work. If there is anything we have learnt from Sir Henry Maine, it is that intimate alliance between comparative and historical research is not only natural and desirable, but necessary for either branch of work being efficiently done. If there is any book to which a modern teacher would point as a typical example of what is meant by comparative jurisprudence, it is this very series of lectures on Village Communities in the East and West. Maine's hesitation seems to have been a kind of expiatory offering to the ghosts of those mechanical and external conceptions of human institutions which he did so much to destroy—if indeed there can be ghosts of vain shadows that never had any life.

No doubt the method is important and not the name. It makes no great difference whether we speak of historical jurisprudence or of comparative jurisprudence, or, as the Germans seem inclined to do, of the general history of law.[1] What does matter is understanding that comparison of institutions is profitable only when we take account of the stage of civilisation and of special development to which the

[1] Die Universalrechtsgeschichte, die man auch vergleichende Rechtswissenschaft zu nennen pflegt, hat die Aufgabe, wo möglich die Rechte aller Völker zu erforschen, der lebenden wie der toten, und diese Rechte zu erforschen, nicht nur was die objektive Rechtsordnung, sondern auch was die Betätigung der Rechtsordnung im subjektiven Rechtsleben betrifft.—J. Kohler in *Encyklop. d. Rechtswissenschaft*, 6th ed., 1902, pp. 17-18.

terms to be compared belong. The mere order of time has next to nothing to do with it, as one or two examples will readily show.

If we compare the Roman law of property which Papinian administered at York seventeen centuries ago with the English law of real property which the Court of Appeal now administers in London, it will be for the purpose of throwing light not on anything in the past history of English law; but on what English law may tend to become in the days of our children or grandchildren; for the classical law of Rome is, in all essentials, far more modern in everything relating to the ownership and disposition of landed property than the mediæval system, eked out with cumbrous and piecemeal alterations, which still serves our turn. On the other hand, the commercial law of the Roman Empire under the Antonines and even under Justinian was archaic and rudimentary as compared with the modern development of the law merchant. Ulpian would have stared and gasped alike at a strict settlement and at a debenture payable to bearer, but for wholly different reasons. If, again, Papinian could have been transported from York to India, he would have found millions of men living under systems of family law so ancient that only faint vestiges of a corresponding stage could be found in Roman traditions and forms; and if he could now visit "Agra and Lahore of Great Mogul," he would find the same rules still being administered by English judges, having indeed suffered something of secular change, and more in some provinces than in others, but little changed on the whole in comparison with their world-wide difference from any modern Western law. To compare the institutions of Indian law and custom directly with modern English law can lead to nothing but ludicrous if not dangerous misunderstandings; as indeed happened in at least one celebrated instance.

It is true that, as Maine said, the provisions of different systems, taken at stages of development sufficiently corresponding to afford a real parallelism, can be compared, in form or on their substantial merits, without any explicit historical criticism. You cannot compare the law of the Twelve Tables as to execution against a debtor with, say, the Indian Civil Procedure Code, except by working through a great deal of intermediate history. But you can compare one modern Western law of companies or of insolvent debtors with another, taking them just as they stand. Even in these cases, however, we shall not find it easy to keep out history. Suppose we are comparing the modern law of bankruptcy in France and England. We cannot help noting the fact that French law makes a sharp distinction between persons engaged and persons not engaged in trade, and English law does not; and the manner in which we account for this difference may (I do not say that it will) have some bearing on our conclusion as to the practicability or utility of assimilating the treatment of insolvent estates under the two systems. Then, if we wish to arrive at the reasons for English legislation and jurisdiction not dealing with commercial law as a thing apart, or at any rate to avoid giving wrong reasons, we may have to go back as far as the incorporation of the law merchant into the Common Law in the eighteenth century, perhaps farther. More than this, the working life of any body of law depends not merely on its authentic texts and the decisions or books that interpret them, but on complex influences of professional training, tradition, and habit of mind. We can appreciate a foreign or antiquated system only by learning to see it in its proper historical atmosphere. Do we say, then, that history is everything and comparison nothing, or that comparative enquiry is merely an application of the historical method? By no means. The merely national or provincial history of an institution is, except by the rarest accident, as little satisfying or intelligible as the anatomy of a single species or the inflexions of a single language. Many parts of English law, taken alone, present in their development what seems to be grotesque aberrations. Such is the manner in which the king's judges, at the very end of the Middle Ages, assumed, or rather accepted, jurisdiction to enforce informal promises. At first sight nothing can be more absurd in modern students' eyes than that one of the most elementary duties of civil life and business should have been left for centuries, in its purely religious or moral aspect, to the protection of the spiritual Courts, and then brought within the temporal sphere by a process hardly to be distinguished from fiction in its earlier and certainly involving fiction in its later stages.

When we turn to the antiquities of Greek and Roman legal forms, we find many traces of a period when the obligation of promises could at most be religious, and religious only. It is now accepted doctrine that the Roman *sponsio* was originally a religious ceremony creating a spiritual sanction. We find, in later times, the religious sanction of plighted faith persisting throughout Europe in the Middle Ages, whether derived from popular Roman tradition, or from an independent though similar Germanic origin, or from a conjunction of both. St. Francis not only makes the reconciled wolf give him his paw in token of faith, but repeats the ceremony (like a good man of business, for it is a vulgar error to suppose that enthusiasts are necessarily unbusiness-like) with the witness of the townsmen of Gubbio. And we see that the curious English history of *fidei laesio* and the action of *assumpsit* is part of a normal and widespread process, though belated in time. I have taken a striking example with which I happen to be familiar, as it was in this region that I first learnt the necessity for basing any sound dogmatic theory of modern English law on knowledge of the mediæval authorities. But it must not be supposed that the example is singular. English land law cannot be understood at all without a great deal of historical explanation; it cannot be understood very well without learning how peculiar the English history of land tenure was, from the Norman Conquest onwards —in other words, without comparing the divergent fortunes of English and Continental feudalism.

As the need for both historical and comparative study is most strongly illustrated in the Common Law, so are the consequences of neglecting or underrating them. Blackstone was a respectable historical scholar according to the standard of his time, and much good history is in fact to be found in his *Commentaries.* But there are also several more or less ingenious but wholly groundless conjectures, and, especially in the earlier period, not a few downright errors; and these are, I think, always accounted for by insufficient command of the historical data. I am far from denying that shortcomings of this kind were often excusable, or even inevitable, having regard to the amount and condition of the materials available when Blackstone wrote. Departments of our law might be mentioned in which text-writers have continued, even in our own time, to repeat much less plausible fictions with much less excuse. There is, or was, a still more dangerous temptation —that of regarding comparative illustration as a matter of mere ornament, and omitting to make sure that the less familiar term of the comparison is correctly apprehended. Some of Blackstone's references to Roman law cannot be acquitted of negligence, for they involve misunderstandings of elementary doctrine from which any civilian in Doctors' Commons or at Oxford could have saved him. Warnings on this score, however, ought not to be required by serious workers at this day. The perils that now beset us are more subtle. We may be too eager to see historical affinities between rules or customs which are really the similar but independent result of similar circumstances in distant times and places. An apparent coincidence may beguile us into proclaiming that something in modern usage is a surviving fragment of prehistoric manners, without satisfying ourselves that the supposed survival, as we find it, is general or ancient, or that it has not a discoverable history which our conjecture will not fit. In our desire to have a sort of normal growth of national custom, we may fail to leave sufficient room for the disturbing influence of foreign institutions, and not only for "contamination," as the philologists call it, but for actual deliberate imitation. Errors of judgement are possible in all these ways and more, and there is no royal road for keeping clear of them. Only experience will teach us to feel an instinctive mistrust when we are entering a perilous atmosphere; to work cautiously as miners who have to work underground; and not to deem ourselves shining lights when our lamps are glowing only with the fire-damp of rash speculation, presently to explode and be succeeded by the choke-damp of deserved oblivion.

At present vindication of the historical and comparative method in law and politics may be thought superfluous. We may rather be inclined to ask why its importance was recognised so late. The fact is that the transformation of political science about forty years ago [1] cannot be disconnected from the all but simultaneous putting forth of new and

[1] *I.e.* from 1860 onwards.

far-reaching ideas in the study of organic nature. *Ancient Law* and *The Origin of Species* were really the outcome, in different branches, of one and the same intellectual movement—that which we now associate with the word Evolution. This identity of spirit was not perceived at the time. The same organs of lettered and respectable opinion which gave Maine's work the welcome of just, though perhaps barely just, praise, were still wasting paper and ink on denunciations, as crude as they were ineffectual, of Darwin. The triumph of the constructive historical method had been assured in both natural and moral science by half a century's work of specialists almost unknown to the general public, and seldom acquainted with or interested in one another's researches; and the disclosure of the results, when the time was ripe, came like thunder from a clear sky. Ten years later the lines of thought which had seemed shocking or paradoxical were familiar; after ten years more it was hard to remember that they had ever been strange. We do not know why these things should have happened just when they did. We can say that the historical temper of the nineteenth century was due to reaction against the didactic rationalism of the eighteenth, and that rationalism, again, was provoked by the futile conflict of dogmatic claims in the wars of religion which succeeded the Reformation and lasted till near the middle of the seventeenth century. But we cannot fix more positively the causes which postponed modern historical criticism till our own time, any more than we can fix those which prevented experimental science from making any appreciable progress in the age, at first sight not wanting in favourable conditions, of Augustus or of the Antonines.

Anticipations of comparative enquiry may certainly be found in jurisprudence as well as in other kinds of learning. Many of these were ingenious, and some important; but, so far as they consisted of observation, they were detached and merely empirical, and, so far as they were speculative, they were barren for want of continuity, having no relation with any certain doctrine or method. Some instruction can be derived from considering these earlier attempts. They will show us, at least, what a little way the most laudable curiosity without method will carry us towards scientific results, and how much better an imperfect method is than none.

Probably the earliest form of the comparative study of institutions was the observation that those of another commonwealth were in some way better than one's own, followed by deliberate imitation of them. News did not spread in the ancient world so fast as it is distributed now, but it did spread. The fame of a great legislator travelled, and lost nothing in travelling. Whether the name of Minos contains any historical element or not, we need not doubt that in the prehistoric time of which we are just beginning to learn something the superior civilisation of Crete attracted many pilgrims and ambassadors from many coasts and islands of the Mediterranean. Stories of this kind may be legendary in detail, but are not to be dismissed wholesale as mere fiction. Indeed, their general credibility is increased by the recent discovery that the introduction of writing in Europe dates much farther back than we had supposed. If laws existed in writing, they could be copied. The supposed absence of writing was one of the chief difficulties in believing adoption by less advanced communities of improvements effected in the more advanced ones to have been common in very early times; and this difficulty is now removed. The classical example of the Twelve Tables, at all events, is within historical times and not open to exception. Whether we accept the received account, or are persuaded by the learned and ingenious argument of M. Lambert of Lyons [1] that the Tables are a custumal of the second century B.C., and the decemvirs legendary characters, matters very little for the present purpose. It is certain that the Twelve Tables, whatever be their real date and original authority, show a considerable amount of borrowing from Greek sources, as the Roman antiquaries of the Empire fully recognised.

It is a more doubtful question whether the Roman *ius gentium* was formed by any process that can be fairly described as comparison or selection. We know that it sprang from the necessity of administering justice between parties to one or both of whom the law of Roman citizens was not applicable; we

[1] In the *Revue générale du droit*, 1902–3. This hypothesis was discussed in the legal section of the Historical Congress held at Rome in April 1903. None of the learned Romanists present—French, German, or Italian—were disposed to agree with it. I do not think much has been heard of it since.

may safely guess that in most cases the parties had no desire to be judged according to Roman law. We do not know by any direct evidence from what materials or on what principles a common rule was constructed. But in Latin literature the name signifies generally received custom, as my late colleague, Prof. Nettleship, has shown. It seems probable that the practice of Mediterranean traders had fixed a certain amount of custom for the regulation of their business among themselves, and one would think the Roman magistrate was more likely to adopt and sanction an existing mercantile custom, when ascertained, than to invent some new rule according to his own notions of justice. Professional and scientific development of the rules thus taken into Roman jurisprudence came, as it could not but come, later. In short, it seems reasonable to suppose that the reception of the *ius gentium* in the Roman law was not much unlike the establishment of the law merchant, many centuries later, as part of the Common Law. If these considerations are entitled to any weight, we can hardly give credit to the Prætor Peregrinus for having founded the science of comparative jurisprudence, and we may even think that deliberate comparison and selection had very little to do with the formation of the *ius gentium* at any stage.

Rudiments of both comparative and historical research occur in the works of the classical Roman lawyers. Gaius not only traces imitation of the laws of Solon in the Twelve Tables, but is curious about an alleged parallel in Galatian custom to the

Roman *patria potestas*, and mentions that in early law spoil of war was regarded as the highest form of property (*maxime sua credebant esse quae ex hostibus cepissent*)—a light on the possible origin of private ownership in movables which seems to be in the right direction. But such passages are few and desultory. Homer might now and again furnish an elegant illustration; it did not occur to any one that archaic and provincial usage, whether recorded in literature or surviving in practice, deserved any systematic study. As the forms of imperial government became more and more centralised and official, any such enquiry became still more remote from the probable scope of an educated man's pursuits. No attempt was made to increase Aristotle's collection of notes on the political institutions of many states and tribes, which would have been priceless to modern anthropologists and of great value to legal history. It does not appear that any pains were taken to preserve it. Except for the treatise on the Constitution of Athens, discovered in our own time, we know this part of Aristotle's work only by tradition.

The fall of the Roman Empire restored ample, and more than ample, variety to the laws and customs of Europe; but it is superfluous to point out that the accompanying condition of society was not favourable to disinterested scientific treatment of the material. When learning and speculation were painfully revived in the Middle Ages, and began to assume new forms, the general ideal of thinking men was the restoration of peace by general submission to some superior and universal authority. The champions of the Pope and of the Emperor criticised one another freely, but the criticism was altogether remote from historical investigation. People who quite honestly believe themselves to possess infallible means of knowing what ought to be will hardly spend their time on the humbler task of learning from the experience of what has been. Besides, the professional learning of both theologians and jurists was dominated by the cosmopolitan tradition of Roman law. The case of England was an exception, but exclusive devotion to the Common Law, heightened by not a little jealousy of any attempt at encroachment on the part of either canonists or civilians, was not a direct way to serious comparative enquiry. Still, it is remarkable that the nearest approaches to comparative criticism, down to the seventeenth century, were made by Englishmen. Sir John Fortescue, when he followed his master Henry VI. into exile, considered French political and legal institutions, and recorded his reflexions in his two principal works, on *The Governance of England* and *De Laudibus Legum Angliae*. It is true that he does not at all concern himself to account for the laws or customs of the French monarchy, and compares them with those of England only to triumph over them as in every way inferior; but he does compare them.

In the sixteenth century Christopher St. German, a very learned lawyer, undertook a much more serious and critical piece of work, probably with a view to conciliation. The co-existence of the Common Law with the Canon Law in England had produced a considerable amount of competition for business between the lay and the spiritual Courts, besides the political conflicts which belong to general history. Not the least of the causes of the Reformation in England was the popular dislike of the Courts Christian for their minute and vexatious enforcement of moral discipline. On the other hand, by regarding breach of faith as an ecclesiastical offence, they practically acted as petty civil Courts in many cases where the Common Law, down to the latter part of the fifteenth century, did not provide any remedy. Thus the points of contact and friction between the temporal and the spiritual jurisdiction were many. St. German lived in the heat of the Reformation and wrote his well-known book, *Doctor and Student*, somewhere about 1520. It is now remembered, and is still useful, as a learned and accurate statement of the Common Law as it then stood; but it is in fact a comparative exposition of the two systems, the Doctor of Divinity and Student of the laws of England taking their turns. The general object seems to be to satisfy persons not learned in the Common Law, by detailed examples and illustration, that on the whole it is a consistent and reasonable system, and apparent contradictions of the rule of conscience as it might appear to a canonist are explicable when they are placed in their proper context. There is no historical enquiry and very little direct criticism, but there is comparison of two systems of legal ideas and rules, undertaken with a definite purpose, and conducted by an author well acquainted with both. At the beginning of the next century (1602) William Fulbecke, apparently seeking to improve on St. German's example, produced his *Parallel or Conference of the Civil Law, the Canon Law, and the Common Law of this Realm of England.* This is an ambitious attempt, covering a wider field and expressed in dialogues between several persons, whom the author adorned with such names as "Anglonomophylax" and "Codicgnostes" (*sic*). It is called a comparative discourse in the dedication of the second part to the Archbishop of Canterbury. As a whole the book is tedious, ill-constructed, and uncritical. It never acquired any serious reputation, and there is no modern edition of it. St. German's *Doctor and Student* has not only been many times republished, but is to this day counted by the followers of the Common Law among their "books of authority." I do not think it would be any disparagement to a modern English or American lawyer's learning if he had never heard of Fulbecke.

We now come to greater names. Leibniz, among many other schemes never completed, formed that of a universal historical and comparative survey of legislation (*theatrum legale*).[1] But he never did

[1] *Nova Methodus discendae docendaeque Iurisprudentiae, Francf.* 1667, part ii. § 29, opp. ed. Dutens, iv. 191. His words are: "Ex his aliisque omnibus [the extant documents of all known systems of law] undecunque collectis, Deo dante, conficiemus aliquando *theatrum legale*, et in omnibus materiis omnium gentium, locorum, temporum placita παραλλήλως disponemus." This is only one of about thirty works to be undertaken for the improvement of legal studies.

anything more in the matter, as, indeed, the project was too vast for any one man's lifetime. We must pass on to the eighteenth century to find the great precursor of modern historical and comparative research—I mean Montesquieu. If we hesitate to call him the founder, it is only because neither his materials nor his methods of execution were adequate to do justice to his ideas. He aimed (if I may repeat my own words, first written many years ago) at constructing a comparative theory of legislation and institutions adapted to the political needs of different forms of government, and a comparative theory of politics and law based on wide observation of the actual systems of different lands and ages. Hobbes was before him in realising that history is not a series of accidents, but Montesquieu was the first of the moderns to proclaim that a nation's institutions are part of its history, and must be considered as such if we are to understand them rightly. Much of his history is sound, and many of his judgements are admirable. Yet he failed to construct a durable system, and *L'Esprit des lois* cannot even be called a systematic book. The materials were still too scattered and uncertain to be safely handled on Montesquieu's grand scale. Perhaps he would have done better to confine himself to Western Europe. The main defects of his method may be reduced, I think, to two. First, he overrated the influence of climate and other external conditions, and underrated, if he did not wholly neglect, the effects of race and tradition. Next, he had not even an inkling of what is now a fundamental rule of this kind of enquiry: namely, that there is a normal course of development for communities as well as for individuals, and that institutions which belong to different stages are not commensurable terms in any scientific comparison. This is as much as to say that even Montesquieu could not wholly escape from the unhistorical dogmatism of his time. It is perhaps a minor drawback that he constantly seeks for reasons of deliberate policy to account for seemingly eccentric features of outlandish customs, rightly or wrongly reported by missionaries or others, instead of endeavouring to connect them with their historic and racial surroundings. But the result is that many chapters of his great work amount, taken by themselves, to little more than collections of anecdotes and conjectures in which the most incongruous elements, such as the customs of China and the laws of Spain, are brought together at random.[1] Also Montesquieu is not free from the very common error, especially prevalent in the eighteenth century, of attributing a constant and infallible efficacy to forms of government. In short, Montesquieu saw the promised land afar off, but was not equipped for entering it. I do not wish to be understood as affecting to find any fault with him. The greatness of Montesquieu's conception was his own, and the shortcomings in execution were at the time necessary, or at least natural.

[1] As Amari well says (*Critica di una scienza delle legislazioni comparate*, p. 218): "Lo spirito troppo vivace nuoce sovente al vero, le osservazioni sono più spesso argute e speciose anzichè esatte: vuole porre un principio e scrive un epigramma."

A great Italian thinker, Vico, wrote some twenty years earlier than Montesquieu.[1] It was both his misfortune and that of Europe that for a long time his reputation and influence were all but confined to Italy. Montesquieu, as he did not lack enemies, was accused of having made acquaintance with Vico's work before publication and used it without acknowledgement; but this seems to be mere fiction.[2] Vico must certainly be named among the precursors of historical method on a large scale. It is possible that he may yet indirectly recover his due share in European speculation through the labours of the school of Italian publicists who have been doing remarkable work of late years. With historical and comparative research, as we understand them for the present purpose, his connexion is less close than Montesquieu's; though, like Montesquieu, he was led to political science by the study of law. Vico's aim was at nothing less than a universal philosophy of politics and history; the elucidation of particular problems in jurisprudence or economics by historical study was only incidental, and the use of comparative examples was not as an instrument of discovery but for the illustration of general truths already deduced on metaphysical rather than historical principles.[3] I confess that my acquaintance with Vico's work is

[1] The first edition of the *Scienza Nuova* was published in 1725, the second in 1730; *L'Esprit des lois*, at first anonymously, in 1748.

[2] R. Flint, *Vico*, Lond., 1884, p. 164.

[3] His Latin treatise, *De uno universi iuris principio et fine uno*, is purely dogmatic in form, though it deals with historical problems and contains many brilliant historical conjectures, anticipating, *e.g.*, Maine's doctrine as to legal fictions.

slight; but such is my impression. Perhaps we may say that he was the pioneer in speculation, as Montesquieu in observation, of our modern scientific historians. In the faith that historical changes are not casual, but follow an order capable of rational determination when the conditions are given, these two men stood together far in advance of their generation.

At first sight it is little to the credit of Montesquieu's and Vico's contemporaries that their work was not followed up.[1] But the temper then prevalent among leaders of European thought was not propitious. The men of the French Encyclopædia

[1] Vico had a remarkable successor in the nineteenth century, whose work was published at an unpropitious time, and seems, unfortunately, to have remained unknown outside Italy. I am indebted to learned Italian colleagues for calling my attention, at the Historical Congress at Rome, to Emerico Amari's *Critica di una scienza delle legislazioni comparate* (Genova, 1857: in Brit. Mus. library; an intended sequel dealing more fully with the historical part of the subject seems not to have been published. The only printed information I have been able to find about the author in England is in Vapereau's *Dictionnaire des contemporains*). Amari insists from the first on the importance of combining historical with comparative study, and the insufficiency of any one system alone to provide materials for a philosophy of law or theory of legislation. He gives due weight to the imitation of foreign models as a factor in legal history, and incidentally deprecates the unthinking adoption by Italian states of the French codes with all their faults. He points out that comparative jurisprudence is not merely statistic or dogmatic, but leads to a real "biology of law," and he dwells on the analogy of comparative philology. He was well acquainted with the German historical school, and with the projects of law reformers in the principal countries of Europe; and, writing in the darkest days of Italy and in exile from his own land of Sicily, he never lost hope. One is glad to know that he lived to see better things; he returned to his native city of Palermo and died there in 1870, on September 20, the very day when the Italian troops entered Rome. The only lacuna to be observed in his book, from our present point of view, is that nothing is said about the special study of archaic legal ideas and their survival or transformation in modern law and practice. There is much acute criticism in detail; Amari rightly sees, for example, that Bentham's system is essentially dogmatic. I have quoted one of his remarks on Montesquieu above.

were protesting against the dogmatic traditions of the Middle Ages, but their criticism was itself hardly less dogmatic. They proceeded on a generalised view of human nature which excluded allowances and qualifications, and they were as impatient as any orthodox doctor of taking lessons from history except such as they were *a priori* prepared to accept. Rationalist ethics and politics, as they had grown up in the eighteenth century, culminated in the doctrine of the English utilitarians, perhaps the most dogmatic of all systems of natural law in spite of its professed appeal to experience. Not that I am minded to disparage the services of that school. Every mode of thought has its appointed time, and the work of the Reform Bill period in England could not have been accomplished by historical criticism. As to legal science in particular, its principal task in the eighteenth century was the establishment of the law of nations on the foundations laid by Grotius. Now the method of the publicists who followed Grotius was essentially rationalising, and their aim was uniformity. Study of diversities occurring in actual history was exactly what they wanted to avoid. Vico himself put aside apparent exceptions to the universality of natural law with a certain impatience.[1] The newly constructed law of nations, an avowed offshoot of the old law of nature, had to impose itself on the governments of Europe,

[1] Vel perturbationes animorum, vel barbararum gentium absurdi mores nihil quicquam ius naturae demutant, quod aeterna demonstravimus constare ratione.—*De uno univ. iuris princ.* § xlviii. This is pretty remote from the modern comparative method.

not only by intrinsic merit, but by the weight of uniform authority; the formulated reason of mankind was to command obedience where the Pope and the Emperor had failed. If it could not say of itself *quod semper*, it would assert the right to say *quod ubique, quod ab omnibus.* Any tenderness for local variation, any too curious investigation of historical progress, would have been fatal to its cosmopolitan supremacy. It is true that Grotius collected and used a great number of examples from many authors of many times and countries. But his method in using them was not what we now call historical. They were to illustrate propositions demonstrable by pure reason. From that quarter, therefore, no encouragement would come to comparative studies, in the modern sense, of either politics or law. Moreover, and more generally, people who live under antiquated institutions, and are constantly hampered by them, if not worse, are not likely to consider their origins and historical affinities with such impartial curiosity as modern science, political as well as natural, demands of its followers. It was hardly Voltaire's business to take a scholarly interest in the development of canonical procedure.

Then came the great clearing storm of the French Revolution, and when Europe was at peace again, the works of peace were resumed by a new generation. It became possible to consider with sane judgement and due respect the past that was frankly past, and to treat history as a science. Modern criticism was started anew, or taken up where the precursors had left it. Yet another generation, and the results of the historical method were revealed to the educated public, as I said above, with a kind of explosion. Comparative jurisprudence, however, being versed in profane and to some extent prehistoric matter, did not pass through the stage of being denounced as perilous to religion. It suffered nothing more nearly approaching persecution than a somewhat cold and unintelligent reception from the champions of old-fashioned philosophies of law, and in England, in particular, the surviving high priests of a moribund utilitarian orthodoxy. The complete recognition of the new branch of legal science may best be dated from the year 1869. In that same year the Society of Comparative Legislation was founded in Paris,[1] and Sir Henry Maine was appointed the first Professor of Historical and Comparative Jurisprudence at Oxford. It is proper to record that the foundation of this chair by the munificence of Corpus Christi College was due in the first instance to Wilson, then President of the College, and Sir Kenelm Digby, then a Fellow. Certainly the use of the word "legislation" by the parent French Society, followed apparently for conformity's sake when the English Society of the like name was established so recently as 1896, argues a rather inadequate conception alike of the problems and of the method; but the work of

[1] There was a chair of comparative law at the Collège de France as early as 1830, and another, limited to criminal law, at the Sorbonne; but Littré, writing his great dictionary of the French language about a generation later, made no mention of any such term as *droit comparé*.

both societies has disregarded these verbal bonds. It is impossible to give in a short compass even the most superficial account of the various applications of comparative research, within the last twenty or thirty years, both to jurisprudence proper and to allied branches of political science. For an English lawyer it is hardly too much to say that the methods which Oxford invited Maine to demonstrate in this chair have revolutionised our legal history and largely transformed our current text-books. If you desire to know what is being done by the historical and comparative method in the world of learning at large, you must enquire not of one man, but of many. I name only some scholars whom I have the privilege of knowing personally. You must ask of Esmein and Paul Viollet in Paris, of Brunner and Gierke in Berlin, of Balzani and Boni at Rome, of Kovalevsky and Vinogradoff—not in Moscow, for reasons not to be mentioned here—of Holmes at Washington and Ames at Harvard, of Alfred Lyall in London and Maitland at Cambridge. There is one word of sorrow to add for mighty men who have passed away from us. Lord Acton and Thayer are no longer captains in our host.

We still have to consider why the University is specially bound to welcome this transformation, to be proud of her own share in it, and to render perpetual thanks to the great scholar and publicist who showed us the way to it in this country and place. It is a good thing that lawyers should be better instructed in legal antiquities, and that students, whether they aim at being historians or not, should be delivered from having fictions repeated to them as history. That is matter, so far as it goes, for reasonable satisfaction, but does not seem to have much to do with scholarship and humane letters in general. Surely there is something beyond this, and not the less because additions to positive knowledge are definable, but the spirit of an intellectual movement is not definable. Historical method has indeed given us more than knowledge; it has made our knowledge continuous where it was formerly dispersed; it has set an ideal in the place of a bare multitude of facts.

Maine taught us to find our profit in the ancient treasure of Eastern custom. Let us go to the symbolic aphorisms of the East to learn the final secret of Maine's wisdom. Muhammad Shamsu'-d-dín Háfiz of Shíráz wrote in one of his odes:—

My heart is vexed by the solitude of Alexander's prison;
I will truss up my baggage and get me to the kingdom of Solomon.

(*Dil-am az waḥshat-i-zindán-i-Sikandar bi-girift:*
Rakht bar-bandam u tá mulk-i-Suleimán bi-ravam.)

This couplet signifies, as the commentators tell us, that Háfiz was weary of staying in Isfahán and eager to return to his beloved city of Shíráz. But Eastern poetry is full of double meanings, and it is not hard to discern here a more general spiritual meaning apart from the literal occasion. Alexander is the lord of this world, a conqueror of kingdoms with the sword of the flesh, a bestower of earthly riches;

and Alexander's prison is the illusion wherein those men dwell whose desire is to worldly rewards and honours and all manner of transitory goods, and who deem such things to be of any worth for their own sake. But Solomon is the lord of wisdom and ruler of spirits, having the seal engraven with the Ineffable Name, by whose virtue he can summon angels and control demons ; and Solomon's kingdom is the world of things eternal, wherein whatsoever is true and good and beautiful is worshipped for itself, and not for any temporal profit that it may bring ; and Solomon's men are those who endeavour themselves to pursue that worship, holding the things of this world neither in overmuch honour nor in contempt, but as instruments to be used for higher ends. And the token of a man's allegiance to Solomon is that he knows it is better to be a doorkeeper in the temple than warder of all the prison. Now the prison of Alexander is paved with useful facts. But the pillars of Solomon's temple are ideas, and its headstones are the imaginations of genius which the men of practical sense despised, and the dome is built of the unity of all knowledge. And in the centre of the dome a jewel is set, flashing light perpetually throughout the temple ; and the divers colours of its rays are the wisdom of the wise, but its whiteness is the infinite wisdom of God. And round about the dome is written the saying of the Lord when David asked him, Lord, since thou wast perfect, what need hadst thou to create the world ? and the Lord made answer, I was a hidden treasure and I would be revealed.

Whoever brings a fruitful idea to any branch of knowledge, or rends the veil that seems to sever one portion from another, his name is written in the book among the builders of the temple. Therefore, here in the Faculty of Law, we give thanks because our master Maine brought us into new and closer fellowship with our brethren of History and of Arts, and taught us to understand what it is that we inherit, and what has been the part of the law and of its ideas in the life of our nation.

The work of the present generation in the field of comparative jurisprudence is mostly work of detail. Our great predecessors have annexed realms which it is for us to settle and administer. But there is no rest for knowledge, and for our children, if not for us, there will again be a time of large adventure. They will go forth to new conquests, perhaps armed with the weapons we have forged for them, perhaps with others of such fashion and power as we cannot even guess.

> Alter erit tum Tiphys et altera quae vehat Argo
> Dilectos heroas—

we may finish the line and say "erunt etiam altera bella," for our successors will doubtless have their controversies too. But the contest will be bloodless and harmless, and the victory will be to truth; neither will our sons forget in their triumphs that we wrought, as best we might, to prepare the way for them. The quest will be ever new and the perils ever changing; but the goal will be the same, the temple which is not of the money-changers, but of Solomon in his spiritual glory. For it is also written by one of our own prophets, To labour in knowledge is to build up Jerusalem, and to despise knowledge is to despise Jerusalem and her builders.

II

THE HISTORY OF THE LAW OF NATURE[1]

I

THE term "Law of Nature," or natural law, has been in use in various applications ever since the time of the later Roman Republic. Their variety and apparent diversity have tended to obscure the central idea which underlies them all, that of an ultimate principle of fitness with regard to the nature of man as a rational and social being, which is, or ought to be, the justification of every form of positive law. Such a principle, under the name of reason, reasonableness, or sometimes natural justice, is fully recognised in our own system, but the difference of terminology has tended to conceal the real similarity from English lawyers during the last century or more. The neglect of mediæval learning which followed the Renaissance and the Reformation has also caused us to forget that the Law of Nature has a perfectly continuous history down to the date of its greatest and most beneficent achievement—one might almost say its apotheosis—in the foundation of the modern Law of Nations by Grotius. Much

[1] *Journal of the Society of Comparative Legislation*, 1900, p. 418.

that has been written on this subject, even by eminent authors, assumes or suggests that Grotius revived for his own purposes an almost dormant conception of the Roman lawyers. In fact, the Law of Nature, as Grotius found it, was no mere speculative survival or rhetorical ornament. It was a quite living doctrine, with a definite and highly important place in the mediæval theory of society. What is more, it never ceased to be essentially rationalist and progressive. Modern aberrations have led to a widespread belief that the Law of Nature is only a cloak for arbitrary dogmas or fancies. The element of truth in this belief is that, when the authority of natural law was universally allowed, every disputant strove to make out that it was on his side. But such an endeavour would obviously have been idle if the Law of Nature had meant nothing but individual opinions. I now propose to give a summary view of the origin and development of the doctrine. The facts are not open to doubt, and any current errors are due to pure oversight rather than to misconstruction.

Natural law, as conceived by mediæval scholars, was derived partly from the Aristotelian distinction of natural and conventional justice, partly from the Latin exposition, led by Cicero, of the same idea in its later Greek forms, and partly from the still later special adaptation of it by the classical Roman jurists. The distinction was not altogether new in Aristotle's time; for the present purpose, however, the celebrated passage in the fifth book of the

Nicomachean Ethics [1]—not from Aristotle's own hand, but certainly Aristotelian in substance—may be taken as the fountain-head. Justice, as a necessary element of the State (τὸ πολιτικὸν δίκαιον), is divided into natural (τὸ μὲν φυσικόν, *naturale*) and conventional (τὸ δὲ νομικόν, *legale*). Rules of natural justice are those which are universally recognised among civilised men. Rules of conventional justice deal with matters which are indifferent or indeterminate until a definite rule is laid down by some specific authority. Such are all rules fixing the amount of fines or other money payments. The rule of the road may furnish as good a modern example as any. Reason suffices to tell us that some rule is desirable on frequented roads, but whether we shall take the right or the left hand can be settled only by custom or legislation; and in fact the rule differs in different countries. Thus far Aristotle might seem to be merely noting the fact that some principles of social conduct are admitted everywhere, or at least wherever there is any settled government. But the Aristotelian use of the term "Nature" goes beyond this; it implies the conception of a rational design in the universe, which is manifested though never perfectly realised in the material world. This last qualification is important. Aristotle expressly guards himself against asserting that the rules of natural justice, as actually found in human society, are perfectly constant. General uniformity is enough to show that they exist, as the

[1] C. 7. This is one of the Eudemian books. The Latin equivalents given are those used by St. Thomas Aquinas, from the literal version prepared under his direction.

right hand is truly said to be the stronger, although there are left-handed people.

The Stoics emphasised the teleological and ethical aspects of the Peripatetic doctrine, and fixed on the term "Nature" in this connexion the special meaning of the constitution of man as a rational and social being. Every creature has its own nature and its own appropriate functions, and for man—whose nature is to be a citizen—the Law of Nature is the sum of the principles, founded in human nature, which determine the conduct befitting him in his rational and social quality. No term answering to the Latin *ius gentium* is known to occur in Greek philosophy, but the later Stoics at any rate spoke of νόμος φυσικός (which Aristotelian usage would not allow), and the original Aristotelian dictum was current in the Middle Ages in the form "Ius naturale est quod apud omnes homines eandem habet potentiam."[1]

As to Roman usage, it appears that *ius gentium* was old popular as well as legal Latin, and meant the common law or usage of mankind—the rules which, in fact, everybody recognises.[2] This is very near the φυσικὸν δίκαιον of the Greeks, taken on the practical and directly observable side. *Lex naturalis* or *naturae, ius naturale,* came in, as deliberate translations of the Greek term, in the last period of the Republic. They must have been neologisms in Cicero's time, for in his earliest work, the

[1] Fortescue, *De Laudibus Legum Angliae,* c. 16.
[2] Nettleship, *Contributions to Latin Lexicography,* s.v.

De inventione, as in that of the anonymous *Auctor ad Herennium* whom he follows, the idea is found, but is expressed by periphrasis. The law derived from Nature, as there set forth, is identical, as might be expected, with the morality of a high-minded Roman gentleman.[1] We are not concerned here with the technical history of *ius gentium* as part of the Roman system of law, but only with the reason given for its adoption. Obviously no positive authority could be assigned; and ancient Roman lawyers were no more willing than modern English ones to admit frankly that they were innovating on grounds of convenience. The Greek doctrine of the Law of Nature furnished exactly the ideal foundation which was wanted, and the classical jurists, perhaps with more aid from lost Greek philosophical works than we can now trace, proceeded to identify *ius gentium* with *ius naturale* for the purposes of legal science.

Strictly speaking, *ius naturale* should signify the rules of conduct deducible by reason from the general conditions of human society, *ius gentium* so much of those rules as is actually received and acted upon among all civilised people. We have already seen that not even philosophers expected natural justice to be completely realised in this world, nor can I find any evidence that either philosophers or lawyers believed it ever had been, notwithstanding the modern use of such expressions as "the lost code of Nature" with reference to the Roman doctrine. If they ever

[1] *De invent.* ii. 53, s. 161: "Natura ius est quod non opinio genuit sed quaedam innata vis inseruit: ut religionem, pietatem, gratiam, vindicationem, observantiam, veritatem."

felt tempted to connect the Law of Nature with the fables of a golden age, they were wise enough to resist the temptation.

Thus a distinction between *ius naturale*, the ideal to which actual law and custom could only approximate, and *ius gentium*, the measure of the practical approximation at a given time, was quite warrantable, if not positively required from a theoretical point of view. Such a distinction, however, is but seldom made by the Roman lawyers, and then in exceptional matter, such as the question of slavery;[1] and modern Romanists appear still unable to agree whether passages of this kind represent a received doctrine or individual speculations. There is no doubt that the terms were treated as synonymous in ordinary cases, and it is not difficult to suppose that in such cases the exceptional ones were not present to the minds of the writers, or the tacit exception of them was left to the reader's intelligence.

The compilers of Justinian's *Institutes* adopted from Ulpian a phrase extending the Law of Nature to all living creatures: "Ius naturale est quod natura omnia animalia docuit."[2] This would seem to be merely a piece of over-ambitious generalisation taken from some forgotten Greek writer, perhaps a rhetorician and not a philosopher. It is quite con-

[1] The contrast is most strongly put in a fragment of Tryphoninus, D. 12. 6. *De Condict. Indeb.* 64: "Libertas naturali iure continetur, et dominatio ex gentium iure introducta est." It hardly needs pointing out that this is not an Aristotelian view. St. Thomas Aquinas tries to reconcile the earlier and later philosophers by a distinction of great ingenuity: *Sec. Secundae*, qu. lvii. art. 3.

[2] D. 1. 1. *De Iust. et Iure*, 1, 3.

trary to the Stoic conception of the Law of Nature, where Nature undoubtedly means the reason of the universe as exhibited in the specific moral and social character of man, and "following Nature" means realising, so far as possible, the ideal of human nature; so that the difference between man and other animals is more important than the resemblances. Ulpian's unlucky phrase is alone in the *Corpus Iuris*; Ulpian himself makes nothing of it beyond saying that rudimentary family institutions may be ascribed to irrational animals, and there is no sign of the notion having had any influence in Roman law. Nevertheless, this passage, having been put in a conspicuous place at the opening of Justinian's *Institutes*, and therefore speaking with the highest authority, has given infinite trouble to commentators. Most mediæval writers felt bound to accept—with more or less qualification, according to their boldness and ingenuity[1]—the threefold classification of *ius naturale*, the rules or instincts common to all animals; *ius gentium*, the rules common to all mankind; and *ius civile*, the particular law of this or that commonwealth.

William of Ockham, one of the boldest, propounded a classification altogether independent of Ulpian. *Ius naturale*, he says, may be taken in three senses: (1) The universal rules of conduct dictated by natural reason; (2) rules which would be accepted as reason-

[1] There is some good criticism in Aegid. Rom., *De regimine pr.* III. ii. c. 25. (This book is often cited without the author's name; care is therefore necessary to distinguish it from the other work, partly by St. Thomas Aquinas, of like title.)

able, and therefore binding, in a society governed (or in any society so far as governed) by natural equity without any positive law or custom of human ordinance; (3) rules which may be justified by deduction or analogy from the general precepts of the Law of Nature, but, not being in fundamentals, are liable to modification by positive authority.[1] The "secondary Law of Nature" of later books appears to cover William of Ockham's second and third heads, but may generally be referred to the third. That which modern writers since Rousseau have commonly called the Law of Nature without qualification is nothing else than a one-sided development of the "secondary Law of Nature" as it was understood before the scholastic terminology was forgotten. But we must return to the normal process of mediæval thought on the main lines of the subject.

About the beginning of the twelfth century the revival of Latin learning, which is not unjustly called the "Lesser Renaissance," was fully as active in legal and political speculation as in other directions. The more exciting and more easily intelligible controversies of the sixteenth century have obscured the importance of this movement for latter-day readers. John of Salisbury may be taken as its typical English champion. It culminated, a century and a half later, in Dante. When we call it a revival

[1] Dial. pars III. tr. ii. l. 3, c. 6, at p. 932, in Goldast, *Monarchia*, tom. ii. There is an express claim of originality; the Student says: "Istam distinctionem iuris naturalis alias non audivi." Apparently William of Ockham's dialogue has never been critically edited; it is still practically accessible only in Goldast's enormous volumes.

of Latin learning, we include not only the study of Roman literature and the Roman law, but the study of Greek antiquity and philosophy so far as accessible through Latin. Indeed, there is reason to think that knowledge of Greek, in the thirteenth century at any rate, was not so very rare as has been commonly supposed. We have to remember that, for the mediæval history of the Law of Nature, Aristotle is not less important than Justinian, and Cicero's authority does not come far behind.[1] The heathen philosophers had been so much quoted and approved by Fathers of the Church that they stood in the eyes of mediæval scholars on almost as high a level of sanctity as an orthodox emperor. When the age of chaos was past, and the lawyer and the statesman, after many generations, once more had the means of being humanists, the Law of Nature presented itself with twofold and threefold claims to allegiance. Its authors and vouchers carried a weight second only to that of the law of God as declared by the authority of the Church. Evidently the Law of Nature could not be left out in any systematic discussion of human conduct. Any serious attempt to disparage it was no less out of the question. Even

[1] See the Ciceronian passages collected in K. Hildenbrand, *Geschichte u. System der Rechts- u. Staatsphilosophie*, i. 564. (This volume seems to be all published.) The fragment of the *De republica* preserved by Lactantius probably had more influence than any one passage in the jurists. As it is constantly referred to, it may be convenient to give the leading phrases here :—" Huic legi nec abrogari fas est, neque derogari ex hac aliquid licet, neque tota abrogari potest : nec vero aut per senatum aut per populum solvi hac lege possumus ; neque est quaerendus explanator aut interpres eius alius : nec erit alia lex Romae, alia Athenis, alia nunc, alia posthac," etc. (*De rep.* III. 22). The use of the word " lex " involves the idea of rational design, and is justified by it, otherwise it would not be Latin.

the Church could not afford to set herself against Aristotle, Cicero, and Justinian. The Law of Nature was too firmly in possession to be evicted. Yet the Church had to maintain her supremacy, as custodian of the divine law, in matters of faith and morals.

Only one way was possible. The Romans had already identified their *ius gentium* with the Law of Nature; the process must be carried a step farther by identifying the Law of Nature with the law of God. Philosophers had already used language which pointed that way. The step was taken, in the twelfth century, by the author or authors of the *Decretum* of Gratian, and with a thoroughgoing boldness which almost deserves the name of genius.[1] At the very head of the *Decretum*, therefore at the very head of the body of Canon Law as since collected, we read that the Law of Nature is nothing else than the golden rule, comprised in the Law and the Gospel, which bids us do as we would be done by, and forbids the contrary. It is supreme over all kinds of law by antiquity and dignity; it is immutable; it prevails over both custom and express ordinance. Here, it would seem, English lawyers must be content to find the origin both of the maxim, still received, that a custom cannot be good if it is contrary to reason,

[1] I have looked into the best-known manuals of Canon Law before Gratian (Regino of Prüm, Burchard of Worms, Ivo of Chartres) with the aid of the excellent indices to them in Migne's *Patrologia*, rather expecting to find the doctrine in an earlier stage, but have found nothing like it. Apparently Gratian makes a wholly new departure. There is reason to believe that the *Decretum* was strongly influenced by Abelard (see Thaner, *Abälard und das canonische Recht*, Graz, 1900); but whether there be anything to our immediate purpose in Abelard I must for the present leave to be verified by better mediævalists than myself.

and of the doctrine—now rejected, but current (though never put in any effectual practice) in the sixteenth and down to the eighteenth century—that a statute may be held void for being repugnant to reason or "common right." The Law of Nature, however, is not absolutely co-extensive with the law of the Church or with the rules revealed in Scripture. For even revealed precepts, though of unquestionable authority, may and often do deal with matters not fundamental in themselves, but appertaining to ceremonial and positive regulation. It is assumed, rather than directly laid down, that the Church is the authentic exponent and interpreter of natural law. The assumption, however, is obviously required by reasons of discipline. It would never do for bishops and archbishops to claim practical independence under pretence of following the rule of natural reason at their own discretion. But the Law of Nature in the hands of an ultimate authority may be an effective solvent in many cases. A bishop who obstinately relies on a local custom against the general usage of the Church will find himself kicking against the pricks, not merely of official superiority, but of a law which he must needs recognise as paramount.[1] Truth before custom: had not Augustine said it? Thus the Law of Nature, as the eldest branch of the divine law, goes hand in hand with the no less divine authority of the Church to judge all the earth and do right. Such is, in outline, the

[1] If any one should think the reinforcement superfluous, le him remember that the discipline of the Church in the middle of the twelfth century was not what it is now, or what it had become even a century or two later.

system which has never been substantially departed from by orthodox canonists. It is true that the *Decretum* of Gratian has not, in Canon Law, the same binding force as the later Decretals.[1] But if authority were wanting to Gratian's enthronement of the Law of Nature, it was amply supplied by Aquinas, who set his stamp on the doctrine in the next century.

The relation of natural law to divine law in general is more fully defined by St. Thomas; they are not substantially different, but natural law is divine law so far as revealed through the medium of natural reason, "participatio legis aeternae in rationali creatura."[2] This identification was carried over by the glossators into the teaching of Civil as well as Canon Law. Thus Azo explains Ulpian's *natura,* in the perplexing dictum already mentioned, by *id est ipse Deus.*[3] It is needless to dwell farther here on the passages of St. Thomas Aquinas touching the Law of Nature, as they have been cited by recent English writers (Professor Holland and others) and are comparatively well known. Mediæval writers often speak for brevity's sake of divine law, without qualification, when they mean specifically revealed rules of conduct, and of positive law when they mean positive or conventional rules of human ordinance. Hence a current division of all law into divine, natural, and positive, where the first and last of these epithets must be understood to be used

[1] See F. W. Maitland in 2 *Encycl. Eng. Law,* 356, 357.
[2] *Prima Secundae,* qu. xci., art. 2.
[3] See F. W. Maitland, *Bracton and Azo* (Seld. Soc., 1895), at pp. 32, 33.

in the compendious manner just explained, and not to imply ignorance or doubt of the propositions, perfectly well known to the writers, that all natural law is divine, and some divine law is positive.[1]

The full adoption and glorification of natural law by the *Decretum* of Gratian was, as above said, a master-stroke of policy. We may doubt whether it aimed so high as securing supremacy for the Church over the temporal power, or making the Church the arbiter in questions of secular government. Designs of that magnitude were then hardly formed. The Church was clearly bound to uphold the fundamentals of Catholic faith and morality against all earthly powers; we need not suppose that Gratian intended to go farther. At all events there was no way of making political speculation wholly subordinate to theology. It was not long before ingenious controversialists discovered that the supremacy of the Law of Nature was a double-edged weapon. For the Law of Nature, by its very definition, was a rule of life and society discoverable by human reason apart from any special revelation or the decision of any particular authority. When discovered, again, it was admitted to be absolutely binding. Natural law could not be in conflict with divine law, for it was part of the divine law. The intentions of Nature, as philosophy calls them, are nothing else than the intentions of

[1] Selden's brief remarks in his *Table Talk*, s.v. *Law of Nature*, seem to ignore these distinctions. Denial of any natural law apart from a specially sanctioned revelation appears to be the substance of the dictum as reported. But this would make Selden more Hobbist than Hobbes himself, and we cannot suppose that he would have expressed his considered opinion in such terms.

the Creator. As Dante puts it:[1] "Manifestum est quod Deus finem naturae vult." So William of Ockham: "Omne autem ius naturale est a Deo qui est conditor naturae."[2] Whatever, therefore, reason can establish as part of natural law may be used as a touchstone for propositions enounced by any particular person or body and purporting to be deduced from the specially revealed part of God's law. Such propositions, if contrary to natural law, must be erroneous. Nor could theologians or official persons of any kind claim a monopoly of natural reason. Even if the Church were the ultimate interpreter, the authentic voice of the Church could be found only in a General Council; for in the Middle Ages the infallibility of the pope, so far from being a dogma, was barely allowed to be a plausible opinion. Thus a wide field of speculation was kept open, and guarded by the Law of Nature, through the action of the Church herself. Not even a William of Ockham could think of going behind the notorious elements of orthodox belief; and indeed the Law of Nature could obviously have little application, if any, to purely theological argument. But, apart from the fact that some dogmas, or opinions which have since become dogmas, were still plastic, there was much to be done without any such extreme adventure. There were a great number of questions interesting to both Church and State, such as we now call constitutional, which remained legitimately

[1] *De monarch.* 3, 2.

[2] Dial. III., ii. 3, c. 6, at p. 934, in Goldast, *Monarch.* t. ii.

open. One might not derogate from the law of God as expressed in Scripture and laid down by the Church. But in the case in hand the revealed law of God might be wholly silent, or it might be ambiguous, or authentic texts admitted or alleged to be applicable might be capable of widely differing interpretations. When once there were plausible grounds on either side and no decisive authority, the Law of Nature—like the king's ultimate power of doing justice in default of an adequate ordinary jurisdiction—could always be invoked by way of supplement. It might furnish a rule where no rule had been declared, or might guide interpretation where the application of the rule was not certain. Moreover, as we have pointed out, it was not free to a mediæval disputant to traverse the authority of the Law of Nature itself, but only to deny the correctness of the adversary's formulation or application of its rules in the particular case.

A weapon of controversy so tempting and lying so ready to hand could not fail to be freely and eagerly wielded. In fact, we find the Law of Nature, through the Middle Ages and down to the Renaissance, called in aid of many and various contentions, sometimes on the side of the opinions most favoured in high places, but as often on the contrary. Most chiefly it was an inexhaustible topic in the standing controversy for dominion between the Empire and the Papacy. Rival claims to supreme jurisdiction, urged with abundance of plausible authority on behalf of potentates who owned no common earthly superior, furnished exactly the field in which the Law of Nature might be used with brilliant dialectic effect as a *deus ex machina.* So the champions on either side constantly endeavoured to turn the scale by demonstrating to their own satisfaction that the Law of Nature supported, as their case might be, the pope or the emperor. Imperialist arguments were not wanting in boldness. William of Ockham maintains that the people of Rome have probably a divine, certainly a natural, right to elect their own bishop, and appeals with confidence to natural reason to show that a heretical or otherwise incorrigibly evil pope may lawfully be deposed.[1]

On all hands it was admitted, even by extreme partisans, that both pope and emperor were subject to the Law of Nature, though it might be and was urged that one or the other of them was more likely to form a correct judgement as to what its dictates were. As the champions of the Curia suggested or assumed that the official head of the Church was the best exponent of natural law, so the Imperialists maintained that it was the safe course to follow the emperor's judgement in case of doubt, and rash to dispute it unless it were so contrary to settled principles as to be manifestly erroneous.[2] English lawyers accustomed to weighing the relative authority of decisions will readily see how natural and indeed inevitable these positions were in a controversy where

[1] Goldast, *Monarch.* ii. 568, 934.

[2] "Error principis probabiliter ius facit": William of Ockham, Goldast, *op. cit.* at p. 924.

jurisdiction was the principal or only matter really in difference.

It was no less inevitable that the appeal to the Law of Nature as the ultimate ground of decision between the conflicting claims should often become indistinguishable, to modern eyes, from a pretty frank appeal to expediency. We find even the language of modern utilitarianism anticipated, for *communis utilitas* is a quite current term. If Bentham had known what the Law of Nature was really like in the Middle Ages, he would have had to speak of it with more respect. It has been pointed out before now that in any case utilitarianism is just as much a system of natural law as any other dogmatic system of ethics or politics. Indeed, the political principles of the Imperialist doctors come very near to the well-known theistic form of utilitarianism, according to which utility is the test of right conduct because God wills the happiness of his creatures.

The Law of Nature being for the most part an engine of dialectic, we have no cause to be surprised at not finding much mention of it by name in official and authoritative documents. On occasion, however, it might serve the purpose of a prince who wished to assign imposing reasons for a bold reform without derogating from his own supremacy. Thus Philip the Fair of France in 1311 rested the enfranchisement of the bondmen on the Valois domain upon freedom being the natural birthright of man, and brought in the common profit of the realm (following the utilitarian tendency noted above) as a secondary motive.

"Comme créature humaine qui est formée à l'image Nostre Seigneur doie generalement estre franche par droit naturel et en aucuns pays de cette naturelle liberté ou franchise par le jou de servitute qui tant est haineuse soit si effaciée et obscurcie . . . nous meus de pitié pour le remède et salut de nostre ame et pour consideration de humanité et de commun profit," etc.[1] The example was followed by Philip's son, Louis le Hutin. A high authority has seen here a misunderstanding or misapplication of the Roman dictum, "Omnes homines natura aequales sunt."[2] But in the first place it is not clear that there is any reference to Roman secular law. The tone of this preamble is more ecclesiastical than civil, and the Church had always stood for freedom and favoured manumission. Again, it was considered perfectly fair throughout the Middle Ages to apply any text of authority in any sense it could be made to bear, without regard to what the original historical sense might have been. The more authoritative the text, the more applications were presumably to be discovered in it; and the most far-fetched use of a text is no proof that the writer had misunderstood its primary meaning. Besides, if Roman texts are in question, there are express dicta in the *Digest* to the effect that the Law of Nature does not recognise slavery, and it would be enough to rely on these without saying (as the ordinance does not say) anything about equality. I do not know whether it

[1] *Ordonnances des Rois de France de la troisième Race*, xii. 387. Maine, *Ancient Law*, 94, refers only to Louis le Hutin's later ordinance.

[2] Maine, *l.c.*

was open to a French lawyer in the fourteenth century to argue that a wholesale emancipation of this kind was beyond the power of the Crown, or, though not invalid, censurable on constitutional grounds. If any such objection could be expected, nothing could be more aptly framed to meet it than the king's appeal to the Law of Nature as the paramount reason of public policy.

In the sixteenth century the controversies incident to the Reformation gave a singular impulse to speculative political discussion. It would be difficult to name any modern theory of sovereignty, of the State, or of the origin of society, which is not anticipated somewhere in this mass of polemics;[1] and in particular the foundation of civil government was quite commonly referred to some kind of contract. The terms of the contract, and still more its implied conditions, varied according to the opinions of the disputant. But this did not materially affect the importance of natural law. For, since the original contract had in general no historical existence (however the ingenuity of dialectic might strive to disguise this), its terms could not be proved as a matter of fact. They could, therefore, only be presumed to be what they ought to have been; and what they ought to have been was eminently a question of natural law. More than

[1] This is well noted by the late Professor Brissaud, of Toulouse, in his interesting study of the liberal movement in France (*Un Libéral au XVIIe siècle : Claude Joly, 1607–1700*; Paris, 1898), p. 5: "Si l'on se reporte par la pensée à la fin du seizième siècle, on est tout surpris de trouver, au lieu d'une seule foi politique, une véritable mêlée des esprits : théorie du contrat social, théorie de la souveraineté populaire, systèmes aristocratiques, ou même démocratiques, c'est une confusion extrême."

this, it was a prevalent opinion that the original contract itself was of the nature of positive law, and subject to the Law of Nature, like all other branches of law. This or that particular State might be instituted by convention; but, a State being once established, its rights and powers, it was said, were determined by principles of natural right paramount to all conventions.[1]

The various controversial exigencies of the Reformation and the Catholic counter-Reformation produced endless divisions and cross-divisions among Catholic and Protestant publicists, unexpected or even paradoxical in a modern reader's eyes. We find Dominican and Jesuit champions of the Papacy deliberately referring the foundation of the State to natural reason alone, in order to deprive the prince of any claim to spiritual jurisdiction. This, with the *Decretum* of Gratian still claiming respect, was a perilous line of argument. Again, the principles of the Law of Nature were invoked to moderate the letter-worship of the Reformers: the text of Scripture, the Catholics said, must be taken with, and subject to, the universal principles discoverable by reason, and construed in a manner consistent with them.[2] Further, and this comes very near modern methods,

[1] Authorities and references in Gierke, *Johannes Althusius, passim.* As to the last-mentioned point, see at pp. 105, 106. And see now F. W. Maitland's translation (with an excellent introduction) of the section "Die publicistischen Lehren des Mittelalters" in Gierke's *Das deutsche Genossenschaftsrecht,* vol. iii., *sub tit., Political Theories of the Middle Age,* Cambridge, 1900.

[2] So, in England, Pecock (*Repressor*) as early as 1455. Pecock's arguments were, however, suspected of heresy and indeed formally charged with it, though on this point he seems in accord with scholastic tradition.

it was sought to assure the sanctity of property and contract, including the supposed original contract itself, by representing those institutions as part of the immutable Law of Nature; this view was substantially adopted by Grotius, and has largely entered into modern economic doctrine. The process was made more plausible by identifying the *ius gentium* of the *Corpus Iuris* with the Law of Nature of the canonists. There were even those who dared assert that "Deus ipse ex promissione obligatur." [1]

One much-agitated topic was the relation of sovereign power to natural and positive law. No doubt was entertained that the Law of Nature was in some sense above all earthly potentates. This did not obviously decide the question whether a subject could in fact be justified in disobeying his lawful sovereign's commands as being contrary to the Law of Nature.[2] It was admitted that merely consequential or "secondary" rules of natural law, which might be binding in the absence of positive enactment, could be modified or restrained by positive law. St. Thomas was decisive on that point.[3] Subject to this distinction, however, it was the prevalent mediæval opinion that commands of the prince contrary to the Law of Nature were not binding on his subjects and might be lawfully resisted—a doctrine sometimes tempered by advising the subject to presume, in

[1] Gierke, *op. cit.* 270, 271.

[2] No subject, of course, could be bound by his allegiance to commit a breach of manifest elementary rules of faith or morals. Cases of that kind are outside the argument.

[3] *Sec. Secundae*, qu. lvii., *De Iure*, arts. 2, 3.

case of reasonable doubt, that the prince's judgement was right. A more dubious question was whether sovereign power was subject to positive as well as natural law. Did the imperial *potestas legibus soluta* belong of right to all independent sovereigns? In other words, were they the fountain of positive law and above it? There was good authority for saying so.[1] But it was also vigorously maintained that the ruler could be guilty of a breach of positive as well as natural law, full sovereignty being reserved to the people, or in spiritual matters to the congregation of the faithful. Before the Reformation, Marsilio of Padua was the leading champion on this side.[2] This is the distinction of "organic" or "fundamental" from ordinary institutions. It is possible to argue, as Hobbes in effect did later, that such a distinction is incompatible with the Law of Nature. At this day it exists in a large majority of civilised commonwealths.

As Protestant writers did not accept the authority of the Church, of the Canon Law, or of Aristotle, and the Roman disputants of the counter-Reformation were anxious to confute the Protestants on their own ground, the tendency of sixteenth-century controversy, as well as of Renaissance learning in general, was to bring the texts of classical Roman law into greater prominence. Thus a more definitely secular

[1] "Positiva lex est infra principantem sicut lex naturalis est supra." Aegid. Rom. iii. 2, c. 29. This, with the caution that "principans" is the king in Parliament, has long been the accepted English constitutional doctrine.

[2] Gierke, *op. cit.* 266,

and legal cast was given to the whole treatment of the Law of Nature, and the way was prepared for the great construction of Grotius. Not that Grotius has anything disrespectful to say of the mediæval doctors. On the contrary, he ascribes the greatest weight to their agreement on questions of moral principle; when they are found unanimous on such questions, their opinion is more than probable: "ubi in re morum consentiunt, vix est ut errent."[1]

Here we may leave the Law of Nature ready to achieve its development into the modern Law of Nations, and turn to its fortunes in our own country. The Canon Law, as we have seen, was the principal vehicle of the Law of Nature, and canonists were anything but popular among English laymen. In politics they were associated with attempts to encroach on the king's authority for the benefit of foreigners, in common life with the meddling and vexatious jurisdiction of the spiritual courts. Talking of the Law of Nature, therefore, was not a good way to most English ears, and it is not strange that we find little about it in English authors. William of Ockham, of whom we may justly be proud as our countryman, can still hardly be counted for this purpose. There is nothing particularly English about his career or his work; he is cosmopolitan, like all the great mediæval doctors.

One English royal judge, Sir John Fortescue, did commit himself a century later to treating of the

[1] *De Iur. B. et P. Prolegg.* s. 52.

Law of Nature by name, but the case is in every way exceptional. His book, *De Natura Legis Naturae*, was a plea for the Lancastrian title to the crown of England, addressed to Continental readers in the hope of obtaining Continental support. It is at best the artificial performance of a champion wielding unfamiliar arms in a strange field. Compared with the work of trained dialecticians, it is of slight interest and of no value.[1] What little is said of the Law of Nature in Fortescue's principal and really interesting book, *De Laudibus Legum Angliae*—a book also intended, it would seem, for Continental readers—is ornamental, and of no greater importance.

We might expect to find the mark of the regular scholastic doctrine in the early history of the Court of Chancery, but there are only occasional references to law *and reason*—we shall see the importance of this term presently—as the standard of decision. The current form, "for God and in the way of charity," is an appeal to the divine law of the Church rather than to natural law properly so called. Express invocation of the Law of Nature seems rather to have been purposely avoided. Probably it was felt that it would do more harm than good. The king's discretion was understood to be supreme in "matters of grace," and especially large wherever the profit of the Crown, or the rights of any one claiming by grant from the Crown, were affected. Any deduction of it from the Law of Nature would

[1] Mr. Plummer's account in his introduction to *The Governance of England*, at pp. 82-84, is enough for most purposes.

have looked like an attempt of canonical formalists to regulate the king's prerogative in some outlandish fashion of their own. After the Reformation it was a harmless exercise to identify the Chancellor's equity with the Law of Nature or with a Roman prætor's jurisdiction. I do not know of any example earlier than the seventeenth century.[1] Moreover, the administration of equity in anything like the modern sense was, in the fourteenth and fifteenth centuries, by no means the sole or chief business of the Court of Chancery.

For distinct English recognition of the Law of Nature we must look to such law and jurisdiction as had an avowed cosmopolitan character, and principally to the law merchant.[2] This was always understood to be founded on general reason and convenience, evidenced by the usage of merchants. "The law merchant, as it is part of the Law of Nature and Nations, is universal and one and the same in all countries in the world."[3] In 1473, it was said by Stillington, Edward IV.'s Chancellor, in the great case of larceny by a carrier "breaking bulk," that the causes of merchant strangers "shall be determined according to the Law of Nature in the Chancery." Foreign merchants put themselves within the king's jurisdiction by coming into the realm, but the jurisdic-

[1] See Malines, *Lex Mercatoria* (A.D. 1656), 311.

[2] The law of the Admiralty stood too much apart to be specially considered here. There were mutterings of insular pride against its cosmopolitan jurisprudence as early as the fourteenth century. See the very curious gloss quoted in Maitland's *Bracton and Azo* (Seld. Soc., 1895), at p. 125.

[3] Sir John Davis, *Concerning Impositions*, c. 3, "dedicated to King James in the latter end of his reign," first printed 1656.

tion is exercisable "*secundum legem naturae* que est appelle par ascuns ley marchant, que est ley universal par tout le monde."[1] It is said that the practice was to refer such causes to merchants by commission from the Chancellor.[2] In the ordinary jurisdiction of the king's courts we find a trace, but only a trace, of common lawyers envying the dialectic resources of the civilians and canonists. Yelverton said that he did not see why, in the absence of authority, the king's judges should not also "resort to the Law of Nature, which is the ground of all laws."[3] It is just possible that some design for enlarging the king's power through judicial discretion was at the bottom of this; it is all but certain that in the following century Henry VIII. had a plan to compass the same end by favouring the study of the Civil at the expense of the Common Law. Nothing came of it in either case, and the Tudors showed their wisdom by working out their practical despotism in other ways and under more national forms.

Theological and political tracts of the fifteenth century[4] just enable us to say that the proper English translation of *ius naturale* was "law of kind." "Doom of natural reason" is used as a synonym, and we have also the fuller expressions "moral law of kind, which is law of God" (the regular equation of *ius naturale* with *ius divinum*),

[1] Y.B. 13 Ed. IV., 9, pl. 5.

[2] Malines, *l.c.* In the thirteenth and fourteenth centuries suits between merchants could be pleaded in the king's ordinary courts according to law merchant: Y.B. 21 and 22 Ed. I., 75; 32 and 33 Ed. I., 377.

[3] Y.B. 8 Ed. IV., 12.

[4] Pecock, *Repressor; Dives and Pauper*, printed 1536.

"law of kind, which is doom of reason and moral philosophy."

We do find the Law of Nature making a considerable figure in the argument of two well-known cases of the late sixteenth and early seventeenth centuries —*Sharington* v. *Strotton* (the case of "Uses" in Plowden), and *Calvin's* case (the *post nati*), 7 Co. Rep. 12 *b*. Both of these were highly exceptional, of the first impression, and argued throughout on general principle. As already hinted, there was no longer any risk in using the Law of Nature to adorn an argument, and the new learning of such civilians as Alberico Gentili was making it fashionable again. No light is thrown by such peculiar examples on the usual habit of mind of English lawyers.

But there is a real link between the mediæval doctrine of the Law of Nature and the principles of the Common Law. It is given by the use—correct in both systems, though constant, indeed exclusive, in the Common Law, and rather sparing in the Canon Law—of the words "reason" and "reasonable." This was pointed out in the first quarter of the sixteenth century by that very able writer, Christopher St. German, who must have been at least a fair canonist as well as an excellent common lawyer. In the preliminary part of *Doctor and Student*, after the Doctor has expounded the species of law according to the regular method of the schools, the Student gives the law of reason as the first of the general grounds of the law of England, and, in answer to the Doctor's enquiry where he puts the Law of

Nature, explains that in the Common Law that term is not in use, but that where the canonist or civilian would speak of the Law of Nature, the common lawyer speaks of reason. Once pointed out, the analogy is obviously just, and a real connexion at least probable, for we are not to suppose that the judges and serjeants never knew any more of what the canonists were doing than is disclosed by the Year Books. In our own time, before the Judicature Acts, it was the judicial etiquette for Common Law and Equity judges to assume, whether they had it or not, a more than modest ignorance of one another's doctrines. Yet this striking passage of St. German has been completely overlooked in modern times. It would be easy not to discover from current accounts of it that the *Doctor and Student* was anything more or other than a text book of Common Law. We can account for this only by the Reformation having broken up the scholastic tradition, and made it the fashion to despise the Middle Ages. Sir Henry Finch, writing early in the seventeenth century [1]—say in the third generation from St. German—had quite lost the thread; what he says of the Law of Nature is mere confusion. He actually makes out the law of reason (by which he seems to mean something approximating to the "secondary" natural law of the schoolmen) to be something different. Not a lawyer, but a divine, Hooker, was the latest English writer who maintained the tradition substantially on its accepted lines, though not without

[1] *Discourse of Law*, first published 1613.

variations and expansions which seem to be his own.[1] An English reader in search of a general exposition of the Law of Nature as understood down to the Renaissance might, indeed, do well enough to take Hooker for his guide.

Hobbes retained the names of natural law and natural right, and (contrary to what is sometimes said by writers who have not studied him adequately) his language as to natural law being immutable and eternal is as strong as anything to be found in orthodox publicists. But by defining *lex naturalis*[2] with reference to self-preservation as the only guiding principle, he broke away from previous authority to work out a method all his own. The practical contents of Hobbes's morality are, nevertheless, not very different from other people's, nor was his political system without forerunners. But this does not concern us here. Richard Cumberland, Bishop of Peterborough, went about to refute Hobbes in the name of the Law of Nature (1672). But he made no attempt to return to mediæval lines. As to authority, he tries to get a fresh start from the Roman lawyers; as to principles and method, he is (as Hallam justly observed) a precursor of the modern utilitarians. By his time the scholastic Law of Nature had finally ceased to count in English speculation. In France it fared no better, if we may judge by Montesquieu, who had lost the historical tradition as completely

[1] *Eccl. Pol.* bk. i. cc. 2, 3, 8, 9, 10, 12.

[2] *Leviathan*, c. 14. Hobbes's *ius naturale* is not a rule at all, but every man's natural liberty to use his own power for his own advantage.

as any insular moralist. He supposed the Law of Nature to consist only of such rules of conduct as would be applicable in default of any settled government[1]—that is, in the fictitious "state of Nature," with which the original Law of Nature had nothing to do.

But the Law of Nature was not dead: it was only transformed into a shape more available for making conquests in the modern world. Its doctrine, purged of clericalism, had been assimilated, through Grotius and his successors, by the modern Law of Nations, and had thus become part of the common stock of eighteenth-century publicists. In that form it was accepted without demur by rationalist philosophers who would have scorned to be knowingly beholden to the Middle Ages. From the Continent it came back to England, rather as an appanage of polite letters than as a constituent of technical jurisprudence. Blackstone made use of it at second or third hand to ornament—though merely to ornament—the introductory chapters of his *Commentaries*. Lord Mansfield took up the rationalising movement as a practical reformer, and under his guidance it left permanent marks on more than one branch of English law. From the *Decretum* of Gratian to the equitable application of the "common counts," on grounds of "natural reason and the just construction of the law,"[2] and the full recognition of the law merchant in the king's courts, may seem a long way. The journey was certainly roundabout; but there is no real break in it.

[1] *Esprit des lois*, l. 1, c. 2.

[2] Blackst. *Comm.* iii. 161.

There is much to be said of the function of natural or universal justice, including the idea of reasonableness in its various branches, in the later developments of our system. In particular an important part has been played by natural law, under the name of "justice, equity, and good conscience," or otherwise, in the extension of English legal principles under British political supremacy, but beyond English or Common Law jurisdiction. But this topic is large enough to deserve separate consideration.

II.—(*continued*)

THE HISTORY OF THE LAW OF NATURE[1]

II

We have seen in the former part of this study that in the course of the seventeenth century the classical tradition of the Law of Nature was broken up after the Reformation controversies, with the result that in this country it has been forgotten or misunderstood ever since. Oblivion went so far that it was possible for Bentham and his followers to suppose quite honestly that the Law of Nature meant nothing but individual fancy. But at the same time that the Law of Nature ceased to be honoured among us in speculation, it was entering on new spheres of practical power. The modern law of nations was founded by Grotius on a revised scheme of natural law, and his foundations have always and everywhere been treated as sound except by one insular and unhistorical school. Grotius's doctrine was expanded and made the common property of public men by his successors; it was accepted in this current form by the English publicists of the eighteenth century, and thus had considerable influence on English and still more

[1] *Journal of the Society of Comparative Legislation*, 1901, p. 204.

on Scottish expositions not only of the law of nations but of public law in general. In the domain of private law the ideas of reasonableness and natural justice, which do not the less belong to the Law of Nature because they have been called by different names at different times, leapt into fresh activity, and created or largely modified whole bodies of doctrine. Later, by a process which at first sight looks paradoxical, the same ideas became the vehicle for spreading the distinctive principles and methods of the Common Law in lands where it did not and could not formally claim any jurisdiction. We shall now try to follow the Law of Nature in these several careers of conquest, of which some at least are far from being closed.

With regard to International Law, it is notorious that all authorities down to the end of the eighteenth century, and almost all outside England to this day, have treated it as a body of doctrine derived from and justified by the Law of Nature. There has been a certain divergence of opinions on the question whether the law is established by the reason of the thing alone—*natura rationalis*, as Grotius says—or by the actual usage of civilised nations. But this divergence is really more in expression than in any fundamental conception. It was never asserted by the most zealous advocate of the Law of Nature that an individual opinion of what is just can, as such, make a general rule. Here, as elsewhere, we must apply the principle of Aristotle, and deem that to be reasonable which appears so to competent persons. There must be a competent and prevalent consent, and the best evidence of such consent is constant and deliberate usage. Discordant opinions as to what is right or convenient could never produce a uniform accepted usage, as, on the other hand, no other reason can be assigned for the general acceptance of certain usages by independent States than that they are generally believed to be convenient and just. In fact, the elements of reason and custom have been recognised by the highest authorities as inseparable, and strengthening one another. Thus the English law officers (among whom Lord Mansfield, then Solicitor-General, took the leading part) wrote in their celebrated opinion in the case of the Silesian Loan that the law of nations is "founded upon justice, equity, convenience, and the reason of the thing, and confirmed by long usage."[1] In the very infancy of the doctrine Alberico Gentili, while he declared that the *ius gentium* applicable to the problems of war was identical with the Law of Nature, and claimed for it the authority of absolute reason, also vouched the continuing and general consent of mankind to witness it; not an imaginary consent of all men at any one time, but an agreement constant and prevalent—in fact, *quod successive placere omnibus visum est.* For all practical purposes we may define International Law, with the late Lord Russell of Killowen, as "the sum of the rules or usages which civilised States have agreed shall be binding upon

[1] This opinion is commonly referred to in the French version given in Martens' collection. The English may be seen in Holliday's *Life of William Earl of Mansfield*, London, 1797, pp. 428 *et seq.*

them in their dealings with one another," remembering, however, that the agreement need not be formal or express. Such rules may, of course, be modified, generally or partially, by convention or usage,[1] in any manner consistent with the objects for which the law of nations exists.[2] This is not only required by convenience, but wholly in accordance with the doctrine of the Law of Nature as received in the Middle Ages, which expressly admitted the validity of positive rules and conventions not contrary to fundamental principle. If any one ever did want to lay down a dogmatic and immutable code of *Naturrecht*, it was not the schoolmen, but the utilitarians.

Some English writers, and even one or two eminent judges, have rather superfluously protested that the opinions of text-writers cannot make law for nations.[3] It is certain, as Lord Stowell pointed out, that they cannot; but the consensus of authors of good repute, or even the clear statement of one eminent author, may be taken as evidence of the accepted practice where practice is not shown to be otherwise. "Vattel," said Lord Stowell in a leading case on the right of visit and search, "is here to be considered, not as a lawyer merely delivering an opinion, but

[1] See per Lord Stowell, *The Santa Cruz*, 1 Rob. Adm., at p. 58; *The Flad Oyen*, *ibid.*, at p. 139; *The Henrick and Maria*, 4 Rob., at p. 54.

[2] All moralists allow that in some cases it is better, or less bad, to break an agreement that ought never to have been made than to perform it. The exception must apply to nations as well as individuals, though *pactum serva* is the rule, and it is not good to dwell on exceptions. A treaty for the partition of an unoffending neighbouring State, for example, is only a conspiracy aggravating the crime.

[3] See Cockburn C.J.'s observations in *R.* v. *Keyn*, 2 Ex. Div., at pp. 202-3, which seem to overlook the true doctrine laid down long before by Lord Stowell.

as a witness asserting the fact—the fact that such is the existing practice of modern Europe."[1] It is equally plain that no State can maintain claims to exercise a novel jurisdiction over citizens of other States by appealing to the Law of Nature in the sense of the opinion entertained by itself alone of what is right and convenient in the case. An argument really of this kind was urged with great ability and eloquence, but without success, by the counsel for the United States in the Bering Sea arbitration. All this, again, is in strict agreement with the general principles of natural law. No particular opinion of this or that learned person, much less of an interested party, can make that reasonable which is not acceptable as such to the general opinion of civilised mankind.

In this country questions of international law have mostly arisen in Admiralty jurisdiction, and our classical authorities consist to a great extent of Lord Stowell's judgements on points arising out of the exercise of belligerent rights at sea in the war against the French Republic and Empire. There is no doubt whatever as to the kind of law that Lord Stowell thought he was administering. It was *ius gentium* in the fullest sense, a body of rules not merely municipal, but cosmopolitan. For him the Court of Admiralty was a court of the law of nations, and of the law of nations only, not intended to carry into effect the municipal laws of this or any other country.

[1] *The Maria*, 1 Rob., at p. 363. To the same effect is the judgement of the Supreme Court of the U.S., *The Paquete Habana, The Lola* (1899), 175 U.S. 677, 700.

"The seat of judicial authority is locally here, in the belligerent country, according to the known law and practice of nations, but the law itself has no locality."[1] As for the opinion that nations are bound by the law of treaty only, and there is no other law of nations than that which is derived from positive compact and convention, Lord Stowell rejected it as fit only for Barbary pirates.[2] We must either admit that modern International Law is a law founded on cosmopolitan principles of reason, a true living offshoot of the Law of Nature, or ignore our own most authoritative expositions of it. In fact, these utterances have been wholly ignored, so far as I know, by English publicists of the extreme insular school.

Although the mediæval mould of natural law was broken, the substance of its ideas passed into the common stock of European publicists through the new learning of the law of nations, and their influence was manifest in a rationalist movement which had many branches — rationalist because the Law of Nature is essentially so. This last statement would have been a truism in the sixteenth century, and is still familiar on the Continent; it may seem a paradox to some English readers nowadays, but it remains true. Scotland, kept by political traditions in closer touch with Continental thought than England, had an important share in spreading the movement in these kingdoms. It was no accident that our two great

[1] *The Maria*, 1 Rob. 341, 350; *The Two Friends*, 2 Rob. 280; *The Walsingham Packet*, *ibid.*, at p. 82.

[2] *The Helena*, 4 Rob. 7.

rational law reforms of the second half of the eighteenth century were carried out by Lord Mansfield, a Scotsman by birth.

First of these must be mentioned, though this is not the place for a full account, the definite adoption of the law merchant as part of the Common Law. That body of custom had anticipated some of the characters of International Law; it claimed an authority independent of any particular local jurisprudence, as being founded on general reason and usage approved as reasonable; in other words, it was a branch of the Law of Nature, and it was constantly described as such. Under Lord Mansfield it was received, not as a collection of rules to which only legislation could add, but as a coherent system which did not lose its vitality and power of development from within because it was incorporated with the law of the land. Such, at least, is the better modern opinion as to its present standing.[1]

Hardly less important was the introduction in Common Law procedure of a liberal and elastic remedy on causes of action *quasi ex contractu*. Blackstone, following Lord Mansfield's creative example as a faithful expositor, said in so many words of this class of actions—those of which the count for "money had and received to the plaintiff's use" is the type—that they arise "from natural reason and the just construction of the law."[2] Thus the whole modern

[1] See the late Sir Francis Palmer's article in the *Law Quarterly Review* or July 1899 (xv. 245).

[2] Blackst. *Comm.* iii. 161. The best-known statement by Lord Mansfield himself is in *Moses* v. *Macfarlan* (1760), 2 Burr. 1005.

doctrine of what we now call quasi-contract rests on a bold[1] and timely application, quite conscious and avowed, of principles derived from the Law of Nature.

One of the most characteristic and important features of the modern Common Law is the manner in which we fix the measure of legal duties and responsibilities, where not otherwise specified, by reference to a reasonable man's caution, foresight, or expectation, ascertained in the first instance by the common sense of juries, and gradually consolidated into judicial rules of law. The notions of a reasonable price and of reasonable time are familiar in our law of sale and mercantile law generally. Within the last century and a quarter, or thereabouts, the whole doctrine of negligence has been built up on the foundation of holding every lawful man answerable for at least the amount of prudence which might be expected of an average reasonable man in the circumstances. Now St. German pointed out as early as the sixteenth century that the words "reason" and "reasonable" denote for the common lawyer the ideas which the civilian or canonist puts under the head of "Law of Nature."[2] Thus natural law may fairly claim, in principle though not by name, the reasonable man of English and American law and all his works, which are many.

Sometimes, though not often, questions have come before our Courts of purely municipal jurisdiction

[1] "Lord Holt used to say that he was a bold man that first ventured on them [the general or common counts], though they are now every day's experience."—1 Wms. Saund. ed. 1871, 366.

[2] See p. 57 above.

which were so much "of first impression" that there was really no applicable authority at all. Upon such questions, topics of argument were necessarily sought in the most general principles of justice and convenience, and discussed and weighed with very little reference to any more specific test. A mediæval lawyer would have said of such questions that, since positive law did not afford any solution of them, they were soluble by the Law of Nature only. The best-known example in this kind is the long-continued controversy on the existence of copyright and other analogous rights at Common Law, independent of legislation—a controversy which produced a great body of ingenious argument and more than one notable conflict of judicial opinions. We have no occasion to say anything here of the merits or of the result, which dialectically was a drawn battle,[1] but only to note that the arguments and opinions on both sides were *Naturrecht* pure and simple.

The principles of natural justice are recognised and applied by name in the class of cases where our Courts have had to review the exercise of quasi-judicial powers by the boards, committees, or other governing bodies, however described, of divers institutions and societies. There is a preliminary question whether the power which the governing body has purported to exercise against an individual was

[1] The last judicial discussion was in 1854—*Jefferys* v. *Boosey*, 4 H.L.C. 815. There the judges were divided, and the House of Lords unanimous for the negative opinion. But the actual final decision was not that copyright did or did not exist at Common Law, but that, if it ever did, it had been abolished by the Statute of Anne which conferred copyright for a term of years.

"judicial" or "absolute." An absolute discretion for which no reasons need be given may be conferred either by Statute or by the agreement of the persons concerned (for example, by the terms on which an appointment has been offered and accepted), and such a discretion, where it has been conferred, cannot be impeached on any ground short of fraud. In other cases the Court will consider whether the rules of natural or universal justice have been observed; the expressions are synonymous and equally current. Those rules are, for this purpose, that when a person is deprived on the ground of alleged misconduct of an office or honourable rank, or of an interest in property administered[1] by an association for the benefit of its members, he must have notice of the charge against him and an opportunity of being heard, and the special rules, if any, governing proceedings of that kind in the institution or society in question must be exactly followed, and the decision must be arrived at in good faith, with a view to the common welfare. If these conditions are satisfied, the Court will not examine the merits of the decision as if it were sitting on an appeal. The jurisdiction is not of an appellate, but of a prohibitory nature; it is paramount to the jurisdiction of the "domestic tribunal," which, on the other hand, is not interfered with so long as it does not offend against the paramount rules of universal justice.

[1] The legal title to such property is of secondary importance. It may be corporate, or vested in trustees, or held in common by all the members.

Even in the case of a summary executive authority founded on necessity (which may be said to be itself a matter of natural right), the rules of natural justice must be observed so far as practicable. The master of a ship has such an authority, and this is perhaps the only known case.[1]

It would be a strong extension of these principles to apply them to the judicial acts of a competent foreign tribunal within its jurisdiction, and it is not known to have been actually done in England. Still, there is some authority for saying that, in an extreme case, a foreign judgement showing manifest disregard of universal rules of justice would itself be disregarded here. In cases where this topic has been suggested, other more definite grounds of objection have been present, such as want of jurisdiction. But judges of great eminence have claimed for our Courts a reserved power of taking the broader ground at need. It is certain, on the other hand, that our Courts do not pretend to review the manner in which a foreign Court administers its own rules of procedure, nor to require that foreign procedure should conform to any of our merely local standards.[2] The exclusion of witnesses on the ground of interest, for example, is a system which we have discarded, but we cannot complain of its maintenance in other jurisdictions, nor, contrariwise, of the admission in evidence of

[1] *The Agincourt,* 1 Hag. Adm. 271, 33 R.R. 717.

[2] See on this delicate subject Westlake, *Private International Law,* 3rd ed. 351; Dicey, *Conflict of Laws,* 2nd ed. 403; *Simpson* v. *Fogo,* 1 H. & M. 195, 136 R.R. 90, the reported case where the strongest remarks occur; *Pemberton* v. *Hughes* [1899] 1 Ch. 781, 790.

hearsay and other matters which we should exclude. In this region of specific regulation the part of natural law is, as the mediæval doctors said, only secondary, and is confined to giving to authentic acts and instruments, in case of doubt, that interpretation and effect which may appear most fitted to work substantial justice.

As to the body of doctrine known under the head of Conflict of Laws or Private International Law, its authority was originally founded on considerations of natural justice, for so much at least is implied in the fact that, though it is not *ius inter gentes*, it has always been deemed to belong to the law of nations in the wider and more ancient sense of *ius gentium*. But it has now for many years been as much part of the municipal law of England as the law merchant, and it becomes daily less and less needful or useful, in any normal case, to cite foreign authorities [1] or resort to general principles of convenience. The ideal is still cosmopolitan; the actual law of the Courts is national; and I believe this is so, or tending to be so, in other countries also.

Students of comparative jurisprudence need not be reminded that there are extensive territories under British dominion in which English law has never been received as a whole, or introduced by any sovereign act except in particular local jurisdictions

[1] This is not subject to any exception as to the ascertainment of foreign law in the particular case; for that, in our system, is matter not of authority but of evidence, though parties may, and often do, agree to put in the text of a foreign Code, or appropriate parts of it, instead of calling foreign experts to prove their law.

and for limited purposes.[1] The most remarkable example is afforded by British India. Here we find that the Law of Nature has played a singular and almost paradoxical part. It has been the means of effecting a large importation of English ideas and principles in regions where any formal Common Law jurisdiction was not only not asserted, but formally disclaimed.

In the early days of our Indian settlements European traders, like all persons in Eastern countries, were presumed to carry their personal law with them. The charter of 1683, principally intended for Bombay, seems to have contemplated a Court administering to such traders, not the Common Law, but the law merchant. If this experiment proceeded at all, as I think it did not, it left no permanent mark. In the following century the Supreme (now High) Courts of the Presidency towns were established by the authority of Parliament to administer English law to European British subjects within limited territorial jurisdictions.[2] Otherwise, neither the King's Courts nor the East India Company's Courts were authorised or, in fact, assumed (after a transitory stage of disastrous experiment) to administer English law as such. They were directed to do justice

[1] In one Crown colony, Trinidad, there has never been any wholesale reception of English law, but a series of enactments has anglicised one branch after another till there is practically nothing else left in either substantive law or procedure. There may be other examples unknown to me, but such cases are of little general importance, and they do not belong to the present enquiry.

[2] For authorities and details see Sir Courtenay Ilbert's *Government of India*, and, for the earlier history of the Supreme Court of Calcutta, Cowell's *Courts and Legislative Authorities in India*, lects. ii. and iii.

according to the native laws of the parties, if applicable rules could be found. But it often happened that no such rules could be found, and some general provision had to be made. A Bengal Regulation of 1793, substantially copied at various intervals of time in the other Presidencies and provinces, laid down that in such cases the judges were "to act according to justice, equity, and good conscience." These words, down to the end of the eighteenth century, could only be read by any publicist or trained lawyer as synonymous with the Law of Nature. But no detailed system of the Law of Nature has ever acquired general authority. We may safely assume that the attempts of European publicists to construct such systems were unfamiliar to the vast majority of the company's officers; we know that English utilitarianism, which its votaries would have been only too eager to turn loose on the *mufassal*,[1] was only just born. English officials in India being what they were, "an Englishman would naturally interpret these words ['justice, equity, and good conscience'] as meaning such rules and principles of English law as he happened to know and considered applicable to the case; and thus, under the influence of English judges, native law and usage were, without express legislation, largely supplemented, modified, and superseded by English law."[2] In our own time this has been judicially approved as the proper course. Equity and good conscience, we are told by

[1] The correct spelling, *mufassal*, has been officially adopted for some time. The common Anglo-Indian form, *mofussil*, is a solecism.

[2] Ilbert, *op. cit.* 394.

the Judicial Committee of the Privy Council, are generally interpreted to mean the rules of English law if found applicable to Indian society and circumstances.[1] The moral predominance thus acquired by the Common Law in British India may be compared with that which was acquired by the Roman law, not as positive law, but as "written reason," in the *pays de droit coutumier* of the French monarchy.

There is a singular case of a British possession in the East having been abandoned (it will be seen that no other term is possible) to the Law of Nature for several years.[2] In 1786 a native Raja purported to cede Penang, then uncultivated and unsettled, to an officer of the East India Company. Possession was taken, under orders from the Governor-General and Council of Bengal, "in the name of his Majesty George the Third and for the use of the Hon'ble English India Company." The intention was apparently to put Penang under the Bengal Regulations, or at any rate the power to make Regulations. But difficulties were raised as to the Governor-General's jurisdiction, and the result was that for twenty years (except for a few provisional directions issued by the Governor-General on emergency)[3] there was no positive law in Penang. At any rate, nobody knew whether there was any, or if any, what; and in 1803 the judicial officer of the island reported that

[1] L.R. 14 Ind. App., at p. 96.

[2] Walter J. Napier, *An Introduction to the Study of the Law Administered in the Colony of the Straits Settlements*, Singapore, 1898, a very interesting pamphlet, from which the facts in the text are derived.

[3] The local Government purported to make Regulations, but clearly had no authority to do so: Napier, p. 6.

the Law of Nature was the only law he could find to guide him. He also found its guidance inadequate for determining questions of succession and administering estates,[1] which, indeed, was exactly what any mediæval doctor (not to say Aristotle) would have told him to expect. At last, in 1807, the Crown came to the rescue, and a regular Court was established by charter.

It would seem, in the light of later authorities and discussion, that the learned magistrate might properly have followed the example of the Company's Court in the *mufassal*, and administered under the name of justice, equity, and good conscience, as much English law as he thought reasonably applicable to the local circumstances. However that may be, the effect of the charter and subsequent legislation and usage was to introduce English law as the territorial law of Penang, and ultimately of what are now called the Straits Settlements as a whole.

[1] "His Excellency in Council has been heretofore informed that Prince of Wales' Island, prior to its cession in 1785 [should be 1786] was under the dominion of a chief who governed arbitrarily and not by fixed laws. It is now become my painful duty to state that it has so continued to be governed without fixed laws; for upon the hour of my arrival on this island, there were not any Civil or Criminal laws then in existence, and there are not even now any Municipal, Criminal, or Civil laws in force on this island. The law of nature is the only law declaring crimes and respecting property which, to my knowledge, at this day, exists at Prince of Wales' Island; and as Judge, it is the only law which I can apply to the Criminal and Civil suits brought in judgement before me. But as the law of nature gives me no precepts respecting the right of disposing of property by wills and testaments, the rights of succession and inheritance, and the forms and precautions necessary to be observed in granting Probates of Wills and Letters of Administration to intestates' effects, or respecting many things which are the subject of positive law, I have often been much embarrassed in the execution of my duty as Judge in the Court of Justice in which I preside; and many cases there are in which I am utterly unable to exercise jurisdiction."—Mr. Dickens' report to the Governor-General, ap. Napier, at p. 5.

But the part of the Law of Nature was not yet played out.

The population of the new settlements included a large number of Malays, Hindus, Chinese, and possibly other Orientals, all of whom continued to observe their native customs in matters of religion and the family. No provision for administering their native personal laws to native suitors was ever made by any charter or other legislative act. The Straits Settlements were, indeed, under the Government of India for more than a generation (1830–1866); but nothing took place during that time which could operate as a "reception" of the Bengal Regulations or any of the Anglo-Indian legislation confirming them. Nevertheless, the need for recognising native custom in matters of family law was practically the same as in India; and, after a good deal of discussion, it appears to have been now settled for many years that in a general way "native customs . . . will be recognised unless they be contrary to justice and general public policy."[1] Now the general rule of our authorities is that only so much of existing English law becomes the law of a new English settlement as is reasonably applicable to local circumstances. This may be said already to involve a reference to the Law of Nature, for the appeal to the test of reasonableness is, as we have seen, really the same thing. At any rate, there is no express grant of jurisdiction to administer any other positive law than our own. Again, it will

[1] Extract from a judgement of the local Court of Appeal, ap. Napier, p. 39.

hardly be maintained that Hindu or Mahometan law can ever be binding on English judges, in the cause before them, by its own intrinsic authority. There seems, therefore, to be no other assignable source of the jurisdiction which is in fact exercised than the Law of Nature ; in other words the judicial conviction of the Court that in a particular class of cases not only is it not reasonable to apply English law, but it is reasonable to apply the native custom of the parties. It remains open to speculative discussion whether we ought to say that in such cases the Court is free to decide according to the Law of Nature because there is nothing in the positive law generally binding on the Court to exclude or supersede it, or that the Court is bound to follow the Law of Nature because, in the local circumstances and in that class of cases, the Law of Nature is embodied in the Common Law. That the law actually administered is not the native personal law itself is sufficiently shown by the care with which the claims of "justice and general public policy" are reserved as paramount. Thus a considerable part of the inhabitants of the Straits Settlements live to this day, and apparently thrive, as to a considerable proportion of their affairs, under a judicial discretion founded on natural equity alone, and, though no doubt becoming fixed in the way of precedent, never defined by any external authority.

III

LOCKE'S THEORY OF THE STATE[1]

LOCKE'S *Essay on Civil Government* is well known, and is probably the most important contribution ever made to English constitutional law by an author who was not a lawyer by profession; certainly there is nothing to be compared to it until we come to Bagehot in our own time. Still I do not know that it has ever been analysed by an English lawyer with reference to its immediate purpose and circumstances. In fact Locke's political doctrine holds quite a secondary place in such accounts of Locke as are generally current in the hands of the educated public. The *Essay on Civil Government* has been overshadowed by the *Essay on the Human Understanding* and the *Letters on Toleration.* This, together with the special occasion,[2] may perhaps be a sufficient excuse for the present attempt.

The first thing to bear in mind about the *Essay on Civil Government* is that it is essentially an apologia for the Convention Parliament, no less than Hobbes's

[1] *Proceedings of the British Academy,* vol. i., 1904.

[2] The bicentenary of Locke's death.

Leviathan and *Behemoth* were an indictment of the Long Parliament. It is true that in the body of the work the language employed is studiously general. But the date of publication, 1690, would alone be enough to remove any doubts of the intention, and moreover that intention is clearly stated in the Preface to the two treatises of which the Essay is the second. It may be well to cite Locke's own words. "Reader, Thou hast here the Beginning and End of a Discourse concerning Government; what Fate has otherwise disposed of the Papers that should have filled up the Middle, and were more than all the rest, 'tis not worth while to tell thee. These which remain, I hope are sufficient to establish the Throne of our great Restorer, our present King *William*; to make good his Title, in the Consent of the People; which being the only one of all lawful Governments, he has more fully and clearly, than any Prince in *Christendom*; and to justify to the World the People of *England*, whose love of their just and natural Rights, with their Resolution to preserve them, saved the Nation when it was on the very brink of Slavery and Ruin." The doctrine which Locke had to confute was, as is well known, that of absolute monarchy; the champion whom he attacked by name and elaborately demolished in the first of the *Two Treatises of Government* was, however strange it may seem to us nowadays, not Thomas Hobbes but Sir Robert Filmer. For us Hobbes is the recognised founder of the English school of politics and jurisprudence; while Filmer, as the late Prof. Croom Robertson incidentally observed in discussing Hobbes (and I see no reason to doubt the soundness of the remark), is saved by Locke from oblivion. In Locke's time Sir Robert Filmer was fashionable among royalists and Hobbes was not. Hobbes's uncompromising rejection of ecclesiastical claims made it, in fact, impossible for a party bound up with Anglican prelacy to have anything to do with him; and his justification of obedience to any *de facto* government in being was hardly less distasteful to maintainers of the divine right of kings. Express controversy with Hobbes was therefore quite useless for Locke's purpose. Nevertheless Locke must have seen that, apart from the party strife of the moment, Hobbes was the really formidable adversary. Moreover Filmer, with all his absurdities, had one fundamental point in common with Hobbes. Indeed he was the only publicist of the time, so far as I know, who mentioned Hobbes with approval, though a limited approval. "With no small Content," says Filmer, "I read Mr. Hobs's Book *De Cive*, and his *Leviathan*, about the Rights of Sovereignty, which no man, that I know, hath so amply and judiciously handled: I consent with him about the Rights of *exercising* Government, but I cannot agree to his means of *acquiring* it."[1] Again: "We do but flatter ourselves, if we hope ever to be governed without an Arbitrary Power. No: we mistake, the Question is not, Whether there shall be an Arbitrary Power; but the only point is,

[1] Preface to *Observations Concerning the Original of Government* (1679).

Who shall have that Arbitrary Power, whether one man or many? There never was, nor ever can be any People govern'd without a Power of making Laws, and every Power of making Laws must be Arbitrary: For to make a Law according to Law, is *Contradictio in adjecto.*"[1] This, I need hardly say, is pure Hobbism. The impossibility of a limited government or "mixarchy"[2] is the very burden of Hobbes's *Behemoth.*

We need not be surprised, therefore, either at the lack of specific dealing with Hobbes in Locke's *Essay*, or at the ample internal evidence that Locke had in fact studied Hobbes's doctrine with quite as much critical attention as Filmer's.

There is no reason for us to trouble ourselves with Locke's polemic against Filmer, even so far as it runs over from the First Treatise into the Essay.[3] King Charles I.'s imaginary title as right heir of Adam is as grotesque to any modern lawyer as Adam's imaginary political dominion over the world can be to any modern publicist. Good Sir Robert wholly failed, as Locke was at the pains to show at large,[4] to prove what was the rule of succession to Adam's original title, why it should have been primogeniture rather than equal division, and whether it is discoverable by the light of nature or imparted to us by any and what revelation. It would be too curious, perhaps, to consider whether he supposed the course of descent

[1] Preface to *The Anarchy of a Limited or Mixed Monarchy* (1679).

[2] This word was restored by Dr. Tönnies from Hobbes's MS.

[3] Chap. vi. of "Paternal Power."

[4] First treatise, chap. xi., "Who Heir?" And see the Essay, *ad init.*

to be in fee simple, tail male, or how otherwise, and whether after the Deluge Noah took by a new grant and became a new stock of descent, or was in as of Adam's old estate. I have known only one man capable of doing full justice to that theme, my lamented and most learned friend Mr. Challis. Locke does point out that the whole of Filmer's theory falls to the ground unless he can make out that Shem was universal monarch.[1] Adam's original title, moreover, had already been relied on to quite the opposite purpose by the section of the Independents known as Levellers. They deduced to all men, as sons of Adam, "a natural property, right, and freedom" which could be duly exercised only in a pure democracy.[2] Sir Robert Filmer, then, is out of the story; nor is it worth while to guess what kind of reply he could or would have attempted if he had been living; and we may proceed to Locke's own account of political power.

At the outset the object of enquiry is thus defined: "Political Power . . . I take to be a Right of making Laws with Penalties of Death, and consequently all less Penalties, for the regulating and preserving of Property, and of employing the Force of the Community, in the Execution of such Laws, and in the Defence of the Commonwealth from foreign Injury *and all this only for the publick Good.*" The last clause, which I have italicised, gives the keynote of the whole Essay. Princes and rulers hold their

[1] First treatise, §§ 139-142; see too §§ 32-39.

[2] Scherger, *The Evolution of Modern Liberty* (New York and London, 1904), p. 130.

powers, whatever may be their legal form, not by an absolute right founded on grant, covenant, or otherwise, but on conditions in the nature of a trust, and under liability to forfeiture if the conditions are not fulfilled. Locke was no lawyer; but it is allowable to believe that the peculiar doctrines of the English Common Law as to conditional estates, and of English Courts of Equity as to the duties of trustees, although the latter was still in its infancy, had a distinct influence in moulding his dialectic. For absolute originality there was no room. Every kind of material for political construction was ready to hand in the polemics of the Reformation controversy, not to speak of the mediæval writers who had become to Locke's contemporaries far more obscure than they are to us. The researches of modern scholars, among whom the first place is undoubtedly Gierke's, have shown that all possible theoretical combinations, except the much later system of Cabinet Government which has democratised our monarchy, were anticipated, if not developed, by the political writers of the sixteenth century. Locke's work was inevitably eclectic, and must have been so even if it had not been conditioned by a definite practical aim. He is so far from professing to be original that he is almost ostentatious in following Hooker, whom he vouches at several points in fairly copious extracts. Hooker, of course, was an authority whom Anglicans were bound to treat with respect. The skill and judgement of Locke's performance were proved in the most conclusive manner by the commanding position which the doctrine formulated by him acquired forthwith and held for nearly a century.

Locke's political system, like all such systems for a long time before and a long time after him, purports to be founded on natural law; that is to say, on rules of conduct which the light of reason, without aid of any special revelation, and without assuming the existence or authority of any form of society, can discover as generally applicable to man as a rational being. This, I think, is a sufficient account for our purpose of what Locke's contemporaries understood by the law of nature, however widely they differed in their methods of ascertaining its principles, and in the results which they derived. Hobbes was as ready as any man to declare that the laws of nature are immutable and eternal;[1] which however did not prevent his laws of nature from being unlike other people's, or other people from regarding several of Hobbes's immutably true propositions as not only mischievous but demonstrably false. It is important for any fair appreciation of Locke to remember that, although the mediæval tradition was interrupted, the mediæval assumption that there is a law of nature, and that when ascertained it is supreme, was still prevalent. This indeed had never been contradicted, save so far as any Protestant controversialists maintained with Dumoulin that the text of Scripture came first. Possibly both Locke and his English opponents would have accepted the

[1] *Leviathan*, chap. xv.

Reformers' position on that point; it was not one which they had occasion to consider. But Locke does not confine the obligations of the law of nature to mortal men. He proves *a fortiori* that those obligations are binding on princes (§ 195). They "are so great, and so strong, in the Case of *Promises*, that Omnipotency it self can be tied by them. *Grants*, *Promises*, and *Oaths* are *Bonds* that *hold the Almighty*." Locke may or may not have read in an earlier writer rediscovered for modern readers by Gierke that "Deus ipse ex promissione obligatur."

Thus Locke was bound to begin with the "state of nature." No other way of answering either Hobbes or Filmer would have given formal satisfaction. But this state, for Locke as for the Schoolmen, is rather a perfectly conscious abstraction than an attempt to construct the actual origin of society. The question is what a man's rights would be in the absence of any positive institutions. Nevertheless an actual state of nature exists between independent princes and rulers, and between any subjects of different states (or jurisdictions) who may meet in a place where there is no civilised government (§ 14). Under what law (to put a modern example) are a Scot and a French Canadian in the Khaibar Pass? Modern jurisprudence can in most cases lay hold of some circumstance to obtain a working answer. But the topic may not be pursued here. Hobbes is met with flat contradiction (though not explicitly, for the reasons already given) at the earliest possible point. All men are equal by nature in the sense that no one man has an original claim on any other's political obedience; not in any other sense, and so far we are at one with Hobbes. Every man is entitled and bound to preserve the existence which God has given him. But (contrary to Hobbes) he is no less bound to preserve other men, being his fellow creatures and fellow servants, "when his own preservation comes not in competition." This amounts to saying that the problem is not to account for the existence of society, but to ascertain its best or normal mode of existence. I should be the first to admit that Locke's way of saying it is both less frank and less sound than Aristotle's. As against the opponents he had to reckon with, it was effective and ingenious, being so framed that no one who accepted the authority of Scripture could well traverse it without manifest risk of impiety. Hence every man's natural power over others is already not arbitrary, as Hobbes would have it, but quasi-judicial. Every man has natural judicial and executive power until such powers are regularly constituted.[1] Hence, again, the law of nature authorises all necessary acts of self-defence; and this, even under the rule of settled law, is the only ground for the jurisdiction of any government over resident aliens: a curious opinion which seems to be peculiar to Locke, and gratuitous; for one does not see why the theory of submission by tacit

[1] There is a strange verbal parallel in that strangest of mediæval vagaries the *Mirror of Justices*, the work, as I conjecture, of some eccentric foreign clerk settled in England, whose authorship and purpose are still mysterious. "Ordinary jurisdiction has every one who is not deprived of it by sin (!), for every one may judge his neighbour according to the holy rules of right." Book IV. chap. ii.

consent, on which Locke has to rely later, is less applicable to temporary than to permanent allegiance. This doctrine of the executive power is doubtless open, says Locke, to the objection that it makes every man a judge in his own cause. That is so, and the use of civil government is to remedy such inconvenience. But absolute monarchy fails just in this respect, for the absolute monarch so dear to Hobbes and Filmer remains in a state of nature with respect to his own subjects, and therefore judge in his own cause.[1]

Further, there is a "plain difference between the state of Nature, and the state of War, which however some men have confounded": for "men living together according to reason, without a common superior on earth with authority to judge between them" may live in peace if they will, and such is their will so long as they are reasonable. "Want of a common judge with authority puts all men in a state of nature"; but it is only some act of aggression, "force without right upon a man's person," that makes a state of war. Political authority is instituted to avoid the risk of a state of war, not to put an end to a state of war necessarily existing. In short, in the state of nature there may be peace, though a precarious peace. This is, of course, intended as a mortal stroke against Hobbes's theory, and implicitly denies his position that the worst of governments is always more tolerable than the state of nature. Slavery is the result of conquest

[1] This argument is developed in chap. vii.

in a state of war; and freedom is not the absence of all rule, but "is to have a standing rule to live by" as opposed to being subject to an arbitrary power like a conqueror's. Not that even a conqueror's power is unlimited of right; for Locke argues in a later chapter, the connexion of which with his main purpose is not made very clear, that a conqueror does not acquire general dominion over the property of the conquered, but is entitled at most to a charge upon it for an indemnity.

Locke thinks it prudent to establish a natural right of property (chap. v.) antecedent to political institutions. His solution of the problem is that appropriation is the reward of labour. A man acquires a right in severalty to that which "he hath mixed his labour with." The preceding assumption that "every man has a property in his own person" appeared safe and easy to Locke, but it is certainly not good law, and was expressly contradicted by Ulpian ("dominus membrorum suorum nemo videtur").[1] The rights of every man to personal safety, reputation, and so forth, are not marketable or transferable, and are wholly distinct in kind from rights of property. Locke's attempt to make an extended conception of Occupation bear the whole burden of Property was eminently that of an ingenious layman. It is far from obvious, assuming Locke's premisses, how any one can claim the sanction of the law of nature for appropriating more than is necessary to support himself and his family. Locke

[1] *D.* 9. 2. ad l. Aquil. 13, pr.

sees the difficulty, but cannot be said to remove it. This economic digression, however, is now of little interest. It is explained by Locke's anxiety to set up as many barriers as possible against arbitrary interference on the part of the State. He seems even to ignore the doctrine of Eminent Domain, of which he must have heard. We cannot suppose that he would have actually denied the moral right of the State to take private property for public purposes on payment of just compensation, but he may have thought it so liable to abuse as to be best kept in the background.

Property cannot be made secure by natural right alone, and for the better securing of their properties men have entered into civil society. The will of the body politic, when formed, is determined by the will of the majority, and of a bare majority if there be no different express agreement. For this Locke does not give any reason but the necessity of the case; it is certain that much worse ones have been given. As a matter of fact, we now know that a majority vote has not been generally recognised in archaic societies; the difficulty of obtaining nominal unanimity was overcome (as in special cases it still has to be) by various methods, including varying elements of force and fiction. This does not apply to the original agreement to form a society, which is assumed to be unanimous, and includes only the actual parties to it. Any one who stands out may go his ways and provide for himself elsewhere. It would seem that the community is entitled to enforce his departure;

it is certain, on Locke's principles, that it has not the right to detain him against his will. Could he agree to stay in an inferior capacity like that of a resident alien? But it is needless to pursue the auxiliary fictions which might be devised. A body politic, then, is formed by consent; the essential term of the agreement is that every member gives up his natural judicial and executive power to the community (not, as Hobbes maintains, to an irresponsible sovereign); and this consent is renewed, tacitly if not expressly, in the person of every new member; for one cannot accept the benefit of a settled government except on those terms on which it is offered. Locke is bold to assert that "a child is born a subject of no country or government," and may choose his allegiance for himself at the age of discretion: this is another opinion which no modern lawyer will accept, least of all a continental one. It is however necessary to Locke's theory, and is one of the many details in which his individualism, and every scheme of individualism, breaks down. He guards himself to a certain extent by adding that a man does not make himself a member of an existing commonweal merely by accepting the protection of its government. Nothing short of "positive engagement and express promise and compact" will confer citizenship.

As to the historical objection for want of proof that governments were in fact originally founded by consent, Locke answers, first that historical evidence of what men did before the beginning of history is not to be expected, and secondly that examples of states being founded by consent, such as Rome and Venice, are not wanting. More recent and more striking examples might have been drawn from the settlement of New England, but the fact that the colonists remained and professed to remain subjects of the king of England would have given too much of a handle for controversy; not to mention that the Pilgrim Fathers, whose deliberate constitution of themselves into a body politic is on record, were not at all like primitive or prehistoric men. This last consideration, however, would have had no weight among seventeenth-century disputants. The general prevalence of monarchy in early times is admitted as a fact, but not admitted to be any argument against the origin of government in consent. Why should not the consent and intention of the founders have followed the precedent set by the existing usage of families? We may suppose if we like that "a family by degrees grew into a commonwealth, and the fatherly authority being continued on to the elder son, every one in his turn growing up under it tacitly submitted to it, and the easiness and equality of it not offending any one, every one acquiesced, till time seemed to have confirmed it and settled a right of succession by prescription" (§ 110). This is of some interest as showing exactly how near Locke could come to a historical point of view.

Summing up his argument (in chaps. vii. and viii.; I have not closely followed the order, as it is somewhat clumsy to a modern reader) Locke states (chap. ix.) the reasons which move men to restrict their natural rights by mutual agreement, and unite into commonwealths "for the mutual preservation of their lives, liberties, and estates, which I call by the general name, Property." In the state of nature this cannot be assured. The defects of merely natural society are—

1. Want of established and known law. "For tho the Law of Nature be plain and intelligible to all rational Creatures; yet Men being biassed by their Interest, as well as ignorant for want of Study of it, are not apt to allow of it as a Law binding to them, in the application of it to their particular Cases."

2. The want of "a known and indifferent Judge."

3. Power to execute sentences; for though every man is, in default of positive law, "both Judge and Executioner of the Law of Nature," the ability is often not proportionate to the right.

Locke, then, admits that mankind are "but in an ill condition" when left to the state of nature; he is not really very far from Hobbes's well-known description of the state of war. Some surrender of natural right is necessary; where Locke differs from Hobbes is in holding that, as the surrender is for a definite purpose, it is not unlimited, but conditional on that purpose being fulfilled. Accordingly the natural powers of self-preservation and punishment are put "into the hands of the Society" not absolutely but "to be so far disposed of by the Legislative, as the good of the Society shall require"; and the power of the Commonwealth or its legislative organ "can never be supposed to extend farther than the Common Good." Whatever be the form of government, it must be administered according to known law, and "directed to no other End, but the Peace, Safety, and publick Good of the People." Towards the end of the *Essay* (chap. xviii. "Of Tyranny") Locke cites an unexpected witness, no other than King James I., in support of this fundamental position.

The legislative power, once constituted by consent, is the supreme power in the Commonwealth, but not arbitrary (chap. xi.). We find the reason of its supremacy given very shortly in a later passage (§ 150): "what can give laws to another must needs be superior to him." But the legislative authority is bound by its trust and by the law of nature to govern by established laws, to act in good faith for the common advantage, not to raise taxes without the consent of the people by themselves or their deputies, and not to transfer its power of making laws (being only a delegated power) to any other hands.

This is the most meagre and least satisfying part of Locke's work. He does not seem to conceive the possibility of a legislature having powers limited by express convention but plenary within those limits; nor does he consider at all the partial exercise of legislative power by bodies having a merely delegated authority. He could not be expected to anticipate the constitutions of self-governing colonies, but he must have known that the University of Oxford and his own House had statutes: and he must have desired to see the latter, at any rate, better secured from arbitrary interference than they had been in his own case. Yet he does make a very apt reference, in distinguishing absolute from arbitrary power, to the example of military discipline, where the officer may have power of life and death over the soldier, but cannot "dispose of one farthing of that soldier's estate, or seize one jot of his goods." Neither does Locke touch at all on what is now called constitutional amendment, except negatively. He seems to assume that nothing of the kind can be done, in any form of government, without express provision for that purpose. What makes the omission of argument on this point the more remarkable is that Sir Thomas Smith, writing a century and a quarter earlier, had enounced the unqualified sovereignty of Parliament in terms so full and explicit that Blackstone, after the lapse of just two centuries, could add nothing to them; while on the other hand the necessity of unalterable "fundamentals" in any scheme of government had been much discussed under the Commonwealth, and maintained by Cromwell himself among others. Sir Thomas Smith's *Commonwealth of England* (at last properly edited since this paper was first published [1]) was more than once reprinted in the seventeenth century, and one can hardly suppose Locke to have been unacquainted with it.

In fact there was in Locke's time respectable

[1] *De Republica Anglorum, a discourse on the Commonwealth of England by Sir Thomas Smith,* ed. L. Alston with a preface by F. W. Maitland. Cambridge, 1906.

authority for three different theories of the supreme power in England. The King was absolute, according to the ultra-royalists and Hobbes: Locke demolished this contention once for all, whatever we may think of his constructive work. Parliament, or the King in Parliament, was absolute according to Sir Thomas Smith and the practice of the Tudor reigns: this view was accepted by Blackstone and has been the only tenable one among English lawyers ever since. According to a third doctrine prevalent among students of the Common Law down to the early part of the eighteenth century, there are bounds set by natural justice or "common right" even to what the King in Parliament can do; that is to say, the judges ought to disregard an Act of Parliament if it is manifestly contrary to natural justice, and perhaps if it attempts to subvert the foundations of the constitution; for example, if it purported to abolish the Monarchy or the House of Commons. Locke's opinion is in substance a less technical version of this last; and it is worth while to observe that existing legal authorities were in his favour. Sir Thomas Smith, whose opinion ultimately prevailed, was not a common lawyer but a civilian.

Locke touches on the separation of legislative from executive power, which was to become a constitutional dogma for his eighteenth-century followers; he gives only the practical reason that there is no need for the legislative to be always in being, but executive power for both domestic and foreign affairs must be constantly ready for action. The foreign department of government is distinguished by the not very happy epithet of "federative," which was not adopted, so far as I know, by any one.

We have now seen the whole of Locke's principles of polity. The last seven chapters of the *Essay* are a justification in detail, but by way of elaborate allusion, of their application to English affairs in the Whig theory of the Constitution, and in particular of the Revolution of 1688. Power being entrusted to rulers only on condition, that condition is enforceable at need, whatever be the legal forms of government: "there remains still in the People a supreme power to remove or alter the Legislative, when they find the Legislative act contrary to the Trust reposed in them." In this sense the Community is supreme, "but not as considered under any form of government, because the power of the people can never take place till the government be dissolved." In other words, the ultimate reserved power is extra-legal and superior to the positive forms of the Constitution. Blackstone, whose criticism of Locke is in the main intelligent and fair, does not do him complete justice on this point. In a constitutional Monarchy the "single Person" at the head of the Executive may "in a very tolerable sense" be called supreme; and he is entitled to personal allegiance not "as supreme legislator, but as supreme executor of the law, made by a joint power of him with others." The "power of assembling and dismissing the Legislative" may be vested in the Executive by the Constitution, but, like all governmental powers, it is held in trust for the public, and abuse of it may justify the people in recourse to their ultimate rights. On the other hand, Locke suggests that the representation of the people in the Legislative may perhaps be amended at the discretion of the Executive, provided that such action is taken in good faith. Parliamentary reform by Order in Council was not so obviously remote from practical politics two centuries ago as it is now; but what English princes down to Elizabeth had done in the way of creating new boroughs was not of encouraging example; and I do not know that Locke's suggestion was taken seriously by any one. The failure of Temple's plan to establish an efficient and independent Privy Council had in truth made it impossible beforehand. It is an important question, but a question of modern politics and far outside Locke's field of view, whether the latent capacities of the Privy Council may not yet be developed for the purposes of co-ordinating the resources of the Empire and giving the self-governing colonies an effective share—all the more effective for not being too rigidly defined—in the handling of affairs of common interest.

Prerogative is identified by Locke with executive discretion, including some (he avoids saying how much) extraordinary discretion in emergencies; tempered, like legislative power, by the possibility of forfeiture. Selden's way with the supposed mysteries of prerogative[1] was more straightforward and profitable; but Locke wanted to conciliate moderate royalists.

[1] *Table Talk*, s.v.

It is obvious that Locke's position as to the reserved power of dissolving government is not formally unassailable. A Hobbist would say that a political power "not as considered under any form of government" is a contradiction in terms, and is not only extra-legal but anarchical. Dissolve existing government, under whatever pretence, and you are remitted to the state of war which we set out to avoid at all costs. Locke's reply is indicated later (§§ 224, 225). Its effect is that neither Hobbes's nor any other dialectic will make men tolerate an intolerably bad government. In extremity they will act on the belief that institutions perverted to ends other than the public good "are so far from being better, that they are much worse, than the state of Nature, or pure Anarchy." To this no further answer seems possible. Nowadays we should all agree with Locke as against Hobbes that government is the instrument and not the creator of society. We should also have something to say of the force of custom as a fly-wheel in the social machine, steadying and maintaining the common course of affairs notwithstanding technical or even substantial abeyance of legality. But of this Hobbes takes no account at all, and Locke only just touches upon it ("People are not so easily got out of their old Forms, as some are apt to suggest," § 223).

The final chapter "Of the Dissolution of Government" undertakes to show, but still under a transparent disguise of verbal generality, that the conduct of James II. was in fact such a breach of "the fundamental Appointment of the Society" as justified the people in exercising their ultimate right of self-preservation. It does not seem useful to follow Locke through the details of his propositions, as nothing short of a minute historical commentary would illustrate them to any material extent.

The subsequent influence of Locke's *Essay* may be traced, as the President of Corpus[1] has hinted, not only throughout the formal political philosophy of the eighteenth century, but in the doctrine received among English constitutional lawyers, and in the principles enounced by the promoters of American independence and the conductors of the French Revolution in its early stages. Blackstone substantially followed Locke, though he borrowed some ornamental phrases, not to be taken too seriously, from continental writers. He was prudent enough, indeed, to repudiate the assumption of mankind having actually lived in a state of nature and proceeded to form society by a "convention of individuals";[2] and, writing as a lawyer, he was naturally more anxious than Locke to vindicate the Revolution settlement as not only justifiable but legal. It is none the less true that Bentham, when he sounded the note of destructive criticism in his "Fragment on Government," was really attacking Locke's theory of the State through Blackstone. Again, Blackstone's *Commentaries* were a vehicle of Locke's doctrine (though not the only one) to a

[1] T. W. Fowler, living when this paper was written.

[2] *Comm.* i. 47; as to the ultimate remedy of dissolving government, *ib.* 162; Blackstone seems to have thought "theoretical writers" a term peculiarly apt to include Locke; as to the Convention of 1688, *ib.* 152.

numerous and public-spirited audience in the American colonies; and that doctrine was at the foundation of the several Bills of Rights of the American States, among which Virginia gave the first example, and of the Declaration of Independence itself. More than this, it has been shown by modern American scholars that these instruments became well known in France, and served as precedents for the Declaration of the Rights of Man.[1] On the whole it seems that Locke had as much to do as Rousseau with the Principles of 1789, or more. The fatal domination of Rousseau's ideas belongs to a later stage. It would be idle to consider what Locke himself would have thought of his latest spiritual posterity.

APPENDIX:

THE SOCIAL CONTRACT IN HOBBES AND LOCKE[2]

From very early times we find in various forms the notion that all government and society depend in some sense on the consent of the governed. In the fragments of Cicero's treatise on the Republic (better, in English, Commonwealth) there is a definition which had great authority in the Middle Ages:

> Populum autem non omnem coetum multitudinis sed coetum iuris consensu et utilitatis communione sociatum esse.
>
> Not every multitude of men gathered together is a nation, but only such as have agreed to live by common lawful rule for the common advantage.

---

[1] See Parts iii. and iv. of Scherger, *The Evolution of Modern Liberty.*

[2] Summary of an University Extension lecture delivered at Oxford in 1907; published in *Journ. Soc. Comp. Legisl.*, 1908, p. 107.

Augustine refused to accept this on the ground that there could be no true law or justice under a heathen government; but he seems to have been singular in his dissent.[1] Isidore of Seville, in the early seventh century, substantially copied the Ciceronian definition, and it was generally accepted.

But it was a long time before any one attempted to work out a definite doctrine; indeed it was not possible before the twelfth century, when the revival of learning sometimes called the lesser Renaissance furnished the materials, and a motive was given by the problem, now becoming acute, of the relations between Church and State. At the time of the later Renaissance in the sixteenth century the problems were more acute and much more complex, because (1) practically no one could identify the State with the Holy Roman Empire: (2) the Reformers, still zealous for ecclesiastical authority, repudiated the authority of the Roman church. Thus, at the date of Hobbes's birth (1588) experiments had been made by reforming and anti-reforming publicists with almost every possible speculative combination.

Several questions present themselves:

Who are the contracting parties? on what do they agree? how is the agreement binding? what was their condition before they agreed?

We have to note that there are two quite distinct types of assumed contract. You may suppose an agreement to form a political society—a covenant of commonwealth, *pactum unionis*: this does not necessarily comprise the definition of any form of government or the choice of governors. You may also suppose an agreement to establish a particular form of government and bear faith to it; and this may comprise a mutual agreement between rulers and subjects. This is a covenant of allegiance, *pactum subiectionis*.

Strictly the term *social contract* is applicable only to the former type: but it is impossible to consider the one apart from the other either dogmatically or historically: the distinction between them is important but easily overlooked.

[1] Still, he allowed that obedience to governors was founded on some kind of "pactum"; see H. Rashdall in *L.Q.R.* xx. 324.

It is possible to construct political theories requiring one of these types of agreement, or both.

In the first half of the seventeenth century the prevailing view was that there were two contracts—of society and of allegiance: and that the latter was a contract of mutual obligation, a bilateral contract as modern lawyers say, between subjects and rulers—a contract therefore which either prince or people might break.

Historical illustrations were not wanting for either kind of contract. Formal compacts between kings and their subjects were common enough in the Middle Ages, and long before Magna Carta:[1] and in 1620, when Hobbes was still a young man, the Pilgrim Fathers did "solemnly and mutually covenant and combine" themselves "together into a civil body politick" and "promise all due obedience and submission" to "such just and equal laws," etc., as they should make. This of course throws no light on the origin of government, as the subscribing parties were already members of a civilised State and expressly described themselves as loyal subjects of King James I.

But history did not count for very much with the sixteenth- and seventeenth-century controversialists except as a storehouse of examples to be used in support of foregone conclusions. They assumed[2] that contract was the most binding form of obligation, and therefore it must be the proper foundation of the Commonwealth, in analysis and in morals if not in historical fact.

There was room for plenty of controversy within these limits, especially as to the contract of allegiance.

Did the people surrender their power to the prince, or only commit it to him on terms? and on what terms, if any?

Did the people delegate their authority to the prince, or only appoint him as a ministerial officer?

Did the people act as a corporate body, so that the agreement was between the people of the one part and the king (or other governor or governors) of the other part?

[1] Mr. A. J. Carlyle, *Mediæval Political Theory in the West*, gives Frankish examples of the ninth century.

[2] Cp. Locke, p. 87 above.

This last is a question which Hobbes met with the most emphatic negative.

Comparison of Hobbes's and Locke's theoretical construction of the body politic will show that Hobbes's doctrine was revolutionary, while Locke worked, in the main, on accepted lines and was anxious to appear as following respectable authority. This was perhaps one reason why Locke's influence on the political thought of the next century was so much greater. Both Hobbes and Locke start from an assumed "state of nature"—a political blank paper. In this they are in no way singular. Observe that their predecessors, being bound to accept the theological doctrine of the fall of man, did not and could not treat the "state of nature" as a golden age. It was the condition of men as fallen, sinful, ignorant and ungoverned creatures. Any virtues it had were negative. Hobbes and Locke, again, are at one in considering the original multitude as a crowd of unrelated individuals: and this is the fundamental fallacy of the Social Contract in every form.

Hobbes's view of "mere nature" is pessimist enough to satisfy any theologian. Without "a common power to keep them all in awe" men "are in that condition which is called war; and such a war as is of every man against every man": and thus there is no security for any life worth living.[1]

The law of nature[2]—*i.e.* the rule of self-preservation dictated by natural reason—dictates to man "to seek peace and follow it," and for that purpose, among other things, to keep faith.

But the law of nature has no adequate sanction.[3] "Covenants without the sword are but words, and of no strength to

[1] *Lev.* i. 13.

[2] Every one admitted that there was a law of nature consisting of rules of conduct binding on men simply as rational beings, that it was ascertainable, and that when ascertained it was supreme: except that after the Reformation some Protestant controversialists put the letter of Scripture first under the name of the law of God. Why did they not say at once that they knew as much about the law of nature as the Pope? Because they were still thinking mediævally, and wanted a show of superior authority.

[3] *Lev.* i. c. 17 init.

secure a man at all." From what sort of agreement shall the requisite "common power" be derived?

The peculiar and fundamental point of Hobbes's construction is the form of his original contract. There is only one contract: it is a contract of allegiance made not between ruler and subjects, but between those only who agree to transfer all their natural right to the ruler or rulers whom they will henceforth obey. The sovereign thus instituted (not necessarily one person, but in any case bearing the person of the commonwealth) is not a party to the covenant. He promises nothing to the subjects, and is bound only by the law of nature to exercise his power reasonably. His right is derived not from any promise made to him, but from the power conferred upon him. Hence there can be no legal limitation of sovereignty, and to talk of a limited or mixed government comes only of confused thinking.[1]

This single original contract must be classed as *pactum subiectionis* rather than *pactum unionis*.

Hobbes, of course, did not lay down this doctrine merely for the pleasure of speculation. He had a very practical object—to prove that Charles I. was of right and in fact an absolute king. The detailed application is to be found in *Behemoth*. Also the practical motive for his conclusions—not only avowed but insisted on—was the conviction that anarchy is necessarily the worst of evils, and any settled form of government, however bad, much better than a revolution.

Locke, forty years later, started with a very different practical purpose. Hobbes was the accuser of the Long Parliament, Locke the defender of the Convention Parliament. Hobbes argued strenuously for absolute power. Locke was abundantly cautious to avoid making any statement or admission which might lead to the inference of absolute power anywhere.

[1] Hence, the sovereign not being bound by law, no one law can be more fundamental than another. *Quaere*, what would Hobbes have made of the constitution of the United States, or Switzerland, or Belgium? The attempts of modern followers of Hobbes to account for "rigid" constitutions have been signal failures.

For Locke the state of nature is not a state of war until there is actual hostility, but only a state in which peace is not secure. The natural law of self-preservation includes a moral duty to preserve the rest of mankind so far as possible (*Essay*, ii. § 6). The natural power of every man has already a moral and even judicial character. Locke is therefore not an unqualified individualist like Hobbes.

Civil society is formed by every man giving up his natural power; not to a sovereign but "into the hands of the Community" or "to the publick." The authority so conferred upon the society is granted only to be used for the public good (vii. § 87). The next step is that the society, being formed, establishes a government with legislative and executive organs by the decision of the majority. The right of the majority is founded simply on the necessity of the case, because otherwise no collective action would be possible (viii. § 96).

Locke does not say in terms whether he regards this as involving a secondary contract or covenant of allegiance (*pactum subiectionis*), and it is difficult to make out exactly what his formal conception was. It would rather seem that he purposely avoids committing himself. On the whole I submit that he does postulate an auxiliary compact of all the citizens to be bound by the government and laws which the society shall establish (viii. § 122). This compact is not made once for all, but is constantly renewed in the person of every man who becomes a subject and member of the commonwealth by promising allegiance.

Locke's view that permanent citizenship depends wholly on the individual's consent—and even express consent—is both unhistorical and contrary to all legal doctrine, as any instructed modern reader will easily perceive.

The persons appointed to exercise legislative and executive authority are of course parties to the contract as citizens. But Locke does not affirm, and he seems by implication to deny, the existence of any further special contract between governors or officers of state, as such, and the commonwealth: and this, although the supposed original contract between king and people had been prominent in the debates on the conduct of King James II. and its consequences. Not that Locke would deny that a king or any other holder of public office was bound by any special oath of office or other express undertaking given by him on his appointment and admission. But in a general way he regards the powers of government not as depending on contract, but as held under a conditional grant, or in trust, from the Commonwealth, and subject to forfeiture if the conditions are not observed. Here we have to note the influence of ideas derived from the English law of property. The fundamental condition is that power so granted is to be used in good faith for the common advantage.

Thus Locke may be said to prepare the way for Rousseau. Hobbes knew of only one social contract, the covenant of allegiance: civil society is constituted by allegiance to the common power alone. Locke holds (as I read him) that there is a primary covenant of commonwealth and also an auxiliary covenant of allegiance: but the chosen rulers are not, as rulers, parties to that second covenant. Rousseau, with great ingenuity, quitted Locke's lines and framed a theory which may almost be called an inversion of Hobbes's. He abolished the covenant of allegiance altogether, as being superfluous. There is only one contract, the covenant of commonwealth: for the commonwealth which it creates is sovereign, and whatever the commonwealth does is an act of sovereignty needing no further confirmation. Thus Hobbes recognises *pactum subiectionis* only; Locke (seemingly) both *pactum unionis* and *pactum subiectionis*; Rousseau *pactum unionis* only.

Hume had in fact refuted the Social Contract before Rousseau's version of it became known: a version which though more brilliant is no more sound than any other. But this had apparently no effect in checking Rousseau's influence in France: nor did it prevent Locke's political theory, which had become part of the regular Whig tenets, from being generally accepted in England till the end of the eighteenth century. Blackstone, while obviously under Locke's influence, repudiated, as matter of fact, both the existence of a state of nature and the formation of society by "any convention of individuals"; thus putting himself to some extent in the right line of criticism. It is very doubtful however whether any of the expounders of a social contract meant to commit themselves to maintaining that states were normally, or ever, created in historical times by an express act of agreement: Locke is interesting and rather peculiar on this point. The doctrine of the Social Contract in all its forms is analytical, not historical.

Hume showed that even as mere analysis the doctrine is useless.[1] It attempts to found political society on the duty of keeping promises. But no reason can be given for keeping the supposed promise of the social compact, or any promise, which is not an equally good reason for maintaining political society and obeying the law, promise or no promise. We have to fall back on "the apparent interests and necessities of human society."

Bentham was fully convinced by Hume's argument, and adopted it in his Fragment on Government (1776). The Social Contract, therefore, has no place in the politics of the English utilitarian school. Burke in his Reflections on the French Revolution and elsewhere treats it as an absurd and contemptible fiction. I am not aware of any serious attempt to revive it in later times.

[1] Essay xii., "Of the Original Contract."

IV

GOVERNMENT BY COMMITTEES IN ENGLAND[1]

ADMINISTRATION by committees has long been an essential part of English public life, and this is no less true of all communities living under political institutions directly or ultimately derived from those of England. It probably tends to be true wherever English political methods have been imitated or have had any marked influence. No Englishman who takes any part in affairs can fail to acquire some practical knowledge of committee work. It is found in every part of our social and political machinery. The executive of the imperial government is a committee. The final court of appeal from all jurisdictions in the British Empire outside the United Kingdom is a committee. The highest administrative function of sovereignty, that of eminent domain, is exercised by Parliament on the advice of committees acting in a judicial manner. Most if not all of the innumerable unofficial associations founded for the most various objects of public interest are directed by committees;

[1] A paper read at the International Historical Congress at Berlin, August 1908; published in *L.Q.R.* xxv. 53.

in fact the appointment of a committee is generally the first step of any number of English people gathered together for any new common purpose. Even legislative powers have been delegated to such bodies. Our code of civil procedure (for we have one, though we do not call it by that name) is the work of a committee of the King's judges. I shall have a word to say later about the manner in which the committee system has made it possible for those unique semi-official bodies, corporations as every one would call them till he discovers that they are not incorporated, the four Inns of Court, to perform their public functions in concert without abating anything of their individual independence. Here I shall speak from my own knowledge, and I may say at once that this will be the only original element in the present paper. For historical research, so far as I can judge, there is no remaining need, and little or no room. The records of Parliament and of the Privy Council are open to the commonwealth of letters, and they have been well sifted by leaders of historical and political science. Living scholars have presented the results with every possible advantage of both accurate and elegant exposition. I have no claim, for example, to add anything to the work of my learned friend Sir William Anson, or, to mention the latest and some of the best additions to our resources, Dr. Redlich, of Vienna, and Mr. Lawrence Lowell, of Harvard. My purpose is only to exhibit the known, I might even say the notorious, facts in a summary and continuous view fitted to bring out the importance of this particular organ in the body politic of England. Such a view may possibly be of some use to students of comparative politics living under other systems; and, at any rate, I cannot doubt that materials for fruitful comparison exist in abundance, though I have not the time or means to attempt anything of that kind myself.

We may do well to pause a moment on the word "committee." Conformably to its etymology, the primary notion involved is that of mandate. A specified business is "committed" to a certain person or persons to be dealt with according to instructions and authority which may be wider or narrower, expressed or implied. Originally "committee" was a singular noun, formed on the same model as "bailee," "lessee," "trustee," and many others, and, like them, having the stress on the last syllable. It is still so pronounced so far as it is applied to an individual: the "committee" of a lunatic's person or estate (answering to the curator of Continental systems) rhymes to "bailee," and this is the only example current in modern usage that I can call to mind. The corresponding active noun would be "committor," like "bailor," "vendor," etc., but I do not know that it was ever a real word. Commonly, however, "committee" is a noun of multitude, construed with a singular or a plural verb at will, and the genius of English pronunciation (often counteracted by a literary influence or reasons of convenience, but always at work in the language) has prevailed in throwing the stress backward, so that "committee," meaning a number of persons, rhymes to "pity."

If we seek the meaning of this collective name in living practice as it may be observed, we find that the composition and the functions of committees may vary without limit. Often a committee is formed by selection out of a large body which appoints it, and this is generally so in the case of committees administering the affairs of an association; but a committee is not necessarily either selected or elective. In cases where a committee is formed to conduct enquiries or arrange executive details requiring expert assistance, it is quite common to name certain persons in the first instance "with power to add to their number," thus making the body to a certain extent self-propagating. An elective committee need not represent one set of constituents only. Joint committees are found of great use for matters in which two or more distinct bodies, it may be railway companies or it may be wholly non-commercial institutions, have common interests. On the greater scale of world politics the Delegations of the Austro-Hungarian Empire are the most conspicuous example. The Hague Conference, again, is in the nature of a joint committee, though a somewhat overgrown and unwieldy one. Then the powers of a committee may be as plenary or as restricted as its creators choose to make them by the terms of appointment. An "executive" committee commonly has full freedom of action in all the ordinary business of the society which it represents. It is responsible to the general body, and may be displaced if it fails to give satisfaction, the situation being, to compare small things with great, not unlike that of the Cabinet with regard to the House of Commons. In some cases the constituent body does not retain any organic unity of its own, and, having perished in giving birth to the committee, leaves it quite independent. On the other hand, a committee may be appointed with strictly subordinate powers or for a strictly limited and temporary purpose; and many public or semi-public bodies have standing committees which are permanent, but whose functions are confined to the administration of special departments. Again, a committee may be empowered to determine and execute, or only to enquire and report for the information of the constituent body or its executive authority. Further, a committee with general powers may, and often does, delegate the study of special matters and the preparation of business connected with them to one or more sub-committees, by whose reports its final judgement and decision are informed. In non-contentious matters the reports of sub-committees are constantly received, adopted, and acted upon without question. Thus we may find among committees every degree of authority and activity from the highest to the least. Some committees encroach, and leave a mere nominal supremacy in their principals; others are idle and, unless they wholly perish for want of use, decline into mere names. The lowest state of all is that of a so-called "General Council" or "General Committee," such as commonly figures in the announcements and publications of the larger political, semi-political, scientific, and philanthropic associations. The only assignable reason for giving these incoherent and inorganic bodies the epithet of "general" is that they are never known to do anything in particular. As a rule they are not even formally summoned to meet. In fact they are nothing but lists of more or less well-known names selected from the members and supporters of the society for the purpose of making a moral impression on the public. To use the language of mediæval law, they are the *secta* of the real managers: but a suit "produced" only on paper. There is not much strength in a multitude of counsellors who are not consulted and committeemen to whom nothing is committed, but the practice is common and accepted. It seems to be accounted for by degeneration from the type of constitution in which an executive committee is associated with a large deliberative council, and that council does meet and determine questions of policy. Under such constitutions I have known the council to overrule the proposals of the committee; on the other hand, I have also known it fall into a condition of atrophy.

We find in yet another direction some approximation to the vanishing point of a committee's vitality. There is a class of not infrequent cases where a real executive committee contains an inactive element of nominal members entitled to attend, but not required or, in ordinary circumstances, much expected to do so. In few committees, indeed, are all the members equally active; but in some the non-effective ones are a considerable proportion, and they may even be a majority. Most busy Englishmen of the educated classes have at one time or another held such a position somewhere. The existence of these habitually passive members may be justified as affording some check on abuse of authority by a bare majority or an active minority; to be sure, a rather precarious one, but better than none in those cases where, for one reason or another, very few persons can be found to attend regularly to the business, and all the work is practically left in the hands of the chairman and the secretary.

Such is the versatile power of this administrative instrument as it presents itself in the unsought and rather unwilling experience of one English citizen, whose first impulse, for the most part, is to say *nolo delegari*. Its growth has been rendered much easier by the conspicuous absence of governmental requirements and regulations in every part of our public life outside affairs of State. We do not speak here of bodies having essentially the nature of committees which have become integral parts of defined legal institutions, boards of directors in companies established by special Acts of Parliament or formed under the Companies Acts, and the like. At the same time precedent and analogy may be found in English public law, taken in the strictest sense, for almost every one of the various applications of the committee system in our conduct of unofficial matters. As I have already hinted, there are two great committee-forming authorities in our Constitution, the King's Council and Parliament. It is needless to remind any student of English history that Council and Parliament themselves were formed by processes of specialising and reinforcement from the original Curia Regis. Again, the superior courts of Common Law might fairly be described, in their earliest stage, as expert committees of the Curia. Not till the seventeenth century did the indiscreet ambition of James I. provoke a positive declaration that the powers of his judges, once conferred, were plenary and not merely delegated, and the King could neither sit in judgement in person nor divert the established course of justice according to law. If the Curia Regis can now be said to survive anywhere, it is in the formal meetings of the Privy Council when the King in Council receives the reasoned reports of the Judicial Committee and makes them operative and final judgements by issuing Orders in Council following their Lordships' humble advice. It would not be profitable, however, for the purpose in hand to go back to the first beginnings. We may take the Council and Parliament as they existed from the latter Middle Ages onwards, and consider their activities apart.[1]

There is some reason to believe that the Court of Chancery, the source in later times of a branch of

[1] Mr. L. O. Pike has lately published a concise and excellent view of the evolution of public offices and departments, illustrated by a graphical chart; the point of view is that of a special student of the public records, but this rather increases its interest and utility (*The Public Records and the Constitution*, London, 1907: see *L.Q.R.* xxiii. 337). [Mr. Pike died in 1915.]

jurisprudence of the highest general importance, and yet so peculiar as to be little understood except by its own special practitioners, was first a Committee of the Council. One suspects, though I am not acquainted with any proof, a time of transition when the Chancellor administered the King's extraordinary justice with the nominal aid of two or three mute councillors, much as, about a century ago, the judicial House of Lords might consist of Lord Eldon and two or three lay peers who sat with him to make a quorum, and voted as he advised them on questions of which they did not understand the elements. However that may be,[1] the Court of Star Chamber (properly the King's Council sitting in the Star Chamber) was certainly a committee of the Council. It is interesting to note that it was reinforced by the addition of learned persons who were not necessarily members of the Council for any other purpose. This practice, if it needed confirmation, was confirmed by a well-known, but still not fully understood, statute of Henry VII., which it would be out of place to discuss here. I will only say that we cannot expect to know more about it than Bacon did, and Bacon's explanation is by no means complete.[2] There is no doubt that when Parliament abolished the Star Chamber it put some very bad history on its roll in the reasons assigned by the preamble. It does not appear that

[1] See now Prof. Baldwin's introduction to "Select Cases before the King's Council," Selden Society, 1918 (in fact 1920), in the light of which I incline to think the Chancellor's assessors, as long as he had any, were some of the King's judges.

[2] See Anson, *Law and Custom of the Constitution*, 3rd ed. ii. 71-74.

the Star Chamber was unpopular, or that its jurisdiction, though exercised through a procedure quite different from that of the common-law courts, gave rise to any serious complaint, until it was employed as an instrument of vindictive prosecutions on merely political grounds. But for this abuse, it might have had a long and useful history; it might well have given us improvements in our criminal procedure for which we have waited till the present day, and have been the parent of an adequate court of criminal appeal. As it was, the Star Chamber, together with its offshoots and satellites, including not only the Council of the North and its like, but the wholly innocent Court of Requests, fell once for all in the mighty fall of Charles I.'s personal government. Its jurisdiction was original, and therefore not analogous to the King's appellate authority over the tribunals of his possessions beyond seas.

That authority grew, as it were, from a grain of mustard seed. The King, as Duke of Normandy, was bound to do justice to the Channel Islands, and they were never included in the English system of government and judicature. In that function, therefore, the King's Council was not superseded by the English Courts, and its jurisdiction expanded, one may say automatically, as the Crown acquired more and more foreign territory.[1] It now goes round the world and covers British India, Australasia, and half the North American continent. The modern Judicial

[1] It is said that appeals to the Crown in Council from parts beyond seas date only from temp. Eliz., see 2 Macq. 620, *n.*

Committee of the Privy Council is in form a statutory creation of the nineteenth century, but the type was not new. As Mr. Pike has well said, "the machinery by which we work has not undergone any radical change of design." In this case Parliament regulated and fortified in 1833 a jurisdiction which had long been exercised through special and occasional committees; the post-Reformation Court of Delegates which dealt with ecclesiastical appeals after the Reformation, and was also absorbed by the Judicial Committee, has a separate history not material for us here.

The Judicial Committee, we need hardly say, is a real and active committee; but its habitual working members are only a fraction of its nominal list. Besides the nucleus of regular attendants, now practically identical with the learned persons who make up the judicial House of Lords,[1] there are some persons, such as former Indian judges, who are summoned only when their special kinds of learning and experience are required; some who are available at need, but as a rule occupied on other judicial or State employments; and some who are retired veterans and retain their membership only as an honorary distinction. The duty of seeing that the Court is properly made up at each sitting according to the nature of the business, colonial, Indian, or ecclesiastical, is performed by the Registrar. Here

[1] The House of Lords sitting judicially is not a committee or a select body, but the whole House. It has been declared only within living memory that peers not learned in the law, though they may sit, ought not to vote; and there is still no positive law to prevent them The Lords of Appeal as constituted in our own time are in strictness only a reinforcement.

we have something analogous to a feature which has already been mentioned as characteristic of many committees in unofficial life, the penumbra, so to speak, of some members whose attendance is not regular and not expected to be so, though they may sometimes attend, and others who in practice are incapable of attending at all. The Council still has some judicial or quasi-judicial functions which are not exercised by the Judicial Committee. When an application for the grant of a royal charter of incorporation is opposed by persons or bodies who conceive that the grant would be to their prejudice, the matter is argued before a special and occasional committee of the Privy Council, which, unlike the Judicial Committee, does not give the reasons of its decision. I have myself appeared as counsel before such a committee.

Passing from judicial to administrative business, we find that about the middle of the sixteenth century the King's Council was distributed into committees, as appears by a paper drawn up by King Edward VI. himself; the term used is "several commissions and charges."[1] The first-named commission was "for hearing of those suits which were wont to be brought before the whole board" (referring to the King's undefined prerogative of justice in the first instance rather than to appellate jurisdiction; the relation of this committee to the Star Chamber is not clear); the second "for calling of forfeits done against the laws" and punishing breaches of proclamations (this

[1] Burnet, *Hist. Reformation*, Oxford, 1865, v. 118.

committee was obviously quite distinct from the Star Chamber, and its functions appear rather inquisitorial than judicial); the third "for the State"—twenty in number, just half of the whole body; the King was to be present at their weekly meetings "to hear the debating of things of most importance," which would cover all "matters of the State" not assigned to any other commission. This may, perhaps, be regarded as anticipating in some measure Sir William Temple's plan of 1679, justly censured by Mr. Dicey on the ground that his Council of thirty was "too large for a Cabinet, too small for a Parliament." A fourth committee was charged with the supervision of judicial establishments and the revenues of justice, and an existing commission for the collection of Crown debts is mentioned. Some kind of small committee for "the bulwarks," *i.e.* land fortification, is hinted at rather than disclosed. It is specially provided "that these councils sit apart." Under this scheme little if anything beyond merely formal action was left for the Council as a whole to do. We are not concerned here to examine for how long or with what exactness Edward VI.'s instructions were carried out. They are important as showing that the method of dealing with business by devolution to committees was already familiar. Neither is it possible within the limits of this paper to enumerate the various committees of the Privy Council established at various later times for special and temporary purposes, of which the traces may be found in political history; I doubt, indeed, whether it would for any purpose be worth the labour. It is noticeable, as a matter of form, that to this day every meeting of the Privy Council at which the King is not present in person is only "a Committee of their Lordships." [1]

In modern times a remarkable example of what I have called the atrophy of committees has been afforded by the transformation of certain committees of the Privy Council into separate departments of executive government. Here we find, or might have lately found, a nominal Board including several high officers, such as the Secretaries of State; but "the Board is a phantom," [2] not meeting even for ceremonial purposes, and the President of the Board acts just like any Minister in sole charge of a department. Thus the Board of Trade is, in its full official style, though the shorter one has long been authorised, "the Committee of the Privy Council appointed for the consideration of matters relating to Trade and Plantations." The Board of Education, now transformed since 1899, was for sixty years the "Committee of Council on Education." The Local Government Board was doubtless framed more or less on these models, but it dates only from 1871, and was never a Committee of Council, though all its members are in fact Privy Councillors; it operates not through Orders in Council, but by rules and orders issued under its own seal.

On the other hand there is a Committee, commonly described as being an informal committee of the Privy Council, whose importance has greatly increased

[1] Anson on the Constitution, ii. 99 (3rd ed., 1907). [2] *Op. cit.* 194.

within living memory, and is still increasing, namely, the Cabinet. The description above mentioned is warranted by the usage of eminent writers on the law and practice of our Constitution; and there is no doubt that the Cabinet was in its earliest form a confidential inner circle, though not a regular committee, of the Privy Council.[1] But Sir William Anson points out that, as it now exists, it does not meet as a Committee of the Council and is not summoned by any of the Council's officers; the summons comes from the Prime Minister and purports to convene "a meeting of His Majesty's servants." Every member of the Cabinet is, in fact, a member of the Privy Council, and the formal reason commonly given for this is that the Privy Councillor's oath of office provides the indispensable obligation of secrecy; but it appears more likely that it is a mere case of historical survival, for we shall see that as highly confidential matters are handled elsewhere without any like sanction. Thus it seems that, properly speaking, the Cabinet is a committee of the leading Parliamentary[2] supporters of the Prime Minister's party, being Privy Councillors. It is created in a peculiar manner, as in form, so far as there is any form, it is nominated by the Prime Minister; there is no such thing as an *ex-officio* member of the Cabinet, though it is well understood that the holders

[1] For the history see Anson, *Law and Custom of the Constitution*, ii. 76 *sqq.* (3rd ed., 1907).

[2] A member of the Cabinet is not disqualified by not having a seat in either House, and Ministers of Cabinet rank have, in fact, been unseated for a time while in the Cabinet, but normally every member of the Cabinet is a member of one or the other House.

of certain great offices of State must, in fact, be included. Not less peculiar are the functions of the Cabinet; it is the real centre of executive power, and the origin of almost all effective legislation, but, having no place in the legal structure of the Constitution, it has no means of doing anything in its own name. Its resolutions take effect through the individual Ministers in charge of the appropriate departments, and, so far as executive acts are required, in accordance with the procedure of each department as established by custom or prescribed by Act of Parliament. In many cases an Order in Council approved by the King at a formal meeting of the Privy Council is the instrument; but the Cabinet does not report to the King in Council; the Sovereign himself is the only person outside the Cabinet who is entitled to be informed of its proceedings. For the resulting action, of course, Ministers are individually and collectively responsible to Parliament. The Cabinet, in recent times, has often appointed committees of its own number to consider departmental questions, in conjunction, if necessary or desirable, with Ministers who are not in the Cabinet, the legal advisers of the Crown, or others.[1] Some years ago there was a Cabinet Committee on Defence: it was freely rumoured that it hardly ever met; in any case very little came of its work, and it has been superseded by the Imperial Defence Committee to be presently mentioned, which is not a Committee of the Cabinet or of any other existing body. While the power of

[1] Anson, *op. cit.* 122.

the Cabinet has been largely increased by the democratic development of the parliamentary franchise and the consequent higher efficiency of party machinery within the last generation, its increasing number, now risen to twenty, seems to exceed that which is suitable for really confidential discussion, and some good judges think that a sort of inner conclave within the Cabinet itself must become not only at times (as it has often been), but permanently, the real directing power. In that event the true seat of government will be more difficult than ever to assign with any approach to verbal accuracy.

A remarkable addition to our consultative organs is the Committee of Imperial Defence, dating from only about the year 1904, and largely the work of Mr. A. J. Balfour. Its object is to advise the Government on such matters of preparation for war and strategic problems as touch more than one department. In some respects it is rather like and in others very unlike the Cabinet. Besides having no executive power in form, it has also no decisive power in fact; it is merely an advising body, containing, however, so many of those whom it advises that but little special communication between the Defence Committee and the Cabinet is required. For it "contains the Prime Minister" (who summons it and presides) "and . . . practically never meets without having the assistance of the Secretary of State for War, the First Lord of the Admiralty, the head of the Army General Staff, the head of the Army Intelligence Department, the First Sea Lord, and the head of the

Naval Intelligence Department."[1] Still this Committee has not *ex-officio* members any more than the Cabinet, and, strictly speaking, the Prime Minister for the time being is the only permanent and indispensable member. Unlike the Cabinet, however,[2] it has a Secretary who is a recognised and permanent official, and its proceedings are recorded in minutes. Again, the Prime Minister may invite not only Ministers of other departments when their departmental affairs are involved—including Ministers of the King's dominions beyond seas—or the law officers of the Crown when there are questions of international law, but any person whatever whose advice may in his opinion be useful; such, at any rate, is understood to be the view of Mr. Balfour, whose authority on the functions of this Committee seems to be the highest; and any person so invited is not a mere witness or assessor, but "a full member of the Committee for a particular purpose." Although the proceedings are highly confidential, it does not appear that any special pledge of secrecy has been found needful, and this tends to throw some doubt on the usual explanation of the necessity for every member of the Cabinet being a Privy Councillor. The Committee does not interfere with exclusively departmental details. Thus it would not discuss the merits of oil fuel for ships from a marine engineer's point of view, which is the business of the Admiralty,

[1] A. J. Balfour in House of Commons, August 2, 1904, Parl. Deb., 4th s. cxxxix. 619; and see cxlvi. 62, 156.

[2] Since the institution of the War Cabinet this cannot be said without qualification. See note at end.

but it might well consider any probable modifications of naval strategy to which extensive adoption of oil fuel may be judged likely to lead. Some fears have been expressed that the Defence Committee might encroach on the executive authority of the departments and enable Ministers to escape responsibility; but they do not appear to be well founded, especially when we consider that at least three responsible Ministers, including the Prime Minister, are, in fact, present at every meeting.

Both official and unofficial proposals have repeatedly been made for establishing a permanent organ of communication and discussion in matters of common interest between the several Governments included in the British Empire. It has been thought that the most natural and dignified way of doing this would be through a new committee of the Privy Council; but there have been sentimental objections (which I do not myself understand) to be set against this preference, and the example of the Defence Committee shows that there would be no difficulty in making such a consultative body both independent of the Privy Council and as elastic in its composition as might be desired. The Defence Committee could not, as one or two publicists have suggested, be expanded into a Council of the Empire, for the simple reason that it exists in order to perform definite and specialised work which a body with more general functions could not perform efficiently.

We have observed that the current description of the Cabinet as a committee of the Privy Council is open to criticism. It has also been called a joint committee of the two Houses of Parliament; but this is even less accurate, and for three reasons. A Cabinet Minister must be a Privy Councillor, but he may be without a seat in Parliament at the date of his appointment, though it would not be practicable for him to remain long without one. Again, the Cabinet is not chosen by the Houses of Parliament or either of them. At most we can say that the Prime Minister, who chooses the Cabinet, is indirectly chosen by the House of Commons. Lastly, "the King's servants" must be members of the party which commands a majority in the Commons, and if we are to consider the relative importance of the qualifications which have to concur, this is the most vital of all. On the whole, then, the Cabinet is a unique political formation; and in passing from it to the governmental functions of Parliamentary committees properly so called, we are passing to a quite different ground. It is not my intention, I repeat, to describe the constitution or operations of Parliamentary committees. There is nothing left to be done in that behalf; and, moreover, Continental observers have not failed to note how the procedure of the House of Commons has been the model, even in minute detail, for that of lesser deliberative bodies. Adding, for abundant caution, that this influence is by no means confined to official bodies, I will make one further suggestion. The practice by which the House of Commons assumes a kind of allotropic form when it leaves debate on principle for consideration of detail, resolving itself into a committee which includes all the members, and resuming its former character at will by putting the Speaker in the chair again and reporting to itself, is not the least singular part of our Parliamentary machinery, though its convenience is acknowledged.[1] It seems to me that it may help to explain the facility with which in unofficial life a number of persons in pursuit of some common object will constitute themselves a committee as the very first step—a "committee of the whole" in fact—reserving any real process of election or selection to be applied when they need an executive authority. Beyond this, it will be strictly within the limits of our subject to remind those who are not specially versed in the history of the seventeenth century—as the writer himself is not—that, in the brief period of experiments which filled the time between Charles I.'s final breach with the Long Parliament and the Restoration, the machinery of committees was adapted to the direct conduct of war and government, and on the whole with considerable success. This, with other inventions of the kingless days, was of course abolished at the Restoration, or rather ignored as never having had any lawful being. But we shall see that a strong and persistent memory of it was left.

[1] Committees of the whole House were developed out of standing committees by instructions that any member who chose to attend might have a voice. See Redlich, ii. 209 (Eng. tr.), and Prof. I. Franklin Jameson, of Brown University, Providence, R.I., on "The Origin of the Standing Committee System in American Legislative Bodies," *Pol. Sci. Quart.*, 1894, p. 245. The reality of the distinction has been illustrated in our time by the repression of a disorderly attempt to make a motion for adjournment in Committee of the whole House.

The King's declaration of war made it necessary for the Parliamentary leaders to devise new forms of executive government, for without the King's personal consent and sanction at every turn the old ones could not be worked. Committees were the instruments of the new method; they had long been known in the practice of Parliament, but now they were applied to various and unexpected uses. A committee of safety, being a joint Committee of the two Houses, was appointed for the general conduct of war and policy. After 1644, when it was reconstituted, its executive powers were comparable to those of a modern Cabinet.[1] Later, the Scottish alliance caused this to be transformed into the "Committee of the two Kingdoms," often called the Derby House Committee, from its place of meeting; after the execution of Charles I. it was superseded by a body called the Council of State (in foreign business *rei publicae Anglicae ordines*) formed by a curious process of nomination and selection, and not being designated as a committee. This body had committees of its own. Other Parliamentary committees dealt with special departments of the public service, mostly in their financial aspect, from 1642 onwards. They worked in concert with the Council of State, which commanded a majority in the House of Commons, and also with committees in every county representing the dominant party, and they had direct executive functions; thus for all practical purposes they were

[1] Gardiner, *Hist. of the Great Civil War*, ed. 1897, i. 307.

irresponsible and uncontrolled.[1] We have no great reason to be surprised when we find, in 1648, the controversial and somewhat eccentric publicist Clement Walker (a special enemy of the Independent party) complaining bitterly that these Parliamentary committees monopolised all government (*The Mystery of the two Juntos*, p. 4).

> Another ambitious aim of those Junto men is their device of referring all businesses of moment to Committees. For the active speaking men by mutual agreement naming one another of every Committee (or at least their confident Ministers) do thereby forestall and intercept the businesses of the House, and under colour of examining and preparing matters, they report them to the House with what glosses, additions, detractions and advantages they please, whereby the House (judging according to their report) oftentimes misjudgeth, and if it be a business they are willing to smother, the Committees have infinite artificial delays to put it off, and keep it from hearing, or at least from reporting. By this means the remaining part of the House are but Cyphers to value, and Suffragans to ratify what is judged by the said Committee.
>
> This usurpation of theirs is much helped by keeping the Doors of their Committee Rooms shut, and dispatching all affairs privately and in the dark: whereas justice delights in the light, and ought to be as public as the common air, it being against its nature to be chambered up and kept from the observation of eye and ear Witnesses.
>
> And by their examining men against themselves contrary to Magna Charta, they much enlarge their power.[2]

Even more naturally we find, some time later, that Clarendon, as Charles II.'s Chancellor, has

[1] For a general account of these bodies see Preface to Calendar of State Papers (Domestic), 1649–1650, ed. Mary Everett Green, 1875. No complete one is possible, as there were many whose order books were not preserved.

[2] Spelling modernised.

misgivings about putting the Treasury in commission. He thinks that commissioners are "fitted to execute all offices according to the model of a commonwealth, but not at all agreeable to a monarchy" (*Life*, *sub ann.* 1665 and 1667).

Further, the tradition of the Commonwealth committees appears to have continued part of the common stock of educated society till the early part of the nineteenth century. In 1818 Lady Susan O'Brien (Fox-Strangways) wrote in a series of notes on changes observed in her own time:—

> *Now* since the French Revolution the topic [politics] is universal. No man of any degree but reads, studys the newspapers, to form a creed for themselves. No ale-house club but meets to descant on the conduct of the Royal Family, or the Constitution. . . . Every parish has its committee to arrange something or other. No committee but call themselves gentlemen, thank their chairman [the innocent vote of thanks to the chairman which is the familiar conclusion of all public meetings], and ape everything of this kind in their superiors. At present (as once before) the kingdom is governed by committees. The consequences may probably be the same. (*Life and Letters of Lady Sarah Lennox*, Lond., 1904, p. 613.)

It is needless to point out that the consequences feared by Lady Susan did not follow. The connexion between the French Revolution and the Local Government Act which established parish councils late in the nineteenth century is somewhat remote, but in any case those bodies have not shown, so far as their life has gone, any marked signs of revolutionary activity.

We have mentioned the Parliamentary Committee of the Two Kingdoms. At this day one of the most important forms of committee work is that of joint committees enabling independent bodies to work together regularly. Now the legal profession in England offers a striking example in the government of the Bar not by two but by four distinct and formally independent powers, the Inns of Court. As a member of the Bench of Lincoln's Inn and of the Council of Legal Education, I have to be familiar with the joint action of the Inns as well as the internal affairs of my own, and it may be of some little interest to make use of this experience for the purpose of concrete illustration.

The four Inns of Court in London are ancient societies of advocates and students of the law. Resembling the colleges of our universities in many ways, they differ from them in being "voluntary societies" without any legal personality, and, what is more in point for us now, not being constituent elements of any larger body. They are allied but not federated. Nothing corresponds to the quasi-federal bonds of Oxford or Cambridge unless the reserved supervising power of the King's judges, never clearly defined and very seldom exercised, can be said to do so. Common traditions and custom, however, have kept the Inns as alike in type as one Oxford or Cambridge college is to another. The form of domestic government in each is a survival of mediæval republican oligarchy, the purest, I should think, to be found in Europe; for the Benchers recruit themselves wholly by co-optation from the barristers of the same Inn. Such a system is, of course, practicable only in a homogeneous community and under the unformulated but effectual control exercised by the professional *esprit de corps.* The result is, I believe, a governing body quite as representative as any scheme of election by the members of the Inns could make it. Within the oligarchic body so maintained we have a thoroughly democratic temper, aptly symbolised in certain festive ceremonies. If a Chancellor or Chief Justice has any special influence as a member of the Bench, it is by reason of his personal qualities and not of his office. Indeed, I am beginning to think that perfect democracy (or it might be more accurate to say perfect isonomy) is possible only within a happily constituted oligarchy. Such, in very brief outline (for I must not be tempted to digress farther), are the co-ordinate powers which within the last half-century have found it necessary to organise joint action without sacrificing their independence. That, I may add, none of them would do save under extreme compulsion. We have nothing to learn about particularism in the Inns of Court. I will add, likewise, to avoid any possible misapprehension, that the "other branch of the profession," the solicitors, have a separate organisation of their own in the Law Society, which, being of modern origin, is incorporated, single, and in some ways more efficient. Probably it was lucky for the solicitors that the old "Inns of Chancery" had lost their quasi-collegiate function, and for the most part degenerated into mere dining clubs, before the Law Society was born.

About the middle of the nineteenth century there arose a demand for a visible and uniform system of qualification for practice at the Bar. Why and how the ancient system had broken down after the Restoration, and practically nothing was put in its place for about a century and three-quarters, are questions I cannot enter upon here. So it was that in the year 1852, not after but before a Royal Commission was charged to report on the Inns of Court, those bodies appointed a joint committee to deal with the legal education of their students. That committee was and is the Council of Legal Education. Nearly twenty-five years ago I served it as a teacher in the Inns of Court; now[1] I serve in it as one of the members delegated by Lincoln's Inn. We are delegates with limited powers, not a federal council. The regulations we administer are made by the authority of the four Inns, and cannot be altered without the consent of all of them. The funds we dispose of are contributed by the Inns individually from year to year. There is nothing, in form, to prevent any one Inn from destroying the whole scheme by secession. But in fact we have lived to see a good many changes in larger political constitutions in every quarter of the world, and we show no sign of instability. When we desire an amendment in our regulations we report it to the four Inns, and if the general sense of the Council is clear in the matter the consent of the Inns is almost always given. Within our prescribed limits we conduct the

[1] [*I.e.* in 1908.]

examinations which admit the successful candidates to practise at the Bar, and provide instruction for all students who choose to avail themselves of it. Our ideals are not all exactly the same; on some points, if we discussed them, I believe I should be in a very small minority. But we represent on the whole what may be called the best average intelligence of the English Bar, and no representative body can, after all, do more. We know very well what is practicable from day to day, and our work is done with so little display or friction that few people beyond those whom it immediately affects know anything about it. Our names are to be found in the semi-official "Law List," but we have no direct communication with any outside authority, though some of the Judges are members of the Council, not as Judges, but as delegates of their respective Inns of Court.

A somewhat analogous body is the Incorporated Council of Law Reporting for England and Wales, which I have served as Editor of the Law Reports since 1895. Until 1865 the decisions of the superior courts were reported in a number of separate publications conducted as publishers' undertakings. One or two reporters were attached to each court and semi-officially recognised by the Judges, but there was no co-operation or common supervision. The bulk, expense, and dilatory issue of these "authorised" reports had become intolerable to the profession, and a committee appointed by a general meeting of the Bar recommended, after thorough discussion, that a uniform series of reports should be undertaken by a Council representing the Inns and the Law Society. Their advice was acted on with remarkable promptitude; the Council was formed as a joint committee of delegates; the new method was at work in the autumn of 1865, and since that time the Law Reports have been regularly issued under the Council's general direction, and their example has been followed in Ireland and in many jurisdictions beyond seas.[1] Gray's Inn, the smallest of the Inns of Court, held aloof for a time, even as Rhode Island stood out from the United States, but not for long. Nearly all the existing "authorised" reporters took service with the Council, and in about two years the old system was extinct. The Council of Law Reporting procured itself to be incorporated, but merely as a matter of administrative convenience. It is, if possible, even less of an official body than the Council of Legal Education. Most valuable aid is given by the Judges to the editor and reporters, but the Law Reports have no monopoly and claim no exclusive privileges. All I need say here of my own experience is that I find the Council a good master, and should be very sorry to have any more official character attached to my post or those of my colleagues. Observe that I say colleagues, for we have no hierarchical formalities. We are all comrades working together for the benefit of our common profession and learning, and I feel that my own share

[1] The first number of the Alberta [Canada] Law Reports comes to hand as I am finishing this paper.

in the work is successful just so far as I remember that I am only *primus inter pares.* We are responsible to the Council and to the Council only, though professional criticism is, as it should be, free both in public and in private, and often of great value. Of official precedence or rank there is absolutely no question, and I hope it may long continue so. There is a partial exception to our non-official character in the case of the reporters in the House of Lords, who are appointed by the House itself and not by the Council, but this makes very little difference in practice. In this almost informal fashion the development of the Common Law by judicial decisions, which is as active and, I believe, as sound as ever, is recorded both for present use and for posterity. These things may seem strange. Some of them, possibly, may seem hardly credible to some of our Continental brethren. I can only vouch for their truth.

It may not be strictly in order to draw a civic or political moral from facts which in a historical congress ought to be treated in a purely historical manner. But my attempt to do so will be so short that at worst it can hardly offend. *De minimis non curat lex.* Experience has shown, during quite three centuries of English life, that committees are, on the whole, the least cumbrous and the most flexible organs of almost every sort of common business and common interests. Like all human instruments, they have their weak points and their besetting risks. If it is too large, a committee may degenerate into officialism; if it is too small, it may be captured by a despot; in the latter case the evil is less. For in a society ruled by a small committee we can at least know who is master, whereas under a large committee, with fluctuating attendance and an inert majority, this knowledge is often hardly attainable except by those in the secretary's private confidence. If the secretary himself does not know, which is a possible though not frequent case, anarchy is not far off. Industry, vigilance, and judgement are needful in this as in other forms of civilised social action, if institutions are to remain efficient for their purposes. Nor is the part of tact and good offices to be forgotten, especially by chairmen. An engine without steam will not run at all, but it is no less true that without oil it will run disastrously.

Note.—Some time after this paper was first published the complicated history of the growth of the Cabinet and its relations to the various Committees of the Privy Council was fully discussed in the *English Historical Review* by Mr. Temperley, xxvii. 682, xxxi. 291, and Mr. E. R. Turner, xxxi. 545. It will be clear to any one who consults these valuable studies that there is nothing new in the process of a small confidential committee being increased in number till it becomes unmanageable, and its work being taken over by an inner conclave, at first informal and unofficial, whose members come, in Bacon's phrase, to sway all the business. It is not possible to add anything here about the War Cabinet and other innovations brought about by the exigencies of the late war, as to which see a parliamentary paper of 1918, Cd. 9005.

V

GIFTS OF CHATTELS WITHOUT DELIVERY [1]

In *Cochrane* v. *Moore*, 25 Q.B. Div. 57, the learned judgement of Fry and Bowen L.JJ. deals with a question on which there have been great differences of opinion ; namely whether a voluntary gift, without specialty and without delivery, of a chattel capable of delivery, be sufficient to pass the property or not. On a review of all the authorities, the Court of Appeal came to the conclusion that it is not, Lord Esher concurring for a distinct but consistent reason of his own. The result is to uphold the authority of *Irons* v. *Smallpiece*, 2 B. & Ald. 551, against later criticisms and decisions which have not followed it. There seems to be little room to doubt that this conclusion is correct. It is not stated in the judgement of the Lords Justices what is the precise effect as between the parties, or as regards third persons, of a parol gift ; neither is it denied that it may have some effect short of passing property. It may be worth while to point out that such an effect is possible, and seems to be indicated by some of the authorities cited.

On principle it would seem that where *A*, by word

[1] *Law Quarterly Review*, vi. 446 (1890).

of mouth, purports to give *B* a certain chattel, this will have the effect of a licence to *B* to take that chattel peaceably wherever he may find it. For it would not be reasonable for *A* to treat *B* as a trespasser for acting upon *A*'s expressed intention. The licence is no doubt revocable until executed, and may be revoked either by the communication to *B*, by word or act, of *A*'s will to that effect, or by *A*'s death (which was the case of *Irons* v. *Smallpiece*), or perhaps by *A*'s becoming insane. If without any revocation the licence is executed by *B* taking possession of the chattel, then, it is submitted, the property is irrevocably transferred to *B*. There would be great and obvious inconvenience in holding otherwise.

What is the position of *A* and *B* towards strangers before *B* has acquired possession ? It seems to be something like that of a bailor and a bailee at will. *B* has an immediate right to possession, revocable indeed at *A*'s will, but sufficient to give him a right of action against a stranger who takes the thing without colour of right. Whether he could bring trespass as well as trover may be doubtful. If his position can be put as high as that of a vendee entitled to immediate possession, trespass might well lie (cf. Sir R. S. Wright in Pollock and Wright on Possession, p. 188). And, as against a mere wrongdoer, there appears no good reason why this should not be so. However, trover at any rate would be maintainable, if *A*'s licence can be deemed equivalent, as against third persons, to a right to possession. The difference could now be material only in a prosecution for theft. *A*, not having parted with legal possession, and having a right to possession which he can make exclusive at his own will, is clearly entitled to bring either trover or trespass. It seems a correct way of expressing the result, though perhaps not the clearest way, to say that *A* retains the general property until the possession is changed by *B*'s execution of his licence to take the thing given, and that meanwhile *B* acquires an immediate special property by the gift. Or, in the words of the note in 2 Williams' Saunders, 90, "it may still be held that a donee, by a parol gift, acquires such a special property as to be able to maintain an action against a mere wrongdoer, though the donor may resume the thing given."

When we bear in mind that from the fourteenth to the seventeenth century the word "property" was constantly used without qualification where we should now say "special property" or "right to possession," we may find reason to think that the view now suggested, and maintained by Sir E. V. Williams, is by no means without authority, and will account for passages in the authorities which are at first sight obscure. Take first the dictum in Jenkins's Centuries, 3rd Cent., Case 9, which the Lords Justices cite without either approving or condemning it. "A gift of anything without a consideration is good: but it is revocable before the delivery to the donee of the thing given." Here "good" can, by reason of the context, only mean "good as against third persons," and, if read as a somewhat elliptical statement of the doctrine above proposed, the sentence becomes clear and consistent.

Then, going back to the *Year Book* of Henry VII. (21 H. VII. 18, pl. 30), we find Rede J.[1] saying, "If I give to a man my cow or my horse, he may take the one or the other at his election: and the cause is that immediately by the gift the property is in him, and that of the one or the other at his will." The Lords Justices seem to think this wrong, and it clearly would be so if the property ascribed to the donee were what we now call general or absolute property. But if we read property in the sense of right to possess, the sense comes out exactly in accordance with what has been suggested as being, on principle, the result of a gift without delivery. What passes by the alternative gift is just the right to take the cow or the horse at the donee's election. Questions might arise whether his election could be finally determined in any other way than by actually taking either the cow or the horse, whether he would be a trespasser as to both if he took both, and (if the gift were by deed) what would be the result of his failing to take either within a reasonable time. It is needless to consider these points now, as my only purpose is to show that there is no necessary confusion or error in the statement. Farther back still, in 2 Ed. IV. 25, Laicon said in argument, "Suppose I give to you my goods which are at York, and before you are seised of them a stranger takes them away, have you not a writ of trespass against the stranger? Yes, sir, for by the gift at once the property"—*i.e.* right to possession—"was in you,

[1] Not the Attorney-General, as supposed in the judgement of the Lords Justices as printed, 25 Q.B. Div. at p. 70.

and the possession by the writ is adjudged in you presently"—*i.e.* immediate right to possess is equivalent in this case, for the purpose of suing a mere wrongdoer, to possession itself. And to this the Court seem to have agreed; but they pointed out (quite rightly, as will appear to the learned reader, if he cares to examine the book at large) that it would not support the plea which Laicon had drawn in the case before them. It is certainly possible, as the Lords Justices suggest, that in these passages the gift is assumed to be by deed; but it does not seem at all necessary so to read them. In the view here taken, it would have made no difference to the points under discussion whether the gift were by deed or not, and there would be no occasion to advert to the distinction. In 7 Ed. IV. 20, pl. 21, it is noted, apparently as new law, that a gift of goods by deed is effectual without delivery, and can be avoided only by the donee disclaiming it in a Court of record.

In the thirteenth century, on the other hand, a gift even by deed was held to pass nothing without delivery; though the mention of homage in the passages cited from Bracton and Fleta show that the writers were thinking chiefly if not exclusively of grants of estates in land. But we know from Bracton that in his time a sale of goods did not pass the property before delivery. Bracton's law of sale is not Roman but Germanic, though in this point the Roman law was the same. And it is equally clear, as the Lords Justices observe, that in speaking of gifts Bracton was not copying Roman law, for he could not have overlooked the rule of the Institutes that a voluntary gift creates even before delivery a perfect obligation between the parties, though it does not pass the property. It may be mentioned that the reference to this point (25 Q.B. Div. at p. 66), though quite correctly expressed in conformity with the terms of the passage of Justinian's Institutes which is referred to, is extremely concise; and a reader ignorant of Roman law might be led to think that the effect of Justinian's legislation was to make a voluntary gift without delivery transfer the property itself. What he did was to make the gift irrevocable, entitling the donee to call upon the donor for delivery, but not conferring on him any real right as against third persons. Thus the law of Justinian is exactly the reverse of the common-law rule which, as I submit, was laid down by Edward IV.'s judges, and has not been overruled by any modern decision.

It will be observed that the discussion in *Cochrane* v. *Moore* deals only with one of several possible cases as regards the possession or custody of the thing given; namely that in which it is not already in the possession or custody of the donee, or of any third person. The other cases must now be considered. Let us first suppose the donee himself to have the thing. If *B* holds as bailee a chattel of *A*'s, it seems obviously required by common sense and convenience that, *A* being minded to give the thing to *B*, the declaration of *A*'s will to that effect, communicated to *B* and assented to by him, should pass the property without more. The case is by no means uncommon. *A* lends *B* a book which is much more useful to *B* than to *A*, and some time afterwards says or writes to *B*, "You will make better use of it than I should, so pray keep it." Surely this is enough.[1] And the rule must be the same if *B* is holding the thing as *A*'s licensee or servant, though in this case there will be a change of possession as well as property.

If the thing is held by a third person, it seems that the rules as to what amounts to "constructive delivery" in the case of a sale, for the purpose of satisfying the Statute of Frauds, will be applicable. Delivery will be complete, and the gift irrevocable, when the custodian either delivers the thing to the donee or agrees at his request made with the donor's authority, to hold it for him instead of for the donor. In the possible case of the like request being made by the donor, it would seem that the donee's general assent to the gift would be sufficient without his express concurrence in the request to the bailee or custodian.[2]

The actual facts of *Cochrane* v. *Moore* presented a case of the kind last mentioned (25 Q.B. Div. at p. 59), complicated by this, that the subject of the gift, not being the whole chattel, but an undivided share of it, was incapable of manual delivery. The actual decision (*ib.* at p. 73) was on the ground that, whatever view were taken of this part of the transaction, the plaintiff, who claimed under a subsequent bill of sale, was intended by the donor to take, and, being

[1] It is now decided that a gift to a donee already in possession needs no further act to complete the donee's title: *Re Stoneham* [1919] 1 Ch. 140.

[2] See now *Kilpin* v. *Ratley* [1892] 1 Q.B. 582, *Cain* v. *Moon* [1896] 2 Q.B. at p. 289.

informed of such intention, did take whatever passed in respect of the share in question, only as a trustee for the defendant.

In the case of *A* making a gift of chattels by deed to *B* and retaining the custody, it may be asked in what capacity he holds them before *B* claims delivery. It would seem that he makes himself a bailee at will, and that *A* and *B* have concurrent rights of action against any trespasser.

Where *A*'s chattel is held adversely by a third person without colour of right, it seems clear that *A* may authorise *B* to retake the thing as *A*'s servant, so far as *A* himself could lawfully retake it,[1] though *B* is not *A*'s servant generally. And it would seem that *A*, if so minded, may no less authorise *B* to keep the thing, when retaken, for himself. Brian C.J. seems, however, to have held that the owner out of possession had a mere right of action which could not be released by parol even to the person in possession. "The property is divested by the taking, and then he [the true owner] has only the right of property, and so the property and the right of property is not the same. Then if he had only a right this gift is void, for one cannot grant one's right": 6 Hen. VII. 8, 9, pl. 4, cf. 10 Hen. VII. 27, pl. 13, where Keble (a serjeant who never became a judge), arguing that the owner of a chattel can give it by way of release,

[1] *Blades* v. *Higgs*, 10 C.B.N.S. 713, goes very far in justifying forcible recaption; but the old law did not allow it, save on fresh pursuit. See Britton, ed. Nicholls, i. 57, 116, according to which the violent recaptor, though not liable to an appeal of robbery, was a trespasser, and lost his property in the goods.

without deed, to a trespasser who has taken it, was contradicted by Brian. Keble's view on this point seems to be allowed in Shepp. Touchst. 240, 241, where, however, it is possible that the word "give" is to be read as confined to grants by deed. Cf. Mr. J. B. Ames's papers on "The Disseisin of Chattels" in *Harvard Law Rev.* iii. 23, 313, 337.

I do not understand any part of the judgements delivered in the Court of Appeal to deny that a parol gift may be perfected by subsequent delivery or authorised entry into possession by the donee (I avoid the word "taking" as having a technical meaning in the law of theft), or that it may be effectual in a case where the donee is already in possession, or that delivery by attornment may be as good in the case of gift as in the case of sale. But if there were any passage conveying such a meaning, I should humbly doubt, for the reasons above given, whether it could be sustained.

The wisdom of the sort of people who sneer at what they call "academical" learning is well illustrated by the fact that Mr. Maitland's researches on Seisin, published partly in this *Review* and partly by the Selden Society, were turned to excellent practical account by the Lords Justices (25 Q.B. Div. at p. 65).

My learned friend Mr. H. W. Elphinstone,[1] with whom I have pleasantly and profitably discussed the subject at many times, allows me to say that he agrees generally in what I have here set down.

[1] Afterwards Sir Howard, *d.* 1917.

I ought to say that another learned friend [1] whom I have consulted declines to admit the first step in the argument, and thinks that the utmost effect of the parol gift, considered as a licence to take possession, would be to enable the donee to bring possessory actions against a stranger *in the donor's name* without objection on the score of maintenance.

[1] R. S. (afterwards Justice) Wright.

VI

HAS THE COMMON LAW RECEIVED THE FICTION THEORY OF CORPORATIONS?[1]

AN affirmative answer to this question may seem, at first sight, to be implied in much of the language used in various English books of more or less weight, and even in some utterances of persons speaking with authority in the full and technical sense of that word as used in English jurisprudence. I can think of no fitter offering to send our honoured master, Dr. Gierke, on the present occasion than an endeavour to show that this first impression, though it may be natural, is mistaken. The truth is, I believe, that we have to be careful to distinguish occasional borrowing of exotic phrases for ornament from the serious reception of a doctrine, and still more from admission of all its consequences. A classical example occurs in Blackstone's pious exaltation of the law of nature as superior to all human laws, obviously copied without reflexion from some fashionable Continental publicist. When he comes to the real business of the English Constitution this does not prevent him from laying down the omnipotence of

[1] From the Festschrift offered to Prof. Gierke for his seventieth birthday (Weimar, 1911): reprinted in *L.Q.R.* xxvii. 219.

Parliament in unqualified terms. And so in the present case my lamented friend, Maitland, was well within the limits of caution when he wrote: "For the last three centuries and more Englishmen have been repeating some of the canonical phrases" of the Fiction theory, "but Dr. Gierke would probably say that we have never taken them much to heart." English lawyers have never taken dogmatic theories of any kind much to heart. Our doctrines get settled either by a gradual process of semi-conscious consent worked out in the solution of particular cases, or by the development, in the same manner, of conflicting tendencies in professional and judicial opinion until at last a decisive practical choice is called for. Possession, for example, is still of the utmost importance in our law of property, and one would think that, among the questions which can arise in dealing with titles ultimately founded on possession, by no means the least practical and urgent was that of the Relativity of Possession,[1] as it has been called. Yet a definite and comprehensive doctrine on that point was first laid down by our Court of Appeal as late as 1897, when my former instructor, Lord Lindley,[2] then Lord Justice, did me the honour of adopting the words in which I had tried some years earlier to formulate the rational result of many authorities, often ambiguous and sometimes conflicting on the first view. We are therefore entitled to say that, if our Lady the Common Law does really

[1] The principle that possession *de facto* creates not merely an interest which the law will provisionally protect, but a right carrying with it all the incidents of a true title as against every one who can show no better right.

[2] *D.* 1921.

stand committed to any definite speculative theory on the nature of an artificial person, her condition of dogmatic beatitude is not normal but exceptional.

It must be admitted, I think, that a modern English lawyer who knew nothing about the controversy[1] would oftener than not be ready to accept *persona ficta* as the proper Latin equivalent of our accustomed term "artificial person"; either because it would not occur to him that anything beyond a question of words was involved (which appears to be still the state of mind even of some very learned writers), or possibly because he might not be familiar with the slightly archaic technical meaning of the word "artificial" itself. That meaning is certainly not "fictitious." It is rather "in accordance with the rules of art"—the lawyer's art, no other being in question—lawyerlike, juridical. A skilfully drawn deed is said to be artificially drawn; the work of a bungling amateur testator or incompetent practitioner is said to be inartificial. Thus it seems that the term "artificial person" in English does not in itself involve any controversial doctrine more or otherwise than "juristische Person" in German. More than thirty years ago, and before the publication of Dr. Gierke's great work, I ventured to protest against the assumption that an "artificial" person must be fictitious in the popular sense.

[1] Those who do know of it seem on the whole to favour realism. See especially Mr. C. T. Carr's concise and excellent book on the *Law of Corporations* (1905); "The Personality of the Corporation and the State," by Prof. W. Jethro Brown, *L.Q.R.* xxi. 365. Mr. Justice Salmond of New Zealand (*Jurisprudence*, 6th ed., 1920), adheres to the Fiction theory.

"Perhaps," I said in 1876, "we may call the artificial person a fictitious substratum or substance conceived as supporting legal attributes, remembering always that we must think of legal fiction as derived from *fingere* not in the modern sense of mere *feigning*, but in the sense of *creating* or fashioning. Nor would it be very difficult to show, were it not a matter of metaphysical rather than legal interest, that what we call the artificial identity of a corporation is, within its own sphere and for its own purposes, just as real as any other identity."[1]

When I so wrote I had read Savigny, and assumed his exposition to be authoritative so far as modern Roman law was concerned. I did not understand the practical importance of the consequences drawn from the Fiction theory on the Continent, and knew nothing of the mediæval controversies. In later revisions[2] I have made it clear that I hold the "realist" theory the more reasonable, and see no reason why an English lawyer should not adopt it. Whether there is any real authority to prevent him from so doing is just the question on which I propose now to say a little more than can be said by way of digression in a practical text-book. I have quoted my statement in its original form not because any special value attaches to it, but to show that in Lincoln's Inn, as long ago as 1876, a young lawyer still fresh from his masters and books was pretty free to think what he pleased about the nature of corporate personality.

In our search for authority, perhaps it will be the safer way to proceed backwards from the nearer and more known to the remoter and less-known materials.

[1] *Principles of Contract*, 1st ed., 1876, p. 81.

[2] 7th ed., 1902; 9th ed., 1921.

For as soon as we come to any decisive opinion, if ever we do, the stages lying beyond that will be matter only for historical curiosity; while the farther we go back without finding any such opinion, or any recognition of an earlier authentic deliverance, the less inclined we shall be to judge that the Common Law has dogmatised on the subject at all. No one who is familiar with the English judicial mind will be surprised at the scantiness of positive utterances on a question of this high order of generality. The nearest approach to such an utterance that I have found within our own time is twenty-one years old, and occurs in a judgement of the late Mr. Justice Cave, a learned and thoughtful lawyer. Counsel had argued that certain retired members of an insolvent building society were liable, notwithstanding their retirement, to contribute to the payment of its debts. The precise question turned on the interpretation of special enactments, the terms of which have no interest for our present purpose. But as to the general principles involved the learned judge said: "A corporation is a legal *persona*, just as much as an individual; and, if a man trusts a corporation, he trusts that legal *persona*, and must look to its assets for payment: he can only call upon individual members to contribute in case the Act or charter has so provided."[1] No such word is here as "fiction" or "fictitious," not even "artificial." It is true that no formal theory was before the Court at all: it is probable that Mr. Justice Cave was not thinking of

[1] 22 Q.B.D. at p. 476 [it is better now to give the actual date, 1889].

the controversy between fictionists and realists; it is possible that he had never heard of it. Still, do we trust a Fiction? and is a Fiction "just as much" a person as a real man? I do not know what inference a Continental jurist might be tempted to draw from the admission that an Act of Parliament or royal charter may displace the usual presumption, "Quod universitas debet singuli non debent." In this country there is no doubt since Blackstone's time, some would say since Sir Thomas Smith's, that the legislative competence of Parliament is unlimited, and there has never been any that the King's discretion as to the terms of the charters he is pleased to grant is very large. An English lawyer will therefore draw no speculative inference at all.

On the other hand, we may certainly find Lord Selborne saying in 1872 that a railway company "is a mere abstraction of law. All that it does, all that the law imputes to it as its act, must be that which can be legally done within the powers vested in it by law. Consequently a thing which is *ultra vires* and unauthorised is not an act of the company in such a sense as that the consent of the company to that act can be pleaded."[1] This might well have been said by a man with his head full of the Fiction theory, and Lord Selborne, who was a scholar, though not very learned in the antiquities of the law, may well have known something of the theory in its earlier forms. But the English doctrine of Ultra Vires, as we call it, does not really go back to any ultimate

[1] *L.R.* 8 Ch. at p. 152.

conception as to the nature of a corporate body. It is a doctrine, to use a convenient American term, of constitutional limitations. If the same authority which created a given juristic person, or authorised the constitution of many juristic persons by the performance of certain conditions, has at the same time set bounds to the legal competence of such persons, bounds which are matter of public knowledge, then acts professedly done in their name and exceeding those bounds are nullities. No English lawyer can question the power of Parliament (of the King without Parliament we do not speak for the moment) to impose such disabilities. The problem is at bottom one of interpretation, to ascertain what was the will of Parliament in the given case or class of cases. By the way, one writes nowadays [1] of the will of Parliament quite naturally, though Parliament is assuredly no corporation in the legal sense. Is that will a real or a fictitious will? If the Lords have amended a bill sent up from the Commons, is it the will of the majority in the Lords, the majority of the Commons, all the members who voted in both majorities, all the members who took part in the divisions, all the members who heard the debates, or the whole aggregate of members of both Houses whether present or not? But this is off our immediate question: only it would appear that in some sense "Imperium habet animum," Baldus notwithstanding.[2]

Now in the great case of the *Ashbury Company*, in

[1] In the Middle Ages it was hardly possible. See Maitland's note Introd. to *Memoranda de Parliamento*, p. lxvii.

[2] See Gierke, *Polit. Theories of the Middle Ages*, tr. Maitland, p. 70.

1875, the House of Lords finally decided that, as regards companies established under the general provisions of the Companies Act of 1862, the Memorandum of Association—(a public and registered document specifying the company's objects)—is a fundamental constitution or "unalterable law" which the company has no power to enlarge. Lord Selborne used more guarded language than he had done three years earlier: "A statutory corporation, created by Act of Parliament for a particular purpose, is limited, as to all its powers, by the purposes of its incorporation as defined in that Act." There is nothing here about "a mere abstraction of law." Lord Cairns, then Lord Chancellor, a much greater lawyer than Lord Selborne, based his opinion wholly on the policy and intention of the Act of 1862, and said not a word about the nature of corporations in general.[1] This was the end and summing-up of a long series of decisions of which it would be out of place to say more here. No doubt the Fiction theory, or something very like it, had been copied[2] by writers who

[1] *L.R.* 7 H.L. 653, 663 (Lord Cairns), 693 (Lord Selborne).

[2] Or even travestied. John Austin, an acute dialectician, but devoid of historical sense and seldom well informed or accurate in the details of either English or Roman law (though he had studied Roman law in Germany), supposed not only *hereditas iacens* but *praedium dominans* and *praedium serviens* to be fictitious persons (Lect. xii.). The former opinion was, I believe, accepted in 1832, when Austin wrote, but I have never heard of any warrant for the latter. Austin held, seemingly without knowing it, the extreme individualist rather than the fiction theory. Legal persons, he said, "are persons by a figment, and for the sake of brevity in discourse. By ascribing rights and duties to feigned persons, instead of the physical persons whom they in truth concern, we are frequently able to abridge our descriptions of them." I doubt whether any competent English lawyer would at any time have admitted this to be an adequate or correct statement of the Common Law.

had read a little Roman law, and through them had come into fashion among company lawyers. In 1850, *Grant on Corporations*, a text-book of learning and repute, had talked of "metaphysical existence," "abstraction of law," "the *ens rationis* called a corporation." Five years later Mr. Lindley, as he then was, a young lawyer who had studied Continental authors and translated Thibaut (afterwards Justice, Lord Justice, Master of the Rolls and Lord of Appeal), had written in an early edition of his book, now classical, on *Partnership and Companies*: "Corporations have no greater capacity than is conferred upon them by their constitution."[1] But this passage was afterwards altered into the different and much less dogmatic form: "*Trading and similar* corporations *which are created for certain definite purposes* have no greater capacity than is conferred upon them by their constitution."[2] Meanwhile both trading and other corporations have been held responsible *ex delicto* for wrongs committed by their agents and servants in the course of their employment to an extent which ought to satisfy the demands of any reasonable realist. A word must be said of this later. What we now learn, on the whole, from the history of the Ultra Vires doctrine is that in 1875 the House of Lords had an excellent occasion for formally adopting the Fiction theory, if its judicial

[1] Cited in the *Ashbury* case in argument in the Court below, *L.R.* 9 Ex. at p. 286.

[2] *Lindley on Companies*, 6th ed., 1902, i. 214. It may be worth while to note that the application of this principle is not confined to incorporated associations: *Amalgamated Society of Railway Servants* v. *Osborne* [1910] A. C. 87, 94.

members had been so minded, and in fact did no such thing.

We may now go back from the third quarter of the nineteenth to the third quarter of the eighteenth century, and see what Blackstone taught at Oxford and revised in the eighteenth chapter of the first book of his *Commentaries*, published in 1765. "As all personal rights die with the person; and, as the necessary forms of investing a series of individuals one after another with the same identical rights would be very inconvenient, if not impracticable; it has been found necessary, when it is for the advantage of the public to have any particular rights kept on foot and continued, to constitute artificial persons, who may maintain a perpetual succession, and enjoy a kind of legal immortality."

All practising English lawyers know very well that it is much more convenient and practicable to do without any formal perpetual succession or legal immortality than Blackstone professed to know. Maitland has fully explained this matter for the special use of Continental readers (*Trust und Korporation*), and it is needless to say more of it incidentally, save that Blackstone, a member and Bencher of the Honourable Society of the Middle Temple, must have strangely forgotten its constitution, or want of constitution, unless indeed it was his purpose to throw dust in the eyes of the lay people. Outside the Inns of Court, indeed, I know of at least one considerable modern association, the London Library, which has weighed the advantages and disadvantages of incorporation and deliberately decided in the negative. Maitland has already called attention to the still more remarkable case of the London Stock Exchange, and also to that of the Selden Society. Let us pass on, however, to Blackstone's words concerning men who are required or prefer to be incorporated.

> When they are consolidated and united into a corporation, they and their successors are then considered as one person in law: as one person they have one will, which is collected from the sense of the majority of the individuals: this one will may establish rules and orders for the regulation of the whole, which are a sort of municipal laws of this little republic . . . all the individual members that have existed from the foundation to the present time, or that shall ever hereafter exist, are but one person in law, a person that never dies: in like manner as the river Thames is still the same river, though the parts which compose it are changing every instant.

What is there about fiction here? Nothing. Is there any warning to the reader that he must understand the "one will" as a mere abstraction, or that the corporation of London has a worse claim to reality than the river Thames? There is none; and surely no man would have us believe that Blackstone regarded the Thames as a mere name of fiction for the locus of a certain volume of moving fluid. I will not go so far as to affirm that Blackstone would have explicitly refused his assent to the Fiction theory. But I think we may say that if he took it up at all he would carry it lightly. Still less would I venture to guess in what manner Blackstone would have applied his general ideas to the trading and industrial companies of our own times. With municipal trade gilds he and his predecessors were familiar enough.

There is yet more to come. Blackstone declares that a corporation, once formed, has certain necessary and inherent rights. "Necessarily and inseparably incident" is his language. He seems to imply that nothing short of the omnipotence of Parliament can prevent them from being attributed to their subject. Here Blackstone is closely following a passage in Sir Edward Coke's Reports which, notwithstanding this conspicuous repetition of its substance, appears to have strangely fallen out of sight in almost all the nineteenth-century discussion previous to the *Ashbury Company's* case. It will be better, therefore, to consider Coke's propositions in their original form; and all the more so because Blackstone's language, whether intentionally or not, is rather wider than Coke's. In so doing we shall be skipping about a century and a half; we shall skip the great controversy in the case of the liberties of the City of London, in which there was more of politics than of law, though we may refer later to one or two passages in that case; but we shall run no great risk of omitting anything important for our general purpose. The last three-quarters of the seventeenth century and the first quarter of the eighteenth were, broadly speaking, as barren in the development of purely legal doctrine as they were fertile in political invention and speculation. Between Coke, the last great lawyer of the Tudor age, and Hardwicke and Foster, the first of the Hanoverian, we mark a few commanding figures of men who have given us classical judgements or treatises; some of good and approved lawyers who never came to the Bench: Hale, Holt, Maynard, and Treby are such, but we may almost call them "rari nantes in gurgite vasto." It was a time of commonplace, indifferently learned, and not always upright judges, who were ill enough reported for the most part, but perhaps no worse than they deserved to be.

The case of *Sutton's Hospital* (afterwards commonly called the Charterhouse), 10 Rep. 23*a*, arose on objections to the validity of a charter granted by James I. in substantial pursuance of a special Act of Parliament, but with a variance of the site contemplated by the Act for the intended foundation.[1] Coke, who took part in the case as Chief Justice of the Common Pleas, thought the greater part of these objections "were not worthy to be moved at the bar, nor remembered at the bench," and no modern lawyer will hesitate to agree with him. They are formalist even to frivolity, and there is nothing to be said of them here. We are concerned

[1] The statement of the facts is even more confused and imperfect than usual in Coke's reports; he probably thought the details not material. The argument proceeded on admission of the facts as found by a special verdict in an action of trespass on a declaration in the common general form and a plea of not guilty; the verdict is set out in the record, 10 Rep. 1*b*. There was also, it seems, controversy about an additional benefaction given by Sutton's will (10 Rep. at p. 20*b*), and see further references in the life of Thomas Sutton in *Dict. Nat. Biogr.*, but Coke throws no light on this. It looks as if in the common report of the time there was some confusion between the charter and the will.

only with Coke's general propositions. He worked them into his report in his usual unsystematic manner, without making it at all clear how far either their matter or their form represents anything that was really laid down by the Court. But it is an accepted professional convention that whatever Coke deliberately says, in season or out of season, may be taken as good warrant for what was understood to be the law in his time, unless it is clearly repugnant to some other authority of at least equal weight; and on the whole it is a reasonable convention, though historical criticism is obviously not bound by it. "Now it is to be seen," says Coke, "what things are of the essence of a corporation." These things are, in brief: 1. "Lawful authority of incorporation": 2. "Persons to be incorporated": 3. A name: 4. A certain place: 5. Sufficient (not necessarily technical) words. We may pause a moment on the requirement of a name. English law was, in the year 1613, still in the archaic stage of looking at justice and judgement mostly from the point of view of procedure. Men are possible plaintiffs and defendants; they have to come, or be brought, before the Court in due form. When John Doe sues out his writ against Richard Roe, there will as a rule not be much doubt as to the persons designated: whether the right plaintiff has found the right defendant may be a grave question of practice or even of law, but is not to the present purpose. In special circumstances, however, occasion of doubt may arise. Richard Roe may conceivably say to the plaintiff who appears under the name of John Doe, "Who gave you that name?" and John Doe may have, metaphorically, to produce his godfathers and godmothers. He may succeed, or, like Arthur Orton when he sued in the name of Roger Tichborne, he may fail. Or the man on whom process is served as Richard Roe may say, "That is not my name"; or, peradventure, "I am not that Richard Roe but another." We are lax about these things in England: at this day John Stiles is no more required, or likely, to have an *état civil* in his pocket than were his Elizabethan ancestors. Nevertheless personal identity may be challenged, and if challenged must be proved, at need, in the old Germanic fashion by the witness of lawful neighbours. Now there comes a writ, let us suppose, in the name of the Governors of Sutton's Hospital.[1] Most naturally the defendant will ask: What kind of name is that? Thomas Sutton I know; few men have not heard of "rich Sutton"; but who are these nameless ministers of Sutton's intent? If they recover judgement against me, to whom shall I satisfy it? If they fail, from whom shall I get my costs? and if they are in mercy (though I have not to teach the King to look to his own) where shall the King's exchequer find the amercement? Clearly Richard Roe, a lawful man of flesh and blood, is entitled to know that he is not fighting with shadows: not to speak of the sheriff, who might demand a substantial nominative to the

[1] This is abbreviated from the corporate name actually given by the charter.

clause *si fecerit te securum* as long as it meant anything. Coke will give defendant, sheriff, and all others concerned their answer in a form which is not the less apt for being quaint, and is for once concise: "In this case Sutton as godfather gave the name, and by the same name the King baptized the incorporation" (10 Rep. at p. 28*b*). A little farther on we learn that other kinds of answer are possible and may be sufficient in law. The Master and Convent of St. Mary's Hospital at Bristol say they were incorporated by that name before the time of legal memory; the Master of the Hospital of Burton St. Lazarus says he and all his predecessors have always been so named (*i.e.* in pleading) and known; citizens may say, "The King has confirmed our franchise to have a gild merchant"; a college of priests may say, "Paulinus the first Archbishop of York founded us as a body of prebendaries consecrated to Our Lady, and that is admitted by divers records." That is what we call in the Common Law being incorporated by prescription; it is the beatitude of possession transferred to things invisible. "Nunquam viderunt aliter esse," as the men of Anglo-Norman inquests used to say. Moreover this is good to remember when we read, as we may, that it is an offence against the King to "assume to act as a corporation." King Henry II. might have fined us, perhaps he did, for having an "adulterine gild";[1] but if we have been let alone a few hundred years we shall be a very good corporation in the eyes of King

[1] Stubbs, *Const. Hist.* i. 418.

James I. Such is the law of England without question. It seems a law not easy to express in terms of the Fiction theory which some learned persons have supposed to be part of it, and which even Maitland was ready to believe we had nominally adopted. We have heard certainly that fictions may pass for facts on the strength of their antiquity. But it would be rather novel to say that facts, when they have existed long enough, become legal fictions, abstractions, *entia rationis*.

It appears then, in substance, that there are two possible and quite distinct methods of justifying what one may call corporate behaviour. The one is to say: The King by his letters patent which we produce, or the King in Parliament by a statute which is of public knowledge, has made us a body politic and corporate. The other is to say: Our existence under this name and with all the usual incidents of a corporation is ancient and notorious. In this latter case we may have to talk of a fiction, but it is a fiction of pleading which is equally well known in other cases of claims founded on long possession or quasi-possession: it is the fiction of a formal origin of title in the shape of a charter which has been lost. Such is the normal use of legal fiction, not, as the vulgar suppose, to escape from the truth of things, but to make room for it by the recognition of pressing facts. In form it may be, and generally is, transparent; but no one is expected to accept it literally. It may be, and often is, clumsy and circuitous; but so is much archaic and even modern procedure which does not involve any fictitious element.

Coke further remarks, again with his usual want of

any discoverable relation to the immediate context, that "three things were observed." The first is a solemn platitude about *prudens antiquitas*, and has nothing to do with any particular rule of law. The second is that no "prescript and incompatible"[1] words are necessary to create a corporation. The third is that when a corporation is duly created, "all other incidents are *tacite* annexed." Coke seems to regard this proposition as in some sort deducible from the last, but also vouches authority from a long fifteenth-century case in the Year Book (21 Ed. IV. Mich. 55, pl. 28), summarised in Fitzherbert's Abridgement (Grant, 30). Coke appears to go a little beyond Fitzherbert, and Fitzherbert a little beyond the book at large;[2] but this, as explained above, counts for hardly anything among English lawyers, and to us, as we are concerned with the opinions actually held by Coke and his colleagues, it does not matter very much. The real point of the earlier case (it would be too long to explain how) is the importance of avoiding variations in a corporate name, whether in the charter itself or in subsequent pleading; but over-nicety in that respect was already out of fashion at the date of *Sutton's* case, for in the same term it had been decided that variances merely *in syllabis et verbis* in a corporate

[1] Something seems to be wrong about the adjective "incompatible." The sense required is "indispensable" or the like. But whatever word the English translator of the report intended to use, it does not correspond to anything in the French of the original edition. The translation was first printed in the eighteenth century, but may have been made somewhat earlier.

[2] I rather suspect Coke of having purposely cited Fitzherbert's much condensed version as giving more ostensible support to his dictum than any one passage in the full report.

name were immaterial.[1] When Coke goes on to say that power to dispose of the corporate property is incident to incorporation, and if the charter provides (as Sutton's charter did) that alienation shall be only in a certain form, "that is an ordinance testifying the King's desire, but it is but a precept, and doth not bind in law," it does not appear that he has any specific warrant at all for the statement. Still it purports to be the unanimous opinion of nearly all the judges of England;[2] and though the words are doubtless Coke's own, there is no reason, in the absence of contemporary contradiction, to believe that he has perverted the substance. We know that some of Coke's expositions were excepted to by some of his colleagues as incorrect, or at least unauthentic, but this does not seem to be one of them. Indeed it is plain, so far as motives of policy had anything to do with the decision, that the Court intended to give a generous support and liberal construction to the charter in favour of a munificent and deserving foundation. Need we say again that this doctrine is wholly repugnant to the first and most important consequence of the Fiction theory, namely, that a corporation has only that capacity which is expressly conferred on it? or that the opposite doctrine last mentioned could never have had the vogue which it certainly did obtain during great part of the nineteenth century, unless the resolutions in the case of *Sutton's Hospital* had been forgotten? It is by no means clear, indeed, exactly how far Coke meant his

[1] The case of *The Mayor and Burgesses of Lynne Regis*, 10 Rep. 122*b*.

[2] See 10 Rep. at pp. 24*b*, 34*a*.

dictum as to "the King's desire" to extend, or to what extent it would be upheld at this day.[1] But what concerns us here is the fact that this opinion was confidently laid down in 1613. On the question of principle, the King certainly cannot confer on any subject any interest in property save one of those which are known and defined by law, nor, while he confers a known interest, add new incidents to it or deprive it of any existing one. In the fourteenth century the King could not have granted land to a subject and empowered him to devise the whole of it by will; at this day he could not restrain him from doing so; and for the same reason, that the expansion of disposing power in the fourteenth century would have been, and the curtailment of it in the twentieth century would be, contrary to the general law of the land. Let us now substitute a corporation for a natural person; can we say that an estate with a specially limited power of disposition is not really an estate unknown to the law, and therefore such as the King cannot grant? It is not that the corporation, as such, has any privilege in the matter, but that the King has no prerogative to alter the course of the Common Law in this more than in any other case. To that extent Coke's position appears to be sound. The worst that can be said about his manner of stating it is that he was still entangled in an inveterate habit of mediæval scholars which was far from extinct in the

[1] See the modern authorities discussed by Mr. Percy T. Carden, "Limitations of the Powers of Common Law Corporations," in *L.Q.R.* xxvi. 320. My present observations are founded on fresh and independent examination of the materials, but otherwise there is nothing new in them.

seventeenth century, the habit of thinking it necessary to produce some show of authority, however novel and open the question might be. In the same generation Grotius made a vast number of citations from both sacred and profane authors which were not more conclusive or relevant than Coke's. As to regulations not at variance with the law of the land, insertion of them in charters of incorporation is every day's practice, and no one doubts that they are binding, whether as an agreement between the Sovereign and the corporate body or otherwise.[1] But this appears to be merely a technical question of English law.

In the report of *Sutton's* case I can see no evidence that any of the judges or counsel showed any acquaintance with Roman law, classical or modern, civilian or canonical, beyond having heard of the term "universitas sive collegium." But it is certain that some five years earlier Sir John Davies was conversant with the canonists, as appears by citations both in the preface to his *Reports*, and in the body of that book. In particular, his report of the case of *The Dean and Chapter of Fernes*, "sive de capitulariter congregatis"(47*b*, 48*a*) vouches Panormitanus (Nicolaus de Tudeschis) as to the powers of a majority.[2] Sir John's

[1] For example, a member of a company incorporated by charter may sue to restrain the directors from acting contrary to the prescribed conditions: *Rendall* v. *Crystal Palace Co.* (1858) 4 K. & J. 326, 116 R.R. 349.

[2] It may or not be significant that Panormitanus was certainly not a partisan of the extreme Fiction theory. In the only work of his to which I have ready access there is a rubric, "Quomodo decernitur excommunicatio contra collegium aut universitatem"; there should be a sentence of interdiction first, and then it seems the head, or individual members, may be personally excommunicated if they persist in contumacy: *Judic. Ord. Processus*, Colon. 1555, 30*b*.

learning was of no common kind. If there was any like person among the judges or counsel who took part in *Sutton's* case, we may be sure it was not Coke. If any one had presented the Fiction theory to Coke and asked him to accept it, suggesting that the King of England's prerogative could not with decency be held inferior to the Roman Emperor's, perhaps Coke would have been willing to do lip-service to it. But I do not believe he would have understood the consequences, and if he had understood them it is not too much to say that he would certainly have repudiated them. Some approach to the current language of the civilians may be found at p. 32*b* of Coke's report, where it is said that "a corporation aggregate of many is invisible, immortal, and rests only in intendment and consideration of the law . . . they cannot commit treason, nor be outlawed, nor excommunicate, for they have no souls, neither can they appear in person, but by attorney. . . . A corporation aggregate of many cannot do fealty, for an invisible body can neither be in person, nor swear. . . ." But all that is involved here is the assertion that the juristic personality of the corporation is distinct from that of any or all of its members, and is not associated with an individual body capable of suffering corporal pain or imprisonment, or with an individual spiritual subject capable of sin and exposed to the censures of the Church. So much is allowed, and indeed required, by the realist no less than by the fictionist doctrine. Two pages farther on it is said to be true that none but the King alone can create or make a corporation (though, as

Coke explains, he can delegate his authority as to details). It seems at least doubtful whether Coke would have relished any such proposition as that the King, or the law, habitually creates fictions. Part of Treby's argument for the City of London, all but seventy years later, in the great *Quo Warranto* case, is little more than a playful variation on this passage of Coke.

> Suppose that they under their common seal should commit treason, and you bring an indictment of treason against the mayor commonalty and citizens of the City of London, what judgement shall be given against them in their corporate capacity? What? It shall be that "suspendatur per collum corpus politicum." And then, what execution shall be done upon that sentence? What? must they hang up the common seal? (8 St. T. 1138).

Observe, he does not say "delinquere non potest," but "suspendi per collum non potest," a very different matter. Treby's interest, of course, was to suggest every possible objection, technical as well as substantial, to penal proceedings against a corporation. The King's advisers, on the other hand, were prepared to go very far in ascribing both wrongful acts and wrongful intention to a corporate body, for they charged the City of London with a malicious and seditious libel. No general inference can be drawn except that there was no settled rule either way to prevent either argument from being plausible.

We may now try to sum up the doctrine as it appears to have been understood at the time, say about 1600, when the Common Law was settled in its classical form and became accessible in print. A body of men claiming corporate personality may rely either on express royal authority (much more on the authority of an Act of Parliament in which the King and the estates of the realm concur), or on ancient and continuous usage. When the existence of a corporation is established in either way, it is a person in law having such capacities and disposing powers as are compatible with an incorporeal subject of rights and duties. These capacities are attributed to it by the general law, and an express grant is not needed to confer them. On the contrary, they can be diminished only by express restriction. The King, or the founder with his assent, can prescribe internal regulations, but the prevalent opinion is that without Parliament he cannot substantially derogate from the corporation's right to do, by means of its common seal, all such acts in the law as a natural man may by deed, nor yet confer on it immunity from an ordinary man's responsibility ; the law will allow the limits imposed in both directions by the nature of things, and it knows of no others. How far exactly these conditions operate, to what kinds of actions and legal process, for example, a corporation is amenable, has to be worked out as particular cases arise. As to what the nature of corporate personality may be in itself, no positive rule at all is laid down. Most of these points could probably be supported at need by a good show of civilian though hardly of canonist authors. Nevertheless the whole does not look to me very like the work of men imbued with the Fiction theory.

Nothing decisive can well be expected, after this, from the Year Books, nor have I found any such matter by pursuing the usual clues. As to saying with any certainty what language may or may not be found somewhere in the Year Books, that is impossible to any ordinary human faculties, and will remain so until such time as the whole of them are critically edited and adequately indexed. In the meantime we may be thankful for the sixteenth-century Abridgements, and Brooke has a pretty full title on Corporations and Capacities. I do not pretend to have exhausted or nearly exhausted that title ; but from such examination as I have been able to make it seems to me that mediæval English lawyers were very like their descendants, and would not commit themselves on an abstract question in a general form if they could help it. They wanted to know what certainty in pleading was required of a pleader handling corporate names ; what remedies were in practice available against corporate bodies and their property ; how far the Court would take notice of the relations between a corporation and its individual members either for its advantage or for its disadvantage. It may be of some interest to give a few examples.

A condensed version of the material passages must suffice.

> 15 Ed. IV. 1, pl. 2 (A.D. 1476). Action of debt against Abbot and convent on a bond under their common seal. *Catesby* (for defendant) : This action will not lie, for this Abbot's predecessor compelled his monks by imprisonment and menaces to execute the deed. *Genney* (for plaintiff) : The plea is bad, Abbot and convent are

one person in law, and the head cannot imprison or threaten the body. LITTLETON J.: For some purposes they are one and for others not. If a monk commits felony he shall answer for it without the Abbot. BRIAN C.J. [a man of legal genius to whom justice must be done by some future editor]: This is no plea. If the Abbot and all the monks individually made a deed with all their names and sealed it with the convent's seal, it would not bind their successors for want of the corporate name. So the convent is not menaced or imprisoned though every one of the monks be so. *Catesby*: If my Lord's law is good, how shall the corporate assent ever be given so as to bind successors? LITTLETON J.: The Chief Justice's case is well put: the Abbot and convent can be bound only by their corporate name; likewise the Mayor and Commonalty of a town. BRIAN C.J.: A man shall not have a writ of trespass against the Abbot and convent, for the convent cannot trespass; nor yet against a Mayor and Commonalty. "Quod fuit concessum per totam Curiam." . . . LITTLETON: If the Abbot and a majority of the brethren willingly bind themselves, his successor shall not avoid it by alleging that the minority were imprisoned (*i.e.* constrained to agree by imprisonment: it is a question of avoiding the deed for duress). And, sir, in Parliament if the majority of the knights of the shire assent to making an Act, and the minority will not agree thereto, yet it shall be a good statute for all time; so in the other case. . . . [The parties went to issue on the question of menace.]

Brian's dictum agreed to by the Court looks at first sight like a strong assertion of the canonist view. But it must be observed that by no means every delict is a trespass. In the Common Law trespass involves physical interference; disturbance of possession or violence offered to the person. An incorporeal person cannot beat or imprison a man or break a close. We say now that both a natural man and a corporation may be liable for such things when done by their servants or agents, and even for wilful and deliberate wrongs if the wrong was committed in the employer's supposed interest, and the act was of a kind which in some circumstances it might have been lawful for the servant to do in the course of his employment. But this is nineteenth-century doctrine; in the fifteenth century the modern law of agency was quite undeveloped. Brian's view, namely that a writ of trespass would lie only against a natural and visible man who actually laid hands on the plaintiff or trod the plaintiff's ground, was almost inevitable at the time.

In another curious case of a dispute between a Benedictine house and the City of Norwich, which runs through many pages of 21 Ed. IV. (A.D. 1482–3), and is too long to extract, Brian seems to hold a rather different opinion.

> 21 Ed. IV. Pasch. 28 *a*. There is a difference according as the corporate name includes several names or only one. Here are three persons in the corporation, Mayor, Sheriffs, and Commonalty, and imprisonment of the Mayor is no imprisonment of the others . . . but if the Chapter of Ripon is incorporated by the name of Chapter, which is an entire body, and any of them is in prison, a deed made by them is wholly void.
>
> *Eod. anno*, Mich. 70. NEELE J.: This is a body politic made up of men like you and me, and if the head is cut off the man is dead. So if the Mayor, who is head of the body politic, dies, the writ abates. A grant by the Commonalty without the Mayor, or the Mayor without the Commonalty, is void. [But this is disputed.] BRIAN C.J.: It is no plea (to an action against the Corporation) to say that one of the Commonalty was in prison, but if

the majority are in prison it is good. . . . If the Mayor is wrongly imprisoned for a cause arising out of corporate affairs, the corporation, being disabled by the loss of its head, may have a writ of false imprisonment in the corporate name.

21 Ed. IV. Pasch. 31, pl. 28. Action brought by a Dean and Chapter. A juror was challenged for partiality, as being brother to one of the Canons. The challenge was disallowed and the case came up on a writ of error by a bill of exceptions. After a long discussion, HUSSEY C.J. of the King's Bench said that it certainly was a matter of partiality: "for the more the Chapter has, the greater the gain of the Canons," who are paid out of the capitular estates. The case was considered important and difficult, for it was adjourned before all the judges in the Exchequer Chamber (fo. 63). For our purpose it is to be noted that the whole discussion turned on the question whether the juror who was challenged really had an appreciable interest in the case. BRIAN C.J.: As to the point Vavisor (or Vavasour, a serjeant, and Justice of C. P. later) wants to make of a diversity between "Dean and Chapter" and "Mayor and Commonalty," say no more of that, Sir,[1] for no man here can perceive the diversity: "quod fuit concessum." Ultimately the challenge was all but unanimously allowed to be good.—It will be observed that the argument proceeded in the main on common-sense lines, and the speculative view that the Chapter has nothing in common with the Canons was rejected.

These samples of Corporation cases in the fifteenth-century Year Books do not pretend to be adequate, but I hope they are fair and typical.[2] I do not at all

[1] This is perhaps addressed to the opposing counsel; a modern judge would say: "Mr. *A.*, we will not trouble you to reply on that point."

[2] Hervey of Stanton is reported to have alleged, in the course of an argument on the franchises of Canterbury, that "comuna non est capax libertatis"; and denied that a corporation could claim a franchise without showing an express grant; *Eyre of Kent*, ed. Bolland (Selden Soc., 1910), p. 130. I have not yet been able to trace his supposed authority.

suggest that Brian or Littleton anticipated Dr. Gierke, but I do think that if they are charged with having saddled modern English lawyers with the Fiction theory, or any dogmatic theory whatever, there is good evidence to go to a jury on the plea of Not Guilty.

As for the question, "utrum universitas delinquere possit," our modern way has been to circumvent it. The real difficulty was to make out how any man, any natural man, could be vicariously liable to pay damages for the wrongful act or negligence of his servant, which he had in no way authorised and might even have expressly forbidden. When this was overcome, the difficulty of ascribing wrongful intention to an artificial person was in truth only a residue of anthropomorphic imagination. Fraud and malice, some learned persons continued to say, belong only to individual men; much as our Germanic ancestors could not conceive any right being transferred without a tangible symbol, and, as late as the fourteenth century, men thought the patron of a church insecure until he had solemnly grasped the handle of the church door. But those learned persons were already a minority half a century ago. The story is well and sufficiently told by Mr. C. T. Carr in his recent book on the Law of Corporations. My only regret is that he asks himself whether "the Fiction theory has been officially discarded." The time has come, I think, to ask whether any English Court ever officially or semi-officially adopted it, and I make bold to answer in the negative.

VII

THE TRANSFORMATION OF EQUITY[1]

EQUITY, *aequitas*, *ἐπιείκεια*, and equivalents in modern Continental tongues, have for several centuries been current terms among jurists and publicists. In England, and in jurisdictions beyond seas which took their law from England, Equity has become, by a peculiar historical development, the name of a special body of judicial rules administered in the exercise of a special jurisdiction which in its origin was extraordinary. Historical students of legal ideas have to remember that this technical use of the word "equity" is much less ancient than the jurisdiction itself. In the proceedings of the Court of Chancery before the sixteenth century the complainants appeal to the Chancellor most commonly in the name of conscience, pretty often in that of good faith, right, or reason, very seldom in that of equity.[2] Perhaps

[1] From *Essays in Legal History* (International Congress of Historical Studies, London, 1913), ed. Paul Vinogradoff, Oxford, 1913. The present paper may be taken as in some measure supplementary to Professor Vinogradoff's on *Reason and Conscience in Sixteenth-Century Jurisprudence*, read at the Berlin Congress in 1908, and published in the *Law Quarterly Review*, xxiv. 373.

[2] See Baildon, *Select Cases in Chancery* (Selden Soc.), 1896, Introduction. p. xxix.

it is not too much to say that the term was only becoming current among English lawyers when St. German discussed it in his *Doctor and Student*, a discussion to which we shall presently return.[1] In the course of the sixteenth century the Greek word ἐπιείκεια was used by a few writers in an Anglicised form (see the *Oxford English Dictionary*, *s.v.* "Epiky"), but the experiment was short-lived. Whatever words are used, the general notion underlying them is that of a doctrine or authority capable of preventing the hardship which otherwise would ensue either from the literal extension of positive rules to extreme cases or from the exclusion, also by a strictly literal construction, of cases that fall within the true intention of the rule.

Such being the purpose of equity stated in the widest terms, there are two quite distinct and almost opposite aspects under which it may be realised. In the first and more ancient of these we find equitable power exercised by some one, usually the king or a great officer of state, who can dispense with rules according to his discretion, conceived as a reasonable discretion but not defined beforehand. The other and modern form is the rational interpretation and qualification of the rules themselves by a dialectic and scientific process.

The first method works by occasional interference; the occasions may be frequent or not, but each interference is still an isolated act. The second

[1] St. German's immediate authority for the Aristotelian doctrine of equity was Gerson: Vinogradoff, *l.c.* 374.

method works, on the contrary, by continuous development. It is by this time almost a commonplace that the more archaic dispensing power, when it falls into a regular course of official administration, loses its arbitrary character and gradually assumes all the features of scientific law, becoming, as Blackstone said a century and a half ago, an artificial system. In the technical English terms, extraordinary jurisdiction ends by being ordinary. So gradual is the change that it is not altogether easy for the modern student to realise its extent or the discrepance of the original points of view.

Let us consider the nature of superior dispensing power apart from any particular forms. It appears to be called for and determined by the nature of archaic legal rules and archaic jurisdiction. Process of law was, in the beginning, a substitute for unrestrained private vengeance or self-help. For a long time there were no regular means at all, and for a much longer time no adequate means, of compelling parties to use it. Hence early legal formulas do not necessarily represent the general sense, at the date of their origin, of what is just and reasonable. They rather mark an outside limit beyond which vengeance or self-help will not be tolerated, and that limit has to be fixed with regard to the passions of ordinary men under provocation. The lawgiver does not advise taking an eye for an eye and a tooth for a tooth; he forbids taking the whole head. In like manner the harshness of archaic law towards debtors is capable of several explanations, and there may well be some truth in all of them. But this one, I think, is fairly certain, that the law had to compromise with creditors on the least amount of power over the debtor which must be left to them if they were to renounce the use of lawless private force. At the date of the Twelve Tables that amount included, in the last resort, the power of life and death, although there is no reason to believe that the *partis secanto* clause was ever executed in historical times.[1] In matters of family law we know that early Indo-European custom hardly touched the despotic authority of the eldest ancestor. Accordingly the just man, in the estimation of archaic morality, is not he who stands on his right and expects others to stand on theirs, but he who knows how and when to forgo the uttermost farthing: and, when once a competent executive authority has been established, the just ruler is he who gives effect to the moral sense of the commonwealth by relaxing penalties in cases of hardship and by putting forth his pre-eminent strength against enormous evil-doers. Such, indeed, is the prevailing sentiment in Eastern countries to this day. Great men and superior officials are conceived not as ministers of rule, but as wielders of a discretion transcending rule. Even educated Asiatics appear to have great difficulty in under-

[1] "Dissectum esse antiquitus neminem equidem legi neque audivi": A. Gellius, xx. 1. 52: his guess as to the original intention of the extreme penalty, "eo consilio tanta inmanitas poenae denuntiatast ne ad eam unquam perveniretur" is of course uncritical, but many modern antiquaries have made as bad guesses or worse.

standing that there can be such a thing as a rule not subject to a power of administrative dispensation in some one. A normal Eastern ruler would find nothing strange in one Pope treating Benvenuto Cellini as exempt from law and another subjecting him to rigorous imprisonment on mere suspicion, and would see nothing in the indignation roused by James II.'s prosecution of the seven bishops but one proof more that all Europeans are mad.

Not that it is an unknown thing in Western lands to sue for personal favour or indulgence unwarranted by rule, but the suitor, unless he is very ignorant, knows that he is begging for something irregular and hopes to persuade the man in authority, perhaps tries to persuade himself, that a small breach of duty will be venial. To find an European parallel to the normal Eastern attitude we must look outside the region of secular law to the popular and still half-pagan cult of the saints in the Mediterranean countries, where, as an ingenious French scholar has shown, the saints have taken up the heritage of the gods. There, to this day, patron and other saints are besought and expected, sometimes on pain of losing their worshipper's devotion, to perform a variety of good offices in the celestial court, often of a kind hardly in accordance with the doctrine or discipline of the Church. Among the more innocent of these favours is that of helping students to pass their examinations, for which it seems Ste. Radegonde of Poitiers has a special reputation. I know not whether the operation is in the nature of strengthening the candidate's brain (which the psychologist may regard as a not improbable effect of his faith) or of softening the examiner's heart. When it comes to invoking St. Antony of Padua to save a man harmless in a duel, in other words to protect him from the temporal inconvenience, and the still graver spiritual danger, of being killed in the commission of a wilful and deliberate mortal sin, the notion of dispensing power appears to be considerably strained. Such a votive tablet, however, I have seen, and I do not suppose they are hard to find in Italy. These archaic observances of imperfectly instructed Catholics may be regarded, it seems to me, as modern survivals from the prehistoric conception of executive authority in general.

To return to the ground of our own faculty, I took the *lex talionis* as a typical example of archaic positive ordinance, although it is strange to our own legal history: for the system of wergild and composition which, at the opening of that history, we find in force among all people of Germanic stock would not be appropriate for the same purpose. It seems to me to belong to a much later and more rational stage of ancient law, for it presupposes a long course of bargaining and settlement of feuds, not so much between individuals as between families and clans; and that again presupposes a more or less effectual desire for peace, not by way of submission to a ruler but by free consent of both parties. We know that such a process took place in the heroic age of Greece. The famous trial scene on the Homeric shield of

Achilles exhibits this at the very moment when public opinion begins to enforce the acceptance of a wergild under proper conditions.

Homer omits to tell us what those conditions were. This is unlucky for our archaeology, but quite right for the artistic purpose, which is to describe not the cause in dispute or the scene itself, but the representation of it. According to the interpretation in which I agree with my friend Dr. Leaf, the question is precisely whether an aggrieved party who refuses the offer of a composition is not bound to accept it: there does not appear to be any difficulty about the amount. The choice on the other side, the man-slayer's or offender's, to pay or to bear the feud, lasted into a comparatively recent period of Germanic antiquity, as is well known. On the Homeric development the curtain goes down abruptly, and when it next rises we are in a different order of civilisation altogether, with very slight materials for guessing what has happened in the meantime. In any case, and even before acceptance or offer of a composition has become compulsory in form or in fact, the existence of an assessable value shows that something has been arrived at corresponding to what we call a market price or a reasonable price in the world of modern business. Thus the wergild presents itself not as the utmost that can be exacted by strict law but rather as an early form of equitable compromise; and the fixed scales of the early Germanic law-books are really codification of a fairly settled customary rule of *aequum et bonum*. It might be shown, I think, without much trouble, that such a scale of compensation was in its time and circumstances a much more sensible institution than it appears to us at first sight; but to pursue this would be somewhat too remote from the argument.

In England the archaic form of equity predominated in the king's administration of special remedial justice during the fourteenth and fifteenth centuries; the sixteenth was a period of transition; before the end of the seventeenth the Court of Chancery was not only a regular court of justice but had started on the road of technical and scientific elaboration.

We have only within the last year become acquainted with a form of this jurisdiction earlier than its exercise by the Chancellor or even by the Council, so early that all remembrance of it was long lost. Mr. Bolland, in the course of editing for the Selden Society the proceedings of Edward II.'s itinerant justices in Kent, found a course of practice of which no intermediate mention is known through very nearly six centuries.[1] Causes of action arising or continuing while the Eyre was in the county were brought before the justices by presenting a bill instead of suing out a writ in the appropriate form of action. Many of these bills are preserved, and they have a marked resemblance in their frame, and in many cases as to their contents also, to the earliest bills in Chancery. To understand the jurisdiction

[1] 2 *Eyre of Kent* (Seld. Soc., 1912), Introd. p. xxi. As to bills on the Crown side, p. xxii.

it must be remembered that the justices in eyre represented the king's authority in a special and eminent manner. If we may borrow a canonical term, they carried with them high legatine powers; they superseded all ordinary tribunals. Only the King's Bench, the Court held in contemplation of law before the king himself, could claim[1] to rank above them. Thus the king's residual or extraordinary function of causing justice to be done where ordinary means failed lay in their hand, and they were not only entitled but bound to exercise it. Students of our legal history do not need to be reminded that this function had been recognised from the earliest times, and was treated as living much later. The witnesses for it extend from King Alfred's companion and biographer, the Welsh bishop Asser, to the Kentish antiquary Lambarde, one of Elizabeth's justices of peace. So the justices in eyre, being such exalted ministers of the king's power, were quite natural depositaries of this royal discretion when as yet the Court of Chancery was not.

Applications to the justices in eyre by way of bill were multifarious enough. Some of those which Mr. Bolland has published are founded on money claims for considerable sums, and the parties appear to be of good standing. But there is also a class of petitions by humble suitors for relief against oppression or extortion, alleging their poverty and inability to cope with their adversaries by regular process of law. This class anticipates, in almost every detail, the

[1] 27 Ass. pl. 1, cited by Willes J. 10 C.B.N.S. 22.

petitions to the Council and the Chancellor of which specimens were published in 1820 by the old Record Commission, and in 1896 by the Selden Society. We find here exactly the same characteristic mark that distinguishes those early Chancery proceedings, but in still greater prominence. In a large proportion of cases the complaint is such as, in the later settled practice, would have justified a demurrer "for want of equity." The justices are not called on to administer any special rules or to recognise rights outside the ordinary law. What the suitor asks them to dispense with is the formality of process; he claims a summary investigation, to use canonical language once more, *sine figura et strepitu iudicii.* Considering the predominant importance of procedure in mediæval law,[1] this again is quite natural. Sometimes the petitions are so illiterate that the manner of the halting Anglo-French is almost more eloquent of the petitioner's distress than the matter. A specially illiterate one, which gave Mr. Bolland and myself a good deal of trouble before we arrived at the true rendering by the help of a French mediævalist, relates the misfortunes of a man who had paid a sum down to secure board and lodging for the rest of his days. Obviously this crude makeshift for a life annuity[2] was at the mercy of the host's good faith; in this case avarice prevailed, and the host not only failed to make decent provision for his paying

[1] The "lex terrae" of Magna Carta, for example, is rather due process of law than the substantive law defining offences.

[2] Similar agreements were still in use in the latest years of the fifteenth century: Trice Martin in *Archaeologia*, lx. (1) at p. 378, where the complaint is of refusal "to fynd or kepe" the plaintiff.

guest, but imprisoned him, tied him up, it seems, with a chain. This, of course, was a plain trespass at common law, supposing the fact to have been as stated. Perhaps the story gained something in the telling ; at any rate the result was a settlement of some kind between the parties. We have said that there was no question, at this time, of applying any peculiar law to the suits initiated by bills in eyre ; but it does appear that the justices, when once they had a case in their hands, could proceed in a summary manner and use a pretty free discretion. They could even interrogate the parties, a thing unknown to common-law process. On the other hand, a case begun in this way sometimes runs its later course to judgement as regularly as if it had started with a writ ; and this may throw some light on singularities of early Chancery procedure to which Mr. Pike had called attention long before we knew that there was such a thing as a bill in eyre.

It is needless to say more here of Chancery suits in the fourteenth and fifteenth centuries, as the information is easily accessible in the Selden Society volume already referred to, and is summarised by Dr. Holdsworth. There is, however, one rather curious head of jurisdiction of which I have found no mention in text-books. It was not very uncommon to apply to the Chancellor for an injunction to restrain the defendant from practising witchcraft against the plaintiff, or, it might be, from making false charges of witchcraft against him. This appears from a group of cases in which clergymen were concerned, printed in 1907 by

Mr. Trice Martin in the *Archaeologia*,[1] as well as from the more generally known publications. If there was any usurpation of jurisdiction in matters of "nygromancy" it was against the Court Christian.

There is no reason to believe that the jurisdiction of the mediæval Chancellors was unpopular. Complaints began to be loud in the sixteenth century, and were heard of earlier.[2] But these were for the most part, if not altogether, made or instigated by practitioners of the common law who were aggrieved by the growing competition of the Chancery. If the competition had not met a public want it would not have been effective. What concerns us to note here is that the grievance was expressly founded on charges of arbitrary and uncertain interference with legal rights; the Chancellor and his officers went, it was said, by their "conscience and discretion," which might mean reasons borrowed from Roman law or anything else they chose. The only final and satisfying answer to such objections in a civilised country was to make it clear that the Court of Chancery was not a fountain of unlimited dispensations, but as regular a court of judicature as any other, a court whose existence precluded the king from setting up any new tribunals with like jurisdiction, or administering its remedies in any other way; and this was in fact the line taken by James I. with Bacon's advice when the conflict became open and official.

[1] Vol. lx. (or 2nd ser. 10) pt. 1, 353; cp. the same writer's miscellaneous specimens in vol. lix. pt. 1, 1 (1904).

[2] Holdsworth, *H.E.L.* i. 246.

Meanwhile Christopher St. German, a writer in advance of his contemporaries in many things, put an explanation of Equity in the mouth of his imaginary Doctor of Divinity,[1] and appropriately so, when it was still exceptional for the Chancellor to be a layman. The Doctor speaks, of course, from the canonical point of view, and does not profess to know Chancery practice. Equity is not yet a term of art among lawyers. The Student knows something, it appears later, about the cases in which the writ of *sub poena* does and does not lie, but does not care to go into details. Now the Doctor quite clearly takes the view that the fundamental principle of equity is not occasional and overriding interference, but enlightened scientific interpretation. I am putting St. German's thought into modern language, but I believe the words bear me out. "Equity is a righteousness that considereth all the particular circumstances of the deed . . . and it is called also by some men *epieikeia*; the which is no other thing but an exception of the law of God, or of the law of reason, from the general rules of the law of man, when they by reason of their generality would in any particular case judge against the law of God or the law of reason—*the which exception is secretly understood in every general rule of general positive law.*" Of these last words it is hardly too much to say that they anticipate the reforming and constructive spirit of Mansfield. The conception of Equity as expounded by St. German was in itself nothing new. He was quite openly following the scholastic tradition which

[1] *Doct. and Stud.* dial. 1, c. 16.

went back partly by direct and partly by indirect ways to Aristotle. But the treatment of it as practically applicable to English law shows a grasp and insight quite exceptional at the time. The Doctor goes on to suggest that there may be "some like equities grounded on the general rules of the law of the realm" and elicits from the Student examples of equitable construction applied within the common law itself. In the next chapter the Student goes so far as to say that the only reason why the equitable relief granted upon bills in Chancery does not count as part of the common law is the absence of a formal record in the king's court. "Forasmuch as no record remaineth in the king's court of no such bill, nor of the writ of *sub poena* or injunction that is used thereupon; therefore it is not set as for a special ground of the law, but as a thing that is suffered by the law."

About a century later the Court of Chancery was solemnly recognised as a perfect and regular court of justice. Yet it was not till the end of the seventeenth century that James I.'s decisive action bore its due fruit. The causes of the check were not legal but political, and are to be found in the controversies between king and parliament, between prelates and Puritans, which led to the Civil War. The Chancellor was still eminently the king's minister; his jurisdiction was practically uncontrolled, for there was no appellate Court; and men saw in the Chancellor's discretion, as they had seen in the criminal equity of the Star Chamber, a power of being abused to political ends. Here, and not in any merely technical prejudice, is the explanation of Selden's famous gibe, "Equity is a roguish thing." It is so because the measure of the Chancellor's foot may go too near to follow the measure of King Charles I.'s foot, peradventure even Archbishop Laud's: and so the fuller working out of equity on St. German's lines had to wait for the settlement of a free political constitution.

So far as England is concerned, the Puritan dislike of Chancery jurisdiction may be taken as belonging to the common knowledge of legal and other historians; and we know in a general way that it was carried across the Atlantic. The full extent of its working on the western continent has been disclosed to the learned world only by pretty recent publications of American scholars. While Story was setting forth the beauties of equity jurisprudence in his most elegant periods, the power of administering equitable remedies was still, in more than one State, altogether lacking or rudimentary. Traces of the old prejudice may be found even in much later American writers. We have to remember, however, that the Common Law itself found but little favour in the eyes of the Pilgrim Fathers and their successors. For a time it was in danger of being replaced by the Pentateuch, and its reception was precarious, even beyond the Puritan commonwealths of New England, down to the eighteenth century.[1] We have also to remember in extenuation that for some little time after the Restora-

[1] S. D. Wilson, "Courts of Chancery in the American Colonies," *Essays in Anglo-American Legal History,* ii. 779; Fisher, "The Administration of Equity through Common Law Forms," *ibid.* ii. 810; Reinsch, "English Common Law in the Early American Colonies," *ibid.* i. 369.

tion English Common Law judges themselves had not got clear of the old notions about equity, and wondered what it should have to do with precedents.

In our own time, it is almost needless to say, courts of equitable jurisdiction wholly disclaim any such roving powers of dispensation and administrative interference as were exercised by the mediæval Chancellors. A judge of the Chancery Division can in plain terms deny that his Court is a Court of conscience.[1] It would be beyond my present scope, and beyond my competence, to look for any similar process of transformation in other systems of law; but the case of *droit administratif* in France is so near at hand and so generally known that I may allow myself to mention it. The semi-political jurisdiction of the Conseil d'État, established under the First Empire in the interest of the Government rather than of the citizen, has by this time acquired a perfectly judicial character, and it is said that the result is at times better for the suitor than what he could look for under the ordinary law.

During the last two centuries the scientific construction of equity jurisprudence in England has been in the hands of a highly specialised section of the Bench and Bar, concentrated in these very precincts of Lincoln's Inn where we are sitting. Practitioners of the common law regarded equity much as the lay people regarded all legal science, that is, as an inscrutable kind of magic, and rather black than white. Even since the jurisdiction of our present Supreme

[1] Mr. Justice Buckley [now Lord Wrenbury] [1903], 2 Ch. at p. 195.

Court in all its branches has been made uniform this frame of mind has hardly become extinct, and there is still something esoteric about the doctrines of equity and conveyancing. The whole of the ground sacred to these mysteries would be included in a radius of five hundred yards, or for abundant caution let us say metres, drawn from this Old Hall of Lincoln's Inn, within or near whose walls the law of the Court of Chancery was discussed and settled by several generations of lawyers.

APPENDIX

A NOTE ON *SHYLOCK v. ANTONIO*[1]

THE law of Shakespeare commentators, among whom at least one or two might have known better, is a marvellous thing. Combined with their determination to take Shakespeare seriously at all costs, even when he is most comic, it has led them strange dances. In the present case they have failed to perceive the very first objection, which of itself is fatal, to seeking in this trial an image of either real or ideal justice. No court in the civilised world ever undertook to administer any such specific remedy as Shylock here demands. What if the penalty of his bond had been of the same kind, but free from any grave harm, such as that Shylock might shave Antonio's head? The Court would have said: "Then you may shave him, and if he brings an action for battery your bond will support a plea of leave and licence. Meanwhile you need no judgement, and we are not to help you to shave him, much less shave him for you. Demurrer allowed with costs." If Roman creditors ever did cut up a debtor (which

[1] 1914, *L.Q.R.* xxx. 175. The latter part of this note, which dealt with a learned contributor's suggestion that Shylock had no real intention of taking the pound of flesh, is not reprinted.

Aulus Gellius did not believe) they did so without aid of the Court. We need not consider whether the Shylock theme comes from some garbled version of that very clause of the XII. Tables, *partis secanto*, or is an independent folk-tale derived from a similar customary tradition. As it stands, in any case, it confounds two different stages in the development of law, those of sanctioned self-help and of judicial execution.

Waiving this objection, assuming the Court to have ample powers of amendment, and going as near the Shakespearian text as justice will allow, one might offer something like the following as an abstract of the proper judgement.

Declare the bond void at law. (No man can consent to be maimed except in the way of necessary surgical operation to prevent something worse. There is no question of equity in any technical sense.)

Judgement for the plaintiff for three thousand ducats and interest at the current rate, as on a simple contract debt.

But, tender of this having been refused in Court, costs to be paid by the plaintiff.

Plaintiff is in contempt for abusing the process of the Court, and liable to summary fine and imprisonment. His contempt is pardoned at the defendant's suggestion on the terms of making a proper settlement on Jessica. There might be a hint that the plaintiff was lucky to escape a criminal prosecution.

Now Shakespeare had picked up quite enough law to know that the Doge's procedure, prompted by the supposed Balthasar of Rome, was absurd from beginning to end. But if a young gentleman of the Temple or Gray's Inn, admitted by favour to a rehearsal, had said: "Master William, there never was a court in Christendom, save our Lord of Misrule's at Christmastide, would serve either Christian or Jew so, and you know it as well as I do," would Shakespeare have been put out? Not at all. I conceive he would have answered in effect: "My dear man, I am a maker of plays, not of law-books; I wanted a good scene, not justice. The people will think it plausible enough for what a Venetian Star

Chamber[1] might have done in old times. Judge it by the performance, and see if I carry it not so that they take it all for law and gospel." (Which they have done accordingly to this very day.)—" But, Will, what of Gratiano's gibe about the twelve godfathers, after Shylock has been condemned by the Doge without a jury? Will you justify that? Come, 'tis a scurvy jest."—" Why, in your ear, so it is. And yet, if you talk law by the card, the Star Chamber can fine and pillory a man, but may not hang him. But what? the groundlings' ears must be tickled, and my Jew must pass with them for a red-bearded villain, such as I took him from the Italian book. 'A grew in my hands, now, to a man, I can scarce tell how, till I could almost love him. Farewell, sir, Burbage calls me."

[Another vulgar error is to take Portia, posing as Balthasar, for Antonio's advocate. She is there as a judicial assessor, and speaks throughout on behalf of the Court: the appeal to Shylock's sense of mercy, being really a judicial warning that he will do better not to insist on the letter of his bond, but falling on deaf ears, is, apart from its eloquence, a fine stroke of dramatic irony.]

[1] If Shakespeare thought of any English court at all as analogous to the Doge's, it must have been the Star Chamber, which used civilian procedure (including interrogatories, see Portia's last speech in Act v.) and inflicted fines and corporal penalties without a jury.

VIII

ARCHAISM IN MODERN LAW[1]

LEGAL solemnities of all kinds are proverbially conservative. In ceremonial acts and observances, in necessary or accustomed modes of expression, in the "common forms," as we call them south of the Tweed, or "juridical styles," as I am learning to call them here, which embody so much learning, caution, and experience of human affairs, in the very outward garb of judges and advocates, one may find, sometimes plainly stamped, sometimes half effaced, the marks of ideas and customs that have long ceased to exercise any practical influence. It would not be difficult to collect examples of this kind on either side of the Border. There are few departments of law where some stubborn bit of archaic form has not stood out, down to times within our own memory if not to this day, like a pile of ancient rock, weathered and denuded, but not yet worn down to the level of the plain where men dwell and work. One of our very commonest English forms, used by thousands of people of every condition and every degree of learning

[1] An address to the Glasgow Juridical Society, Dec. 21, 1892, published in *L.Q.R.* ix. 271.

or ignorance, is the most venerable of all. The words, "With this ring I thee wed," take us back to the oldest Germanic laws and customs of which we know anything. The wedding-ring is not a mere symbol, it represents a vital condition of the contract. It is a *vadium*, a piece of a system in which there was yet no room for the more modern and subtle Roman doctrine of consent sufficing to form an agreement. Our Anglican marriage service dates, in all its essentials, from a time when a contract to be performed in even the proximate future could be secured, so to speak, only by an elaborate system of outworks in the way of surety and pledge.[1] Again, it is pleasing to compare the Northern *ultima ratio* against an obstinate denier of justice, whereby he was "put to the horn" as the king's rebel, with the "commission of rebellion," which formed a part of the old English Chancery process. While these forms existed as part of ordinary practice it might still be said that there was something extraordinary and almost mysterious about the king's justice. Besides the justice which was the common right of the subject, there was a power in reserve to overcome special obstacles and make an example of great offenders who trusted in their greatness to defy the law. When that horn of Scots justice was last really sounded I have not had time to learn, but its name brings before us the days when a whole jurisdiction lay within the compass of a horn-blast, needing no horn of Roland, but only

[1] See the Anglo-Saxon and later Continental forms appended to Sohm's *Das Recht der Eheschliessung*, Weimar, 1875.

such as the plain wayfarer might carry with him to proclaim himself an honest man and no roving cattle-thief. But, however tempting it might be to linger in this region of picturesque survivals, it is not exactly there that I shall invite you to spend this hour of professional diversion (for such are the diversions of lawyers), but among matters of antiquity that have entered more deeply into the substance of the law. Both in Scotland and in England we find inveterate archaisms either existing in rules of the law still in force, or having existed late enough to be set forth by the classical text-writers of the eighteenth century in the full light of their rationalising method. In almost every case it is or has been sought to justify such rules by more or less ingenious reasons of justice or public policy which certainly have nothing to do with the historical origin of the rules, and little, if anything, to do with the fact of their persistence in modern times. Those who rightly perceived that reasons of this kind would not serve nowadays have been apt, on the other hand, to assume that there never were any other reasons. Our ancestors have accordingly been credited with all but miraculous foresight, and charged with barely credible stupidity. Blackstone made them out a little lower than the angels, Bentham little better than the beasts. In truth, I should conceive they were not much better or worse, wiser or more foolish, than we who have come after them, so far as natural ability and good intentions went. Like us, they were pressed with manifest evils of divers kinds, and applied such remedies as their skill and knowledge could devise. Like us, they deemed their burdens greater than those of any former generation, and their inventions more brilliant and beneficent. I need not remind you, the fellow-citizens of my learned friend Mr. Neilson, who has made the subject of Trial by Combat his own, that Glanvill, celebrating the provision of the Grand Assize as an alternative for the duel, is as proud as any modern popular reformer. Like us, in short, our mediæval forefathers made laws and maintained justice as best they could, and when we consider how feeble were the powers in that behalf of any prince or commonwealth in Europe only a few centuries ago we shall be more disposed to wonder how they did so well than that they did not do better. Being mortal, they made their share of mistakes. Like us, they sometimes found them out in time, and sometimes not. Now and again they lived and died in the belief that the worst of their well-meant blunders were their greatest triumphs, and cheerfully left posterity to mend or endure them. Probably they were not unlike us in this respect also, though, by the nature of the case, we shall not know it in this world.

Before we come to examples let us endeavour to realise something of the general features of early Teutonic law. Conceive yourselves, if you can, living in a society where courts are held and judgements given, but the fruits of judgement are left for the successful party to gather by his own efforts. "Diligence" has not become in fact, any more than in name, a specific part of the order of public justice, and even the successful suitor must rely for the most part on his own diligence in the sense of that word which alone is recognised in common discourse. A man who wilfully and persistently refuses to do right to his neighbours or obey the dooms of the Court may be outlawed in the last resort, and dealt with as a public enemy. But great men and their followers will often take this risk rather than submit to an adverse judgement. In Iceland, indeed, we find at a comparatively late period that contending parties may take up arms and break from litigation into petty war at the seat of judgement itself. In Wessex, in Alfred's time, the pursuer of a lawful feud might lay siege to his adversary and deliver an assault if he held out after due warning. Law is not yet the active minister of justice, but rather a formalised voice of the popular conscience declaring to each man the point at which he may without blame use whatever power he has to do himself right. Form is not wanting, far from it. Procedure is elaborate and ceremonial almost in proportion as the direct authority of the tribunal is weak, and proof is as rigidly formal as anything else. Rules of evidence in the modern sense do not exist. It would seem, on the contrary, as if the ingenuity of early Teutonic sages had exhausted itself to avoid the responsibility of forming any opinion whatever on a matter of disputable fact. There is a prescribed way for a party to prove his case or to clear himself. If the fixed conditions are once satisfied, the proof is conclusive.

It may well be that our ancestors of fifteen or eighteen centuries ago would not have accepted any merely human and individual judgement in matters of opinion and belief. It is said that their descendants in the North of England do not always accept the decision of the umpire at a football match. Perhaps the ancient Germans acquiesced in what seem to us arbitrary and barbarous methods of determining an issue, not because they believed in them as guides to the truth[1] much more than we do, but because they could use no process that was not self-acting, and had no practical power of sifting facts. Perhaps the search after truth by any ordinary means of inquiry seemed to them too precarious and complex for the purpose of settling a judicial controversy where the result had to be made, above all, certain. At any rate there was no leading of evidence in the modern sense. Oath was not the warranty or sanction of a witness's account of facts, but an operative proceeding; it might be for the pursuer a necessary condition of his claim to be heard, for the defender (when multiplied by the proper number of oath-takers) a final and conclusive discharge. Most curious of all to modern eyes is the fact that the extreme technicality and rigidity of ancient laws is not the work of professional ingenuity; for there is not any legal profession. There are no trained judges, save so far as bishops and other clerkly

[1] There are distinct indications that the Lombard princes would have abolished trial by battle if they could; and the ostensible reason for introducing it was the prevalence of perjury.

persons in high places may have a tincture of Roman or Romanised learning; and as for advocates, there is so little thought of them as an established order that it is a matter of grave difficulty for any party to appear otherwise than in person.

What has just been stated is, to the best of my knowledge, a sober and unvarnished outline of such judicial institutions as were to be found in this island and the greater part of northern and western Europe about a thousand years ago. Now, let me turn (protesting, nevertheless, that I speak as a layman in Scots law) to the rules of criminal pleading in Scotland as late as the Restoration. I learn from a received text-book[1] that down to the year 1669 it was a principle of the Courts, evaded in practice only by shifts and fictions, that a defence contrary to the averment of the libel could not be allowed. An *alibi* was regarded as a kind of preliminary exception by the prisoner—panel, I should say—and at one time it was actually the practice to take the proof of this or any similar special defence before hearing the prosecutor. And this is Hume's explanation of the rule—"The notion of a conjunct probation of the libel and defences before the assize was thought too dangerous to be admitted. The prerogative of proving, and the choice of the witnesses, were to be assigned to one of the parties only; and on the evidence taken for him the issue must entirely depend." I do not pretend to know the mediæval history of the rule, and if I tried to investigate it

[1] Hume, *Comm.* ii. 297-8 (ed. 1843).

with an English lawyer's imperfect knowledge and appreciation of Scottish authorities I should almost certainly go wrong in details, if not altogether. But, as the thing stands at a time little more than two centuries back, it is a most striking reproduction of the archaic doctrine of proof which was once common to all Germanic law. Proof and evidence are not contentious, not a process of eliciting the truth by examination and cross-examination from the various and perhaps conflicting accounts of witnesses; they are as much one-sided acts of the party as pleading. The party who can first put himself, so to speak, in possession of the Court is in the better plight; for the other has no chance of interrupting him, and if he carries his proof through according to the rules the Court is bound to give judgement for him. If he fails in any prescribed point the Court must equally give judgement against him without regard to the general merits. The whole cause is staked on the issue of the party's proof, just as down to a much later time, in England, it might be staked on the issue of a single point of pleading, remotely, or not at all, connected with the real matter in difference. Quite in the spirit of this view we find that Hume expressly speaks of the *prerogative of proving*. A modern lawyer speaks of the *burden of proof*, and will be astute to find out as much as he can (which, in our latest English procedure, is perhaps more than he ought) of the adversary's intended proofs before he enters upon his own. Here, then, we have in Scotland, long after the Courts have taken upon themselves to brave the perils of a serious endeavour to arrive at the truth of disputed facts, the ghost of the ancient formal and single proof not only walking but giving serious trouble.

An ingenious young lawyer, Mr. Salmond, of the New Zealand Bar, has lately pointed out [1] that even in the latest civil and criminal procedure of the common law the old Germanic notion of judicial proof has left its mark. Trial by jury was, in its beginnings, only one possible mode of proof, and, like all archaic modes of proof, it was conclusive. To this day the verdict of a jury cannot in strictness be appealed from. I speak only of English practice, as that in which the functions of the jury have been most fully preserved. In criminal justice, where archaism is even more persistent than on the civil side, there is no remedy by regular process of law, but only through the pardoning power of the Crown, against a wrong verdict of guilty, and none at all against a wrong verdict of not guilty. The same rule prevailed for centuries in civil causes also, and was evaded first by devices of pleading intended to multiply questions of law for the Court, and leave as little as possible for the jury, and later by the method of ordering a new trial. The judges would not take upon themselves to reverse or annul a verdict which they thought perverse or due to a wrong direction given in matter of law by the presiding judge, but they could and would refuse to give effect by the final judgement of the Court to such a verdict. They

[1] *Essays in Jurisprudence and Legal History*, by John W. Salmond, London, 1891. [The learned author is now on the Bench.]

remitted the case for a new trial, and awaited the result of the whole operation being repeated with another jury. The parties might be saddled with huge delay and expense, but the sanctity of a verdict remained, in the latter, inviolate. At last, under the boldly innovating system of our Judicature Acts, the Court of Appeal has a discretion, though not an unlimited discretion, to give the final judgement which it thinks ought to have been given in place of ordering a new trial.

Again, there is one form of proof or evidence in constant use on both sides of the Border which bears pretty plain marks of its antiquity—I mean the deed or charter. It is not of Germanic origin; indeed, it is clerkly and Roman. Strictly speaking, it is as much an exotic as the methods of your Consistorial Court or our Court of Chancery. But it came in early, and had to be fitted into Germanic procedure while ideas of procedure were still rigid. The charter found its place accordingly as a mode of proof; and it was conclusive, not because it was a specially solemn or considered expression of the party's will, but because degrees of probative force were not recognised, and if admitted at all, it could be nothing else than conclusive. In the time of Glanvill, and of the "Regiam Maiestatem" which attests that down to the thirteenth century English and Scots law had not diverged from their common Anglo-Norman stock, writing and battle, *scriptum vel duellum*, are the two recognised final modes of determining an issue in the King's Court. A deed is not conclusive nowadays, but it still retains peculiar qualities and virtues derived from its earlier history. In England its operation is a kind of standing protest against our modern theory of contract, with which it stubbornly refuses to be reconciled. In Scotland you have been more faithful to the archaic type than we have. With us the attestation of a deed is only matter of habitual prudence and convenience; with you it is a necessity. But when you have got a properly attested deed, I understand that in this kingdom it proves itself without external evidence, whereas in England we have so far forgotten our old lines of judicial thought as to treat the execution of a deed as a fact which, unless admitted, must be proved like any other fact. On the other hand, we have stoutly retained the Anglo-Norman solemnity of the seal. It is true that the whole point of the seal in the twelfth or thirteenth century, and even later, was its individuality; so long as a man kept his seal carefully he was in no danger from forged grants. In modern times the seal has become an empty formalism, and its use has been generally dispensed with by statute in the American common-law states and in our English-speaking colonies. Perhaps we have indirectly derived some good from writing not under seal being left, as a thing of no solemnity, to find its place as best it could among common and modern transactions. Our rules as to the relative value of written and oral evidence are quite rational and fairly simple.

On the other hand, we can boast of having preserved in English criminal law one of the very oldest pieces of Germanic procedure, transformed and recast in the great constructive period of the common law. The grand jury is still an indispensable part of our system, though now scarcely more than a ceremonial one. Sometimes, in the case of a vexatious or hastily undertaken prosecution, it saves an innocent person the pain of a public trial. On rare occasions it may assume a semi-political office and ease off impending friction between the law and public opinion. I well remember one such occasion in 1867, after the Jamaica riots, when certain officers were indicted for murder in trying and capitally convicting the supposed leader of the rebellion under colour of martial law without any regular jurisdiction either civil or military, and on evidence which a Court of law could not have received. The late Lord Chief Justice Cockburn expounded the law to the grand jury with much learning and eloquence, and strongly in favour of finding a true bill. I heard the charge, and very impressive it was, though perhaps the Chief Justice's style and manner were open to the criticism that they were more forensic than judicial. In point of law I believe he was right. But the grand jury threw out the bill, and in point of fact I believe they were right too, for such was the prevalent public feeling, whether right or wrong, that a petty jury would certainly not have convicted, and the trial would only have prolonged a bitter controversy without vindicating any principle of justice. As a rule, however, the grand jury looks nowadays rather like a fifth wheel on the coach, and grave and learned persons have in the course of late years proposed more than once or twice to abolish it. For my own part I am inclined to think that such a measure would do no real good, would do some, though not much, harm, and would offend a far greater number of people than it pleased. At all events one would be sorry to lose, without strong reasons, so venerable a link with antiquity. For the grand jury may be said to represent, in substance, though hardly by direct succession, that accusation by the common report of the country which in the early Germanic plan of criminal justice was no mere ornament or safeguard, but a mainspring of the machine. Among the ordinances made at Wantage in Berkshire by Æthelred and his Witan for the northern parts of England, nearly nine hundred years ago, we find this provision—"Let a Court be held in every wapentake, and let the twelve eldest thanes go out, and the reeve with them, and swear upon the halidome put into their hands that they shall accuse no innocent man, nor conceal no guilty."[1] Now these twelve thanes are certainly different in many ways from what we now understand by a grand jury. The grand inquest representing the body of a county seems to date only from the fourteenth century. These twelve men represent a wapentake (as the jury of accusation under the Assize of Clarendon represented the hundred long afterwards), and it is by no means clear that the law and procedure of the ordinance in which they are mentioned is not Danish rather than English. Still, it may not be an idle curiosity

[1] Æthelr. iii. 3, Liebermann, *Ges. der Angels*, i. 228, cf. the plaintiff's oath in Schmid's ed. *Anh.* x. 41, p. 406, and the witness's oath (13th cent.) in *The Court Baron* (Selden Soc.), p. 77.

to compare the oath prescribed to them with that which I have myself administered on Circuit as judge's marshal, "You, as foreman of this grand inquest for our Sovereign Lady the Queen and the body of this county, shall diligently inquire and true presentment make of all such things as shall be given to you in charge or *otherwise come to your notice* touching this present service." Thus it is contemplated as possible that the grand jury may present offenders of their own knowledge as well as indict them upon the prosecution of some person, and in law there is certainly nothing to prevent them from doing so, though it has long been out of use. The form goes on, "The Queen's counsel, your fellows', and your own, you shall observe and keep secret. You shall present no man for envy, hatred, or malice, neither shall you leave any one unpresented for fear, favour, affection, gain, or reward." This is really nothing else in substance than an amplification of the oath appointed for those twelve leading thanes in the dooms of Æthelred. But what is still more curious is that the ampler form is really the older, for in a Rhenish ecclesiastical manual of the early tenth century we find, in a procedure evidently modelled on the Frankish royal inquests, that the jurors (so expressly called, it appears, for the first time) are sworn to conceal nothing from the bishop or his commissioner, "*nec propter amorem, nec propter timorem, nec propter praemium, nec propter parentelam.*"[1] Mediæval English forms are simpler, so far as they can be

[1] *Regino abb. Prumiensis de synod. causis*, etc., ed. 1840, 207; Brunner, *Schwurg*, 463.

traced.[1] We find in Britton a clause that the jurors shall not omit their duty for any love, hatred, fear, gift, or promise. In other forms there is only a promise to answer truly, and sometimes also to keep the King's counsel secret, of which "the Queen's counsel, your fellows', and your own, you shall observe and keep secret" is the modern equivalent as I knew it. As late as 1649 the form given in a compilation called the Book of Oaths is very short and simple. The longer form, which I have given from memory, was certainly the current one on the Western Circuit a score of years ago. There is also, I believe, a shorter form in common use, containing, however, all the same points in substance. It would seem that the fuller form came in soon after the Restoration, for the language cannot well be much later. I confess myself at a loss, at present, to guess how and where it had been preserved, or from what custody it was produced, when its phrases were restored to English use after an interval of some centuries. Perhaps it was a piece of deliberate antiquarianism; we know that the latter seventeenth century was an age of antiquaries. Probably enough different forms were used on different circuits, and possibly there may have been continuous precedents of the more amplified type in ecclesiastical proceedings. In any case we are sure of two things, and there is something to be learnt from both of them. Notwithstanding the singular resemblance of the oath

[1] *Oaths of the twelve knights before justices in eyre*, Bracton, fo. 116, Britton, i. 22, and the formula, "De sacramento ministrorum Regis" in *Stat. of the Realm*, i. 232.

of the Grand Inquest in its latest form, that to which I can myself bear witness, to the earliest English formula of a like sort, we cannot prove that the two are connected by any continuous history of English usage; the reappearance of these Carolingian clauses would seem to be not a survival, but a revival or outcrop, which may or may not be capable of complete explanation. The second point is that this, like everything else about the jury system, does not belong to the old Germanic folk-law. With the early Westphalian example before us we can have no doubt that the form as well as the substance is due not to the untutored wisdom of folk-moots but to the ordinances of Frankish princes, advised by counsellors whose learning was not Teutonic but Latin. Yet what a pretty story of the fidelity of English custom to primitive Anglo-Saxon usage might we not have made with a little dexterous and almost pardonable omission! We should only have had to minimise the Danish features of the ordinances made at Wantage, to manipulate the thirteenth-century evidence, making the most of Britton and the least of the other books, and to treat the form printed in 1649 as a transient innovation of irreverent Commonwealth men. As for the most fatal piece of evidence, the Westphalian instructions for an Episcopal visitation, it is quite a new-fangled thing for English lawyers, even if they profess a taste for historical antiquities, to wander off to Rhineland monasteries and discover how much business-like writing was done in the so-called Dark Ages. We have now seen how dangerous it is to put one's trust in coincidences between things remote in time and place without verifying the intermediate links. Let us pass to another example.

Our petty jury, corresponding to your assize, has a more archaic appearance in one respect. We do not accept the verdict of a majority, though in a civil cause the parties can accept it by consent, as indeed they can dispense with a jury altogether, a thing which was sometimes done on circuit even before the Judicature Acts. The principle that in the proceedings of assemblies a vote passed by a majority is binding, in the absence of more special regulations, appears venerable to us nowadays. But it is by no means immemorial. We read in Prof. Kovalevsky's *Modern Customs and Ancient Laws of Russia* that "the privilege enjoyed in our days by the majority was quite unknown to the primitive folk-motes." The decisions of the early Slavonic meetings were required to be, or rather to seem, unanimous; "in case of difference of opinion, the minority was forced to acquiesce in that of the majority unless it could succeed in persuading the majority that they were in the wrong." Dissentients might be fined or even beaten. The dissenting juryman, I need not remind you, is one of the stock figures in the humours of modern English procedure. He has been immortalised by a born Scot of whom both kingdoms are proud, by one of the few who could ever boast of having conquered him, by no less a victor and reporter than Thomas Carlyle. Is he indeed the true lineal descendant of the stubborn Slav freeman who was reduced to unanimity by being beaten with rods or thrown over a bridge? One is tempted to say so. But we have here, it seems to me, only another example of the temptations that have to be resisted in the historical study of institutions; and perhaps the example is all the better for occurring in a matter of no great importance in itself. To begin with, the jury is not a primitive or popular institution at all. It has nothing to do with a folk-moot, and it never became naturalised in the old local and popular courts. What is more, unanimity is not required in the grand jury, which is the older institution of the two. There is, indeed, an archaism in this matter, but an archaism of a different order; perhaps it is not less respectable in its way. We have to do with the sanctity of a particular number. Fixed numbers run through all customary laws, and, for some one or more of several possible reasons, we find twelve in special favour among our Germanic ancestors. Even duodecimal reckoning makes a certain place for itself in spite of the fact that we are born with only ten fingers. The long hundred of six score becomes an important factor in land measurement; it is the normal number of acres in the hide (if one will be content to accept the few precise and definite statements we have, rather than construct elaborate hypotheses from ambiguous data, and then reject the definite ones for not agreeing with those hypotheses). A man put to his oath constantly has to clear himself with the twelfth hand, that is, with eleven other men's oaths to back his own. So it came to be held, though not without hesitation and attempts to get an easier rule admitted, that in the oath of twelve men, and not less, a verdict should be established.[1] We know that people had no love for doing suit of court in the Middle Ages, and no more love for being jurors than they have now. The smallest acceptable number of jurors accordingly became the standard and only number in the petty jury from the first or almost from the first. Twelve men sufficed, but the verdict had to be the verdict of twelve, and therefore the twelve must be unanimous. And so they have to be to this day. The law discreetly knows nothing of the dialectic or other processes by which they become so.[2]

Now I take up a specimen of a different kind. It is almost painfully familiar to us Southrons, but for you it may possibly have some little novelty. Thanks to the sages of the law who flourished in the reign of King Charles II., we live under a certain "Act for prevention of Frauds and Perjuries," commonly called the Statute of Frauds. It has been said that every line of it is worth a king's ransom; and it is certain that not a few lines of it have cost some such amount to successive generations of litigants during the two centuries for which it has been in force. According to the recent research of the Dean of your Law Faculty here,[3]

[1] It was only in the first quarter of the fourteenth century that the necessity of the twelve concurring was taken for settled law (Thayer, "The Jury and its Development," *Harv. Law Rev.* v. 296-7). The method originally prescribed for the Grand Assize (Glanv. ii. 17) of adding new jurors till an unanimous verdict of twelve was obtained does not seem to have been extended. Cp. Christian's note on Blackst. *Comm.* iii. 376, whose criticism on this as on many other matters is remarkably sound, having regard to his imperfect materials.

[2] See *Owen* v. *Warburton*, 1 Bos. & P.N.R. 326, 8 R.R. 817—"The Court will not set aside a verdict upon the affidavit of a juryman that it was decided by lot."

[3] Richard Brown, *The Statute of Frauds in its relation to the Law of Scotland*, Glasgow, 1893.

the workmanship is mostly Lord Nottingham's. It does not seem to me to do that learned person much credit. Anyhow, I have always understood that you find life and business in Scotland pretty tolerable without the Statute of Frauds. One of the most important and constantly discussed clauses has to do with the sale of goods. A contract for the sale of goods to the value of ten pounds sterling or more is not "allowed to be good" unless one of certain conditions is satisfied. The making of "some note or memorandum in writeing of the said bargaine" is one of them; I have nothing to say of this at present. The others are as follows:—"Except the buyer shall accept part of the goods soe sold and actually receive the same or give some thing in earnest to bind the bargaine or in part of payment." What is the effect of this? It is a piece of fairly modern legislation, framed by persons who probably knew something of Roman law, and almost certainly knew nothing of Anglo-Saxon or any other Germanic legal antiquities. Yet what it does is just to throw us back to the mediæval Teutonic doctrine of sale, pretty much as we find it in Glanvill and Bracton. Indeed, the statement is not at all unlike Glanvill's. It expresses notions equally unlike those of the Roman law and of the modern Common Law. The contract is real, not consensual. Agreement on the thing to be sold and the price will not make a contract; there must be part performance on one side or the other, or at any rate "something in earnest to bind the bargain" must be given; not as part payment, which is quite another thing, still less as a fictitious or symbolic payment, but as the price of the seller binding himself not to break off before performance.[1] There is not the least reason to suppose that the framers of the Statute of Frauds were Teutonic enthusiasts or had antiquarian intentions of any kind. What they intended, probably, was to make reasonable allowance for the existing habits of English buyers and sellers as they knew them. Those habits had doubtless remained, among country folk, practically unchanged for centuries. Almost a century later Blackstone could speak of shaking hands to bind the bargain as "a custom which we still retain in many verbal contracts." But Blackstone seems to compare this with giving earnest. It really belongs to yet another branch of the history of contract, to the history of troth-plight, *affidatio*, the religious or *quasi*-religious obligation which, after first supplementing the meagreness of secular law, and then, in the hands of the Church, becoming a formidable competitor, was finally merged in the temporal jurisdiction.[2] And this brings us round again to the very ancient marriage forms of which I spoke at the beginning of this address.

The contract of sale, as explained by Blackstone in the passage I have just referred to[3] may give us

[1] In accordance with this conception, the *seller only* was bound by giving of earnest down to the thirteenth century, and then only to the extent of repaying double the earnest money. The buyer merely lost his earnest money if he withdrew. Fleta, however, states a much more stringent custom of merchants imposing a prohibitory forfeiture on the defaulting seller.

[2] Mr. J. H. Round has an interesting note on "affidatio in manu" in the appendix to his *Geoffrey de Mandeville* (Note T).

[3] *Comm.* ii. 448.

a little more food for reflexion. "As soon as the bargain is struck," says Blackstone, "the property of the goods is transferred to the vendee, and that of the price to the vendor." And a few pages above we read that when A. contracts with B. to pay him £100 he "thereby transfers a property in such sum to B.; which property is however not in possession, but in action merely, and recoverable by suit at law." Now Blackstone certainly knew as well as we do (and his own explanatory words would prove it if proof were needed) that A.'s promise to B. to pay B. £100 cannot make B. the owner of any specific money of A.'s. What then does he mean? He is simply true to the old principles of all Germanic law, which still underlie the common law and its remedies in matters of property, however much our modern language and habits of thought may obscure them. Blackstone thought and spoke in the terms of a system to which the Roman *dominium* was foreign. The leading idea of Germanic property law is not ownership, but possession and rights to possess. Glanvill talks, it is true, of *proprietas* in connexion with the writ of right, but what he means is the right to be put in seisin. Strictly speaking, the common law has no form of action which can be compared to the Roman Vindication. The claims to property which it recognises are founded on disturbance or denial of possession, and it arrived only by artificial methods at giving any remedy at all to an owner who had never had possession. It would require too much time and would take us too far into purely English technicalities to enter here on the proofs of this. But, whether the statement seems novel or not, the conviction of its truth has grown upon me steadily for some years, and I have no doubt that the ancient Germanic notion of *gewere* or seisin —possession warranted by law—is still at the bottom of our common-law doctrines. Refinements and expansions have come inevitably. When once you begin to protect and enforce a *right to possess* apart from actual possession you are tending towards *dominium*. We have refined in various ways on the right to possess—making it for certain purposes, by benignant fictions, equivalent to possession itself—until there remains about it little or no practical difference from ownership as conceived by a Romanised philosophy of law. Still the relation of the two orders of ideas is more like that of a hyperbola and its asymptote than that of two roads which, coming from different directions, ultimately coincide. I must give warning, in passing, that for my part I am not prepared to admit that our Germanic point of view is really less philosophical than the Roman. You will hardly expect me to draw any definite conclusion from these desultory instances. Perhaps we have seen enough to show that tracing the pedigree of legal ideas is ticklish work. The most tempting resemblances of modern to ancient forms are often fallacious, and ideas which are really of great antiquity may, on the other hand, lie comfortably concealed in modern terminology. One way and another there is a great deal of ancient human nature about man, and it does not forsake him when he determines to be rational and a lawyer.

IX

JUDICIAL RECORDS[1]

If you open the current *Law Reports* at a venture, you will see just under the names of the parties at the head of a reported case a collection of symbols like this—

[1912 H. 938],

which presumably conveys no meaning whatever to the lay people. This is what we call the "reference to the record." It is the key to the original and authentic documents containing the official history of every step taken in the action from the issue of the writ to the final judgement or other determination; a history which may cover a period varying from a few weeks in a matter of a simple money claim (though such cases, I need hardly say, do not concern the *Law Reports*) to several years if it is a complicated administration suit in the Chancery Division. For twenty years these originals are to be found in the vaults of the Royal Courts; afterwards they pass into the custody of the Master of the Rolls at the Record Office, where they are permanently

[1] A lecture delivered before the Faculty of Law in the University of London, February 26, 1913. Printed in *L.Q.R.* xxix. 206.

added to a series of judicial records unrivalled in the world for their extent, antiquity, and continuity. The selections of criminal and civil pleas which were among the first publications of the Selden Society contain entries of the year 1200. Through seven hundred years and more there has been change of many kinds external and internal; and yet no violent breach, unless the change from Latin to English in the eighteenth century be counted for such; but still change enough. An ordinary English scholar who knows classical Latin can no more read a judicial roll of our antique fashion than he could read a Hebrew roll of the Pentateuch, and an ordinary English lawyer would have but little advantage over him. First the script has to be mastered (and handwriting varied through the centuries, not for the better); then the business Latin of the Middle Ages, quite a living tongue in its day, very different from the Latin of the schools just because it was alive; and lastly the matter has to be understood. At this last lesson we are still working.

Conversely we may guess that a thirteenth-century judge, assuming him to have learnt modern English and to be reconciled to the innovation of printing, would be no less bewildered at the sight of our twentieth-century files. I am not so sure, however, that the guess would be right without qualification, for in some things the whirligig of time has so brought us round that we are much nearer than Blackstone was to our mediæval ancestors. If Henry of Bratton could be taken through the rolls of the subsequent centuries he might well shake his head at the stiffening technicalities of the fourteenth century, grumble at the flamboyant over-subtlety of the fifteenth, and cry aloud at the enormous verbosity of the sixteenth. When he came to the latest forms of Common Law and Chancery pleading in the eighteenth century—the time when Blackstone thought everything almost perfect—he might peradventure break out, clerk in orders and archdeacon though he was, into such oaths as are reported a little after his time in the mouth of Hervey de Stanton, nicknamed Hervey the hasty: "*Par le sanke qe dieu seigna!* if any pleader had tried to pass off such a heap of jargon on us, we should have said, and in rounder French than your English, that if he did not tell us something better in five minutes we should give judgement against him." The guide (whom we must suppose conducting the learned and Elysian author, not without aid of supra-mundane speed and ease, through a series of typical rolls picked out for his inspection in the Record Office) would explain with deference that nowadays pleadings are not settled by discussion in Court. "So much the worse," Bracton (to give him his conventional name) might reply: "all that writing with no prompt judicial check has spoilt your pleaders' common sense." Nor would he be wholly mollified by an account of the modern interlocutory proceedings in judges' chambers which have taken the place of the old dialectic passages between the Court and counsel, so far as the place is supplied at all. We may as well go on overhearing the conversation between Henry of Bratton and the twentieth-century lawyer; it may be the shortest way to realise that there were many modern points about the thirteenth century.

Henry of Bratton. Then I don't see where or how your young men learn pleading.

Guide. Well, sir, to be quite frank, they do not learn it; but then there is very much less of it to learn.

H. of B. How is that? Here is a roll of Queen Elizabeth before me, three centuries after my time, and so far I can only see that the tangle gets worse and worse. And such writing! we wrote a good business hand, both justices and clerks, and set no store by the fancy tricks of the papal chancery, though I had to know those too.

G. Truly, sir, I am no great expert, and yet I can make shift to read the rolls of your masters and companions; but I have known it three men's work to make out a roll of King Charles II.

H. of B. What was the Chancellor about that he did not amend these matters? It was his duty to keep the forms of the King's Court in order, so that the king might do true justice, as we read in some mighty pretty verses writ by John of Salisbury, who was a great clerk—but perhaps you have no memory of him?

G. Now I am sure you are jesting or trying to catch me out in ignorance. If you and your companions hear anything in Elysium you must have heard that John of Salisbury acquired a European reputation and was quoted by learned Italians as Policratus Anglicus; and our news travels slow if you have not yet heard that his *opus magnum* is excellently edited by an Oxford scholar with all the honours of the University press. But for the Chancellor, sir, there were stiff-necked folks who would not let him invent anything: it was so already in your time: surely you remember the Provisions of Oxford and the oath by which the barons tied him up? And so he had to get a jurisdiction and a court of his own, about which I suspect you know more than you let me see, and the proceedings, while they were never so formally precise as those of the Common Law, became even more long-winded and cumbrous, and quite as captious.

H. of B. So it seems, indeed. Here is eighteenth-century writing; it is from the time of my successor Blackstone, who had the advantage of using his mother tongue as a polished literary language, and so surpassed me greatly in form. But when you talk of mistakes in Roman law, now, you must remember in charity that Exeter was a very long way from Rome, and I had to puzzle out my Azo mostly by myself. Really I think Blackstone's dogmatic and historical mistakes about Roman law had less excuse than mine, for surely he might have consulted doctors of the Civil Law at Oxford.

G. Very true, sir, but I could show you one place where Blackstone was misled by a more learned man than himself, no less a man than John Selden.

H. of B. Certainly we are all fallible. Anyhow

my brother Blackstone was too easy-going when he tolerated this monstrous overgrowth of parchment.

G. Suppose we skip a century or so; you may find something to please you better.

H. of B. Why, this is printers' work; plain enough to me too, for it is not much unlike my grandfather's writing; and the pleader sets out to tell the story so that one can see at least what the suit is about; and most of the rubbishing jargon is done away with. But at Westminster they are still writing on parchment late in Queen Victoria's time, it seems, and their forms are only in part more intelligible. The Chancellor had got some way ahead of the king's judges—I mean the queen's. But what is this title of his that catches my eye at the head of a printed bill? Lord High Chancellor—of Great Britain.

G. By your favour, sir, he had been so for about a century and a half.

H. of B. Yes, I remember now, but the name of Great Britain is a strange mouthful to a thirteenth-century Englishman. We old fellows can hardly get over our surprise at the Bishop of Durham no longer being a great frontier chief, with the cares of a secular principality, and Scottish foemen to provide against. It was little I heard tell of Scots in Devonshire, but I met north-countrymen at the King's Court and listened to their tales of border feuds and forays. Well, the kingdom has grown out of all knowledge, and our children have played, up and down the world, the part of the *gens robusta et longinqua et ignota* foretold by Jeremy the prophet; I have heard talk of your judges having to learn strange heathen laws.

G. That tale is elsewhere, sir. Of the King's Council and what has sprung from it we can hardly speak now, for it is a long matter. Let us pass on to the latest records.

H. of B. Well done, young fellows; this is better still. I should not have thought you could clear yourselves of all those cobwebs, and make for the simplicity I was trying to attain in my own time. So you have got rid of the diversities of Courts, and restored our lord the king in possession of his one *Curia Regis*. Well done, I say again.——

G. Now, sir, let us go back to your old rolls for a moment. See here your own marks, which have been brought to light again in these latter days, in the margin of the cases you took out for your Note Book.

H. of B. A good sight; and better to see that book well handled and made free of the world of letters; and best of all that the work was done by a fellow west-countryman, almost a neighbour of mine.

G. I should guess, if it were lawful to guess, that you have already had right good talk with Maitland.

H. of B. My young friend—for even when your hair is turning grey you all seem very young to me—you shall not imitate the pleader who wanted to be *plus sage qe Dieux.* We may not report the matter nor the manner of our heavenly converse; and you would not understand it if we might. This visit of mine is exceptional enough of itself, such a thing as does not happen *nisi aliquando de gratia.* But you may salute for me the good clerk who found my book, Paul the son of Gabriel whom Oxford has captured from the far land of Muscovy. . . .

When that guide awoke he felt certain pricks of conscience, wondering whether he ought to have produced the Rules of Court and the White Book, and how far Henry of Bratton's approval of our simplified pleading might be damped by the contemplation thereof. But it is certain in any case that the White Book is not of record; and therewith his conscience was pacified.

This imaginary dialogue, which might be indefinitely extended, may serve as well as any other device to recall to us in a summary way what an immense amount of legal and political history the records of our courts have embodied, and the fact that for much of it they are the real ultimate authority. I will mention here a little technical point for the sake of any student who may be puzzled by it, as I was for a time. Sir G. Jessel once committed himself to the statement that the Court of Chancery was not a court of record.[1] The only reason he gave was that the records were in the custody not of the Chancellor but of the Master of the Rolls. The statement is directly contrary to Blackstone's,[2] and, with great respect, the reason is doubly wrong. First, according to general understanding and practice the Master of the Rolls was only the Chancellor's

[1] *L.R.* 20 Eq. at p. 347.

[2] *Comm* i. 68.

deputy, though this was not free from controversy. Secondly, the decisive mark of a court of record, according to Coke's opinion given in two places, is not that the judges of the Court keep the record, but that the record itself is the only authentic and conclusive proof of what the Court has done. It is a minute question, for nobody doubted the power of the Court of Chancery, but still worth clearing up. Coke might just possibly have denied the name of a court of record to the Court of Chancery in its equitable jurisdiction on the ground that its procedure was not according to the course of the common law. This would obviously not apply to the functions of the Court in the issue of writs and the like, as *officina iustitiae*, or as holding pleas in its "ordinary" legal jurisdiction.[1] He might also have taken the still more technical exception that the Chancery proceedings were not entered in Latin on a parchment roll like those of the Common Law Courts.[2] Both these reasons would have involved an equal refusal to call the Star Chamber, a very exalted Court according to Coke's own statement in the Fourth Institute, a court of record. In point of fact I do not find that Coke said or suggested any such thing with regard either to the Star Chamber or to the Court of Chancery.

We have lived so long with our unique wealth of documents that we take it as a matter of course and

[1] Bl. *Comm.* iii. 48, 49.

[2] St. German seems to have thought the difference merely technical, *Doct. and Stud.* 1, c. 17. Lord Langdale doubted, see *First Report of the Commission on Public Records*, 1912, pt. 2, p. 10.

fail to be duly thankful for it. Let us consider for a moment the state of modern Romanists, and what they would give for a tithe of our resources. Many scores of learned volumes have been written about the procedure of republican and early imperial Roman law. No small amount of what had been written before the nineteenth century was rendered obsolete when the Verona palimpsest of Gaius gave up so much of his buried text as could be painfully revived. But how much greater would our enlightenment be if we could recover a complete record of the proceedings in a single action under the formulary system. It is hardly uncharitable to suppose that about three-quarters of the learned monographs would lose their importance, be it greater or less. Reports of Roman forensic oratory we have, and at great length; but they are insufficient not only because Roman advocates, it seems, allowed themselves great latitude in deliberately talking bad law to an unlearned court, but because their speeches assumed the very things to be known which the modern Romanist does not know and would like to find out. Not that the official record alone, in any system I have heard of, would tell us the whole practice. But a report alone, official or unofficial, will even less enable us to understand the whole matter without authentic knowledge of the formal procedure. Our experience with the Year Books has given ample proof that in the case of a report made by private enterprise the record is of the utmost value as a check. I say private enterprise, for, with all respect for Mr. Pike's ingenious attempt to save the face of Bacon, Coke, and Blackstone, I hold that the legend of the Year Books having had an official or even semi-official character (which I tried to find credible as long as I could) is now finally exploded. The check in question is likewise applied from time to time by the Court itself, as every habitual reader of the current reports knows; and seldom without profit. Neither is this practice merely modern; we have at least one case, at present accessible only in Brooke's Abridgement,[1] where the judges corrected an erroneous account of the actual decision in an earlier Year Book by comparing it with the roll.

Accordingly the fathers of English reporting, Plowden and Coke, writing in the days when there were no published books of practice, were at the pains of setting out at the head of their reports a copy of the record itself or at least the pleadings. Considerable extracts from the pleadings, I need hardly remind this audience, are quite common in modern common-law reports; and similarly in equity cases, where the exact form of the decree is often material, the minutes of decree were frequently added. It depends on the nature of the case, and the procedure applicable to it, how much or little information about the facts in evidence and the reasons for the decision can be derived from the official documents.

A learned person lately said of the rolls of our Courts as distinguished from reports that "the

[1] Tit. *Executor*, pt. 22.

objects of the record are science and jurisprudence." That is exactly what officials and archivists would deny. The business of the record, they would say, is to show what was officially done, and nothing else; or if it does show anything else, that is a superfluity which were better done away with. We are to learn from the roll what rights were asserted and denied by the parties, what was at issue between them in fact or in law, and what judgement was given. How far any rule of general importance was laid down, to what extent received opinion or current practice is affected, whether the facts were of a familiar kind or novel, these are things we must find other ways of learning. Hence the distinction of which we are aware from our earliest student days between a record and a report. The record is authentic; a report has not, in this jurisdiction, any authentic or even official character, and can always be contradicted by a more accurate report or even by the clear recollection of the Court or counsel, though this does not often happen. Lines of technical distinction are in law, as in other sciences, more clearly and sharply drawn in later than in earlier days; and so we need not be surprised when we find that in the middle of the thirteenth century the Westminster record may tell us a good deal of what the case was really about, but in the middle of the eighteenth century it will, oftener than not, tell us nothing. The mediæval fashion may be conveniently seen in Maitland's edition of Bracton's Note Book, and that of our great-grandfathers in the forms printed by way of appendix in the older and genuine editions of Blackstone's *Commentaries*: forms which ought to be studied, as well as the untouched text of the author himself, by every one who desires to understand the history of modern English law. In Chancery proceedings, on the other hand, all the facts relied on had to be asserted in the course of pleading, and therefore we have the story, though in a form which became more and more cumbrous and involved as the Court of Chancery developed a fixed procedure, and was reduced to rational order and dimensions only in the middle of the nineteenth century. Neither in common law nor in equitable procedure were the reasons for the ultimate decision apparent on the record itself, though in many cases a competent lawyer with the pleadings before him could form a pretty safe guess as to the point or points on which it turned. This, I think, may safely be said to be characteristic of the English judicial system, though I have no such extensive knowledge of foreign procedure as would justify me in either affirming or denying that our usage is singular.

It may be supposed that judicial records have lost much of their importance by reason of formalism having been abolished, or at least having greatly declined, in modern procedure. Such a view, I think, would be superficial. It is true that slips in procedure are no longer fatal, and that it is not necessary to disguise questions of principle under apparently technical controversies as to the proper form of action. But it is impossible to conduct the business of administering justice without rules of some sort; those rules have to be interpreted; and the necessity for applying them to unforeseen facts may raise questions that go much deeper than form. A dispute whether a writ can be served out of the jurisdiction, for example, must not be assumed to be merely technical. It may depend on a determination of nationality, and require the Court to consider and review principles not only of general but of cosmopolitan interest. On the other hand, the manner in which questions of this kind arise, and the fact that they arise at one time rather than another, must in large measure depend on the structure of legal procedure even in the most modern and rational system. Roads are for the sake of traffic and not traffic for the sake of roads, and yet when a road is made the traffic has to follow it. So do the conditions of procedure, once established, determine the form of substantive legal problems and the lines on which they can be solved. The framework of procedure supplies the conventions without which no art can be practised; for in truth all art, from dancing to pleading, is conventional, and innovators who speak brave words about doing away with convention are only setting up some new convention of their own, which may be good or bad as it happens. Thus every new legal form and every material modification of an old one is a possible nucleus of further development which may very well be more than formal. It is also to be noted that many questions are on the borders of procedure and substantive law, questions of parties for example. Whether any man has done me a wrong, or owes me a debt or an account, and who, is certainly a substantive question, and finding the right man to sue can hardly be called an affair of procedure. But then questions may arise, in affairs of a certain complexity, whether other people are not necessary parties, whose business it is to bring them before the Court, and in what form ; and if these are not matters of procedure it is difficult to say what is.

There is a great harvest of knowledge yet to be gathered from our judicial records and the documents associated with them, and so far the labourers in any one generation have been few. Some difficulties are in the way, but not comparable to those that have been overcome in many other fields of scholarly research. It is simply a matter of having enough competent workers and encouraging them to carry on the work. The method and instruments are sufficiently known, and there are masters willing to teach, but they want more learners. Is it not fit to be considered what can be done in this behalf by the young and vigorous Law Faculty of a University established here in London, within easy reach of the centres of legal and mediæval learning and the Record Office itself ? Perhaps it may not be presumptuous to suggest that the local circumstances afford good reason for some special determination of your University's higher legal studies in this direction. There is the certainty of dissertations being required for the higher degrees, and candidates are often glad to have some guidance in choosing their subjects. There is the possibility, I should hope some probability, of a Seminar such as my friend Prof. Vinogradoff is already conducting at Oxford. Moreover, although for anything I know this may be, for the present, a counsel of perfection, I do not see why candidates for the higher honours of the Faculty should not be expected to show some acquaintance with the language and the materials of our mediæval law. It is unhappily true that in the Inns of Court it is quite possible, partly for the hardness of men's hearts and partly for accidental reasons not necessary to mention here, to satisfy the requirements of the Bar Examination, which include Roman law, without being able to construe a sentence of Latin. But surely there can be no need to exhort a University audience to regard that state of things as warning rather than example. Many years ago I was examining for the Law Tripos at Cambridge, and overheard some examinees discussing a paper set by myself the same morning. Their judgement was unfavourable. "I thought we should have questions on history," said one of them, "and they set a lot of beastly Latin." It is precisely the vocation of a Law Faculty which takes its work seriously to make it plain to students that without the "beastly Latin" they cannot have any history deserving the name, and without adding mediæval French to the Latin they cannot have any opinion of their own worthy of being considered by scholars, or even classed by examiners, on any part of the history of English law before the nineteenth century. My ideal Bachelor of Laws should be able to read the usual constitutional and legal texts in Latin, and to make out plain Year Book French with the aid of Horwood's and Maitland's editions. My ideal Doctor of Laws would not necessarily be able to read an original roll or a Year Book MS. with certainty, but I should like him to know what they look like, and I should certainly want him to be able to check a translation from either in print, short of the really obscure passages where translation has to be more or less conjectural. This involves, no doubt, a fair knowledge, and the more all-round the better, of both mediæval Latin and mediæval French: I do not see why that is too much to expect. For a man, at all events, who has already grappled with the niceties of classical Greek and the intricate structure of Latin, the task cannot be deemed formidable; and it seems likely that for some time to come our scholars in legal history will be mainly recruited from those who have passed through some classical training. Moreover, I think the suggested requirement would be well fitted to discourage amateur antiquaries from trying to pose as jurists; and I really do think there is less danger to legal science from the frank and shameless ignorance of the illiterate practitioner than from the sciolism and wild guesswork of the half-trained amateur. Great is the wilderness wherein the wild mare maketh her nest, and many there be that find it. What is more, the lay people may take those deluded adventurers for real explorers and discoverers, as like as not; for most laymen believe all law to be so absurd that no doctrine in or about it can be too absurd to be probable.

We have, besides our judicial records proper, large classes of official and administrative documents more or less closely connected with judicial proceedings, and at times so much mixed up with them that it is hard to say where the judicial character ends and the merely official begins. An obvious example is afforded by the revenue side of the Exchequer. The reasons for seeking to increase the knowledge of these records, and the profit to be derived therefrom, are much the same as in the case of records actually belonging to courts of judicature, and most of what I have said is equally applicable to the semi-judicial or quasi-judicial archives.

As to the actual denominations, distribution, and custody of our judicial and official records, it may be useful to some of my hearers to indicate very briefly where the proper information can be found. Everything necessary for the student's guidance, except the elements of history, law, and politics on the one hand, and detailed instruction in language and palæography on the other, is given in Mr. Scargill Bird's *Guide to the Public Records* and other Record Office publications, the article "Record," by Mr. Crump of the Record Office, in the eleventh edition of the *Encyclopædia Britannica*, Mr. Hubert Hall's *Studies in English Official Historical Documents* and the accompanying *Formula Book* (1908–9), and (by no means least, though it is quite a short tract) Mr. Pike's Oxford lecture on *The Public Records and the*

Constitution (1907). Mr. Pike's article on the Record Office in the *Encyclopædia of the Laws of England*, and the *First Report of the Royal Commission on Public Records* (1912), may also be consulted.[1] This is very far from exhausting the profitable literature of the subject, but it is enough to begin with. In this lecture I have purposely avoided any fragmentary presentation of facts which have been methodically and fully set out by men acquainted with them at first hand, and which mostly do not admit of profitable or safe abridgement.

[1] There is now a most useful compact summary, the *Repertory of British Archives* (Part I., England), edited by Mr. Hubert Hall for the Royal Historical Society, Lond., 1920.

X

ENGLISH LAW REPORTING[1]

THE English Council of Law Reporting has before now been represented at meetings of the American Bar Association by some of its most distinguished members. I do not think, however, that they said anything about the *Law Reports* or the English system of reporting; and I believe this is the first time that an editor of the *Law Reports* has the honour of being your guest. Indeed, I am the first editor of the *Law Reports* as a whole, for until 1895 there were three (originally four) independent editors under the general supervision of the Council. For this reason, and also because anything I say here is bound to be quite different from the lectures I am invited to deliver in October to the law schools of certain universities, it may be appropriate to the occasion to tell you something of the business I have been charged with now for eight years and a half. I need hardly premise that we, the staff of the *Law Reports*, consider ourselves as exercising an office of trust on behalf of the legal profession not only in England, but in every jurisdiction where the common law is received or its

[1] A Paper read before the American Bar Association at Hot Springs, Virginia, August 26, 1903; printed in *L.Q.R.* xix. 451.

authorities quoted. Still less is there any need to imitate the panegyrical and not wholly felicitous prefaces of Coke or his demonstration that Moses was the first law reporter. Neither shall I dwell on the intimate and necessary connexion of law reporting with the authority of judicial decisions in the common law. That, I conceive, is fully understood by all here. I will not speak, again, of the history and merits of the early reporters, for therein your countryman, John William Wallace,[1] is our master; it was one of our greatest common-law lawyers, the late Mr. Justice Willes, who sent me to "Wallace on the Reporters" more than thirty years ago. Nor yet will I set forth the virtues of a good reporter so far as they are common ground to us all. You know them well enough; probably there are many here who have practised them; certainly there are more who have stimulated them by the frank exhibition of critical interest. We are here as men of business; let us come to business and consider those points about law reporting in England which may be less familiar here than the general historical or doctrinal aspects of the subject.

First, our law reporting is unofficial, as it has been ever since the commencement of modern reports. It is more than doubtful whether the year books were the work of official reporters. Internal evidence is distinctly unfavourable to the tradition, for it looks like a professional tradition, which Bacon and Plowden

[1] Reporter of the Supreme Court of the United States, 1863–1875. His classical work on the early reporters is unfortunately scarce, even in the comparatively recent edition by F. F. Heard, and is, I believe, not so familiar as it deserves to be.

accepted. Bacon would be a better witness if he had not used the story to support a scheme of his own for official reporting; and Coke's enormous credulity makes his repetition of it worthless.[1] In any case the later reports which we call authorised were produced by private enterprise and enjoyed only a personal authority given by the judges of the several courts to the several reporters, which, down to the institution of the *Law Reports*, and in some cases a few years longer, procured them certain exclusive advantages. In the eighteenth century judges now and then took on themselves to discredit particular books of reports; James Alan Park, J. (not to be confounded with Parke, afterwards Lord Wensleydale), said in 1830, "Lord Kenyon reprimanded me when I was at the bar for citing Keble."[2] This is perhaps later than any of Wallace's examples. But, according to modern custom, any report vouched for at the time by a member of the bar may be used in court for what it is worth, although the citation of an unpublished report is not at all common nowadays. The multitude of independent reports for several courts, and competing authorised and unauthorised reports in the same court, gave rise to inconveniences which have often been described, and in 1865, as the result of much professional discussion, meetings of the bar and other matters of inducement, all which are fully set forth in Daniel's *History of the Law Reports*,

[1] I now think that Mr. Maitland's critical investigation of the year books of Edward II., forthcoming in a Selden Society volume, finally makes the legend untenable. [His Introduction, now classical, was published in 1903.]

[2] *Adams* v. *Gibney*, 6 Bing. at p. 664, 31 R.R. at p. 521.

the Council of Law Reporting and their reports came into existence. That body is not a Government or official institution. It has no legal privileges and does not claim any monopoly ; the freedom of citation which I have just mentioned remains unimpaired. In fact it is a joint committee of the Inns of Court, the Law Society[1] (representing solicitors, who, with us, as you know, are a distinct branch of the profession), and, of late years, the Bar Council. One can easily imagine how differently this would have been ordered in any other European country, supposing our system of the eminent and exclusive authority of judicial precedents to have obtained there. If England were a German kingdom, I should undoubtedly be an official person, probably rather a considerable person, with some such title as *Königlich-Obergerichts-Archivs-Direktor*, and a *Geheimrat* or *Justizrat* to boot. As it is, I am nothing of the kind. My learned colleagues on the staff of the *Law Reports* and myself are not an official hierarchy. We are not members of the civil service. We have no insignia, no precedence, no title to be invited to state functions. The lay public is hardly aware, if aware at all, of our existence. We are even among the few things in the British Empire unknown to Whitaker's *Almanack*, that compendious and almost universal book of reference.

If these be drawbacks, and I doubt whether most of us would count them such, we have our compensations. Disciplined co-operation is, of course, a necessity ; though some learned persons, when the

[1] The addition of " incorporated " is now dropped.

establishment of the *Law Reports* was under discussion, did not see of what use an editor would be. But our bond is more like that of a college crew than that of a Government office. What rules we have, outside matters like the dates for returning proofs, really belonging to the printing and publishing more than the reporting department, are mostly unwritten. I admit that I set some value on two rules I have made for myself, to give my colleagues as free a hand as possible and never to write a formal letter when I can help it. My successor will not find much in the way of demi-official archives. We confer freely and confidentially, as occasion requires, with the judges, with the counsel engaged in cases to be reported and with one another. Any suggestion from the judges is, I need hardly say, most respectfully considered, and observations from the profession at large, whether constructive or critical, are welcome. I have known five minutes' talk with a learned friend, of which there was no written record whatever, lead to a modest but useful typographical improvement. But all this is quite unofficial. We are answerable to the council who appoint us,[1] and to the council alone; and in the most improbable case of an attempt at formal interference from any other quarter, I should have no hesitation in telling the intermeddler, however exalted his professional or official position might be, to mind his own business, and I should do so with the full

[1] There is one exception to be noted here. The appointment of reporters in the House of Lords is made by the House itself, practically by the Lord Chancellor [now on the nomination of the Council of Law Reporting]. The editor has nothing whatever to do with the appointment of reporters in any branch.

assurance of being supported by the council. In short, we imitate on our small scale that method of proceeding by customary and unwritten understandings and settling the really important matters, so to speak, out of court, which is the pride of Anglo-Saxon political institutions and the despair of almost all foreign students. There is a growing tendency among our people to multiply rules and administrative machinery and demand what is called organisation. No one who has had much to do with the English universities any time the last twenty years can have failed to observe it. Broadly speaking, I think it is a mischievous tendency and ought to be resisted. Some rules are certainly necessary for every society not of a domestic and intimate kind, and combined work must certainly be organised if it is to be effective. But this does not mean that it is reasonable to hamper business with an excess of minute regulations or to paralyse discretion, fritter away responsibility and, worst of all, waste the energy of men fit for better things by imposing a complicated routine on even the simplest affairs. As a matter of fact, the precautions that such routine is supposed to embody are very seldom, if ever, of any honest use. If it is intended to make certain things really difficult, such as changes in the nature of constitutional amendments, there are plenty of known and tried ways of doing this openly. Making everything, great and small, difficult just to the point of cumbrousness and vexation, but not difficult enough to secure a considered and solemn decision of the greater matters, is the worst way of all, though unhappily not uncommon. But I am digressing.

Having thus endeavoured to show you the spirit of the *Law Reports* and to prevent misunderstanding of the form, I will speak of our actual constitution and operations. Reference to the Weekly Notes, digests and other auxiliary and occasional publications of the council, is omitted as not likely to be of much interest here. We have to provide reports of cases decided by the following tribunals :

The House of Lords (including appeals from Scotland).

The Judicial Committee of the Privy Council.

The Chancery Division of the High Court of Justice.

The King's Bench and Probate Divisions of the same court.

The decisions of the Court of Appeal are attended to (with a minute exception in bankruptcy cases) by reporters attached to the division from which they come. You may see the number and names of the reporters, and their usual distribution among the courts, printed on the covers of the current numbers of the *Law Reports*, and it would be idle to repeat those particulars. What does not appear on the face of the cover[1] is that the Chancery reporters communicate direct with the editor, the House of Lords and King's Bench reporters with my learned friend Mr. Stone, the assistant editor, and the Privy Council

[1] [The arrangement here described has been much simplified. In 1915 Mr. A. P. Stone retired, and his post was not filled; all the reporters now (1922) communicate direct with the editor. Also the reporting in the House of Lords is all in one hand.]

reporter with the editor, enjoying, however, this peculiar franchise (a relic of former absolute autonomy) that his MS. does not pass through the editor's hands. The reasons for these diversities are partly too local, personal and otherwise accidental to be worth stating, and partly unknown to myself. I do not know, for instance, why there is only one reporter for all the colonial and Indian appeals before the Judicial Committee and a separate reporter for Scottish and divorce appeals in the House of Lords; still less do I understand the reason of this last conjunction, but so I found it. Probably our want of logic would shock a learned Frenchman somewhat, and our laxity might shock a learned or military German more. Being an illogical folk, we do well enough on the whole with all our anomalies. All the proofs, however, are seen by the editor, including those of the Indian appeals, a distinct series of which there are probably not many copies on this side of the Atlantic. As to these last I have a particular little grievance, not remediable except by the Indian courts themselves. The High Courts of the Indian Presidencies are independent. Each of them has its own fashion, mostly barbarous and antiquated, of transcribing Indian proper names and words of art. Perhaps the extreme case is that of a beautiful Sanskrit compound which becomes "Chuckerbutty" in the Anglo-Bengalese dialect, suggesting some grotesque personage in Dickens. The practical result is that the same name may be written in three or four different ways in the documents which come before the Judicial Committee and has to be indexed accordingly as if it were as many different names; and also, though this is of less importance, that many common terms of tenure and agriculture are so written, oftener than not, that a merely English reader is almost sure to mispronounce them. If the Indian courts would agree to adopt any one tolerable and consistent plan of transliteration, the Indian appeals would cease to present a ridiculous appearance to every one even slightly acquainted with any of the classical or vernacular languages of India; but I know of no reason to expect any amendment.

As to the matter of the reports, there is no fixed rule for deciding what cases are to be published. Utility to the profession is the only test. We do not necessarily report a judgement because it is written, still less omit to report it because it is delivered off-hand. The judges themselves are under no rule as to reserving or writing their judgements, and any hard and fast distinction founded on judgements being written or oral, considered or not considered, would lead to absurd results. The late Sir G. Jessel, one of the strongest judges we ever had, very seldom wrote his judgements. In the Court of Appeal written judgements are naturally more frequent than elsewhere, but there need not even be uniformity in the same case. For the most part separate opinions are delivered, and one member of the court may write his judgement while the others do not write theirs. I may mention that even when judgements are wholly written they are still actually read out in court: I do not know to whom this is of any use; certainly not to the reporters. In this respect our practice is somewhat peculiar. In some jurisdictions the appellate courts are bound to put their judgements in writing; in many, I believe, it is the practice to report all written judgements. With us a much greater burden of discretion is thrown on the reporter. An elaborately argued case involving large pecuniary interests, and requiring a very careful judgement, may be of no general professional interest whatever, and turn wholly on special facts. Of this kind are many patent and trade-mark cases. On the other hand a very brief and off-hand judgement may settle a vexed point of practice or even of law. A wide field seems to be open; but on the whole the trained perception of the reporters, assisted by the keen but quite friendly competition of other publications, is very seldom at fault. I venture to say that, with few and accidental exceptions, that which neither the *Law Reports* nor the *Law Journal* (our chief competitor) report is not worth reporting. Occasionally there may be reasons of an extra-judicial kind for reporting a case, not so easily known to the reporter as to the editor. Once I caused a decision of the Court of Appeal to be reported, though it did not add anything to what we already knew at home for settled law, because I happened to know that the case and the points involved in it had excited a good deal of interest in the West Indies; and once or twice I have thought that a case was not to be discarded merely because it had become notorious among the lay public on professionally irrelevant grounds. The responsibility of suppressing a case sent in by the proper reporter is evidently much greater, and I cannot remember ever having done such a thing against the reporter's persistent judgement. Here the reason is plain. In case of doubt, it is safer to report a decision than to leave it aside; and the fact that a skilled person specially charged to form an opinion does think a particular decision reportable is of itself good evidence in its favour. Holding back a case which is to be the subject of an appeal is quite a different matter, and depends on a variety of considerations, as does the further question whether, in a consolidated report, the judgement below shall be set out or only its purport stated. On such points of discretion, which may be rather nice, an experienced reporter's opinion is always valuable and often conclusive.

The reporting of arguments and of oral judgements is doubtless the most skilled and difficult part of an English reporter's task. Arguments have to be exhibited fully enough to explain the points made, the line of reasoning, and the authorities relied on, but not at superfluous length. You must remember that printed "briefs" or expositions of counsel's arguments are not in use in England. It is true that the procedure of the House of Lords and the Judicial Committee requires printed cases to be lodged. But these documents are anything but a certain guide to the points which will be really insisted on; they are in a narrative form, concluding with a short statement of reasons, but giving no clue to the authorities. Nothing but careful attention to the argument as it actually takes place, not forgetting judicial interlocutory remarks, will produce an adequate report. In dealing with oral judgements the reporter's aim is to give the spoken word a becoming written form without substantial change of sense. More or less editing may be wanted; some judges are more careful or more concise in their language than others. But the cases are rare indeed in which a mere verbatim note of anything said extempore, however good it may have been to hear, can be accepted as readable English. Our labour is lightened by the favour of the judges, most of whom (in the Chancery Division all) revise their judgements in proof; but I do not think that would justify us in giving them a crude shorthand note to work upon. Further, some things are useful for the judge to say in court which are superfluous for the reader of the report, having the facts and arguments in print before him; so that here there is a good deal of literary as well as legal discretion to be exercised, and moreover it is the editor's duty, without prejudice to any genuine individuality, to secure a certain uniformity and maintain a due standard of language. On the split infinitive, for example, I do my best to wage a war of extermination. Another pest of law reports, derived I think from ill-penned statutes and conveyancing forms, is the slovenly misuse of "such" as a mere demonstrative. As for example: "The plaintiff's yellow dog, being, as was alleged by the plaintiff, muzzled, bit a dynamite cartridge belonging to the defendant. Such cartridge exploded, and after such explosion it was not found possible to reconstruct either such dog or such muzzle." This likewise I endeavour to extirpate. But some weeds are very hard to grub up finally.[1]

Addition of special notes by the reporter or the editor, or both, is a matter of occasional convenience for which there can be no dogmatic precept. No one would think nowadays of imitating the disquisitions appended to their text by the very learned Serjeant Manning and some of his predecessors, though one or two of them have become classical. But little pieces of information, not strictly part of the report, are at times apposite and useful. Several times I have found it desirable, if not absolutely necessary, to correct the singularly bad translations furnished for the use of the court by persons, I know not whom, generally incapable of writing intelligible English and

[1] It is not relevant to the issue before us—but the temptation is irresistible—to consider what pleadings might arise on the facts I have suggested, in a jurisdiction such as New Jersey or Vermont, where the pure word of the common law still prevails. There might be a plea to the effect that the plaintiff's dog was unlawfully at large without a muzzle, contrary to the ordinance in that behalf, and that he, therefore, bit any goods of the defendant wholly at his own peril; to which plea there would be a demurrer, on the ground that it amounted to an argumentative general issue. There might also be a special plea in confession and avoidance, alleging that the plaintiff's dog was unlawfully at large with intent to steal, take and carry away goods and chattels of the defendant and of divers, to wit, two hundred other lawful citizens of the United States whose names and residences are to the defendant unknown; that the dog, attempting to execute such unlawful intention, did with his mouth seize, bite and apprehend a certain dynamite cartridge of the goods and chattels of the defendant, which cartridge, thereupon, in self-defence, and being unable otherwise to prevent the commission of a felony, did, a little and moderately, and without unnecessary force, detonate, burst and explode, and then and there did, a little and moderately, the said dog of the plaintiff disperse, scatter and destroy, as for the causes aforesaid it lawfully might, which is the trespass complained of; without this, that the defendant did kill and destroy the plaintiff's dog in manner and form alleged. To this plea there would be a replication *de injuria* and probably a demurrer thereto. I leave it to this court to say what the proper judgement would be.

often capable of misunderstanding the original. One would think that a person rendering a French or German legal document into English ought to have some rudimentary knowledge of the words of art of both systems, but this appears to be considered quite unnecessary. There was a case, not many years ago, where a translator's mistake in French—an elementary mistake too, and not depending on anything technical —might have really embarrassed the court if Mr. Justice Wills, being an excellent French scholar, had not promptly corrected it. A particular kind of note forming a category by itself is the incidental report of a decision which was relied on in the principal case, and of which the published report or reports are imperfect or inaccurate. Search by counsel or judges in the records of the court sometimes throws quite a new light on old and scantily reported cases. We have had a very recent example.[1]

It may be of some little interest to state the regular course of dealing with a reported case from delivery of the MS. to publication. I take the Chancery Division as being that in which the material is under my own eye at every stage. In the last days of one month and the first of the next the MSS. on hand are sent on to the printers after a summary inspection. The reports on which any question arises at this stage are very few, and it often happens that a reporter's copy is in my custody only for some hours. In favourable circumstances a short case decided near the

[1] See the corrected report of *Palmer* v. *Young*, 1 Vern. 276, in the note at the end of *Re Biss* [1903] 2 Ch. at p. 65.

beginning of a month may be reported within a week, sent to press with the current batch, and published in the very next number. It is not so very long since our present speed would have been thought impossible or hardly decent; but I have not observed that promptitude leads to any falling off in accuracy. Indeed I think the work is likely to be better, if anything, for being put through while the memory of all persons concerned is fresh. About two months, however, is the more usual lapse of time between the date of a decision and that of its appearance in the *Law Reports*. A longer interval, when it occurs, may be due to the preparation of the report having been unusually laborious, or to unavoidable delay in obtaining the necessary papers from counsel and solicitors, or in the return of proofs by the judges, or to time having been taken to consider whether the case should be reported, or to pressure of matter at certain times of the judicial year compelling the postponement of something. The numbers published immediately before and in the long vacation (August, September, October) may be treated, for practical purposes, as one number divided into three for technical rather than professional reasons.

To return to the normal history of a Chancery Division case, the first proof comes from the press in the second week of the month. A duplicate is furnished to the judge, or one to each judge if it is a Court of Appeal case. The corrections of the reporter and the judge are worked in; and here I must repeat that the obligation of the reporters and the profession to the learned judges for the time and care they bestow, purely as a matter of grace, on the revision of their reported judgements, and not infrequently on valuable hints for the improvement of other parts of the report, is far greater than any one could guess who does not see the work done. Then, for greater certainty, all references and quotations are verified by a sub-editor specially employed for the purpose. About the middle of the month the slips go back to the press, and the final proof in pages comes to the editor in time to be passed with about a week to spare, from the return of the latest sheets, for the mechanics of striking off and stitching. As a rule there ought to be, and is, next to nothing to correct in the final proof, but sometimes an elucidation of fact, name or reference turns up at the last moment, or a manifest error is discovered which has contrived so far to escape several pairs of trained eyes. I may observe, as the result of a pretty long experience of press corrections, that the more manifest an error is the greater chance it has of continuing to escape when it has escaped once. The reason is that even a skilled proof-reader may unconsciously read with his mind's eye what ought to be there instead of what is; and if he does it once, he is as likely as not to do it again. A familiar and annoying example is the accidental transposition of the words "plaintiff" and "defendant," a blunder which I conceive every one of us must have unconsciously committed in his own work at some time or other, and as unconsciously failed to correct.

We do our best to provide a series of checks. First

there is the reporter's eye; then the judge's; then the editor's and his clerk's (and my clerk has read proofs for and with me for twenty years); then the sub-editor's; and finally the reader's in the printing office. Yet with all this we cannot wholly avoid errata. Speaking to those who know how special and complex is the typography of the footnotes in a law report, which may at any time include unfamiliar abbreviations and outlandish words and names, I make no apologies. But I believe that the number of misprints at all likely to mislead any reader to whom the references are significant is in truth exceedingly small. And so the reports go forth on the first day of the month; I will not say "on or about," for we allow ourselves no days of grace unless the first of the month is a *dies non*, and any other kind of accidental delay is a matter for searchings of heart. Strict punctuality is what we aim at and usually attain.[1] Our work is quite unknown to the general public; it is perhaps rather obscure even to a large number of the profession; a great deal of what we publish is, by the nature of current litigation and legislation, merely local and transitory. What is to you here, for example, the statutory definition of a "new street"? Nevertheless you know and we know that we are about a work the English-speaking world cannot do without. In our modest and ministerial field of operation we are helping to maintain a national and more than national heritage, the ancient and still vital growth of the common law.

[1] [It is now (1922) pretty well restored after some inevitable shortcoming under war conditions.]

XI

LAY FALLACIES IN THE LAW[1]

My purpose is to speak of certain false opinions which are suggested, if not asserted, by the language of more than one old-fashioned textbook; I mean such as were still in vogue less than half a century ago. When I call them lay fallacies I do not mean that they have not deceived, or may not deceive, unwary members of the profession, but that they are signs of failure to give due attention to the peculiar nature of legal science and the proper attributes of legal justice, and are such as easily occur to the first thoughts of a reasonable but uninstructed layman, even if he has not been dabbling in the works of learned persons whose conventional rhetoric, easily discounted by professional readers, he has innocently taken at the face value. Mistakes of this kind are not altogether trivial or harmless. Lawyers know pretty well in a general way what courts of justice are capable of performing and what not; but the citizen who confidently aspires to make the world better in his own sense, not being restrained by practical sense born of experience, will often require

[1] From *Legal Essays* in honour of John H. Wigmore, Chicago, 1919.

the law to perform impossibilities; and when his expectation is disappointed, as it has to be, he will denounce judges and lawyers as if they were in a wilful conspiracy to pervert natural justice. Ancient wisdom has defined justice as the constant will to give every man his due. Whatever may be the shortcomings of this definition, its framers were discreet in not adding any warranty of complete power. Successors who have expanded their words have not always been careful enough to follow their discretion.

I

The most fruitful of these fallacies, if indeed it be not the common root of them all, is the assumption that the law of the land purports to be a general guide for the conduct of life. Viewed in that fashion, it must be admitted that the commandments of the law come sadly short of being adequate. We lawyers know very well, and may find high judicial authority for it if required, that life would be intolerable if every man insisted on his legal rights to the full. It does not take much reflexion to perceive that human action cannot be reduced to complete mechanical uniformity, and the most rigid custom, the most minutely framed enactment, must leave a certain margin of discretion; also that, when once discretion is admitted, it may be exercised for better or for worse. But as the greater part of mankind do not reflect adequately, and many not at all, it is easy to take the hyperbolic language of orators and text-writers literally and suppose legal justice competent, and therefore bound, to cover the whole field of conduct.

Misquoted or misunderstood utterances of famous authors have had much to do with the prevalence of false notions in law as in other sciences. Two or three words of Cicero's current in our books are probably answerable for a great crop of confused thought. He spoke of law, or rather of legislation, as prescribing what is of good report—"iubens honesta"; so it is commonly quoted, but the text[1] reads *imperans* (the similar phrase "iubet ea quae facienda sunt" does occur in another passage).[2]

Now Cicero was never esteemed an authority in the Common Law, but that is no reason why we should leave him under suspicion of having written nonsense, or something dangerously like it. Many readers of Cicero and other Latin authors (or retailers of fragments from them) forget that words often have much more definite implications in classical Latin than their nearest English equivalents will carry. The conception at the root of the word *lex* in all its uses is that of willed design, whether the designer be a God, or a legislator, or the framer of an express condition in a private transaction, as in the very common phrase "ea lege." It is hardly too much to say that the primary content of the word is the reason or intention of him who prescribes a rule rather than the matter prescribed. Therefore Cicero's dictum, even when torn from the context, does not

[1] *Phil.* XI. xii.

[2] *De legg.* I. vi. 18.

mean that legal ordinances, as formulated, purport to cover the field of morals. Its point is something very different and much more reasonable, namely that, so far as legal precepts positively command anything to be done, their ultimate justification is the authors' conviction that what they command is politically and morally right. But let us take a step farther and look at the context (*Phil.* XI. xii. 28). What is Cicero talking about? Is he engaged in defining terms of art in jurisprudence? Is he dealing with ordinary legal categories? Is he thinking as a lawyer at all? Quite the contrary. He is arguing in the senate as a statesman and defending a formal irregularity by an appeal to the higher law of moral necessity. A commanding officer and provincial governor has acted outside the limits of his command on emergency. What is to be said for him? Here are Cicero's words:

> Qua lege? quo iure? Eo, quod Iuppiter ipse sanxit, ut omnia quae rei publicae salutaria essent legitima et iusta haberentur. Est enim lex nihil aliud nisi recta et a numine deorum tracta ratio, imperans honesta, prohibens contraria. Huic igitur legi paruit Cassius quum est in Syriam profectus, alienam provinciam si homines legibus scriptis uterentur, his vero oppressis suam lege naturae.

Cassius committed an excess of jurisdiction; according to the usual rules of his service, if they are to be applied to the case, it certainly was so. But the situation called for prompt action to redress the violent wrongdoing of a public enemy, and he followed the higher law of righteousness and the common weal. In so doing, Cicero goes on to say, he was only anticipating the certain judgement of the senate, as both he and Brutus had done in like cases before. Compare the sentence a little earlier, xi. 27: "Nec enim nunc primum aut Brutus aut Cassius salutem libertatemque patriae legem sanctissimam et morem optimum iudicavit." Nothing could be more widely removed from the sphere of common official or judicial usage, not to speak of technical definition. We may note by the way that there is nothing specially mediæval, or "monkish," as our great-grandfathers used to say, in the scholastic doctrine which reckoned the law of nature as a branch of divine law. It is in exact accordance with the original classical significance of natural law as declared by Cicero. The soundness of Cicero's opinion, as applying to the special circumstances, does not concern us here; but it appears that the senate agreed with him.

The parallel passage already mentioned is in the *De legibus*.[1] It is expressly concerned not with the specific contents of any system, but with the law of nature as the ultimate groundwork of all legal institutions: "Penitus ex intima philosophia hauriendam iuris disciplinam putas," as Atticus is made to state Cicero's object. Cicero professes to follow the best authorities, meaning undoubtedly not Roman lawyers, but Greek philosophers.

Igitur doctissimis viris proficisci placuit a lege: haud scio an recte, si modo, ut iidem definiunt, lex est ratio summa insita in natura quae iubet ea quae facienda sunt prohibetque contraria.

[1] I. vi. 18.

It is plain from the whole context that Cicero regarded the working out of these universal principles in any particular body of laws as belonging to a quite different order of discussion; and the fact that he was neither an original philosopher nor a profound lawyer does not make him less competent as an expounder of the views accepted by the leading members of both faculties. To represent him as capable of the sort of confusion between the ultimate standards of jurisprudence and the actual contents of legal systems which is too common in modern books would be to talk mere nonsense. The passage in *De legibus* is earlier than that in the *Philippic*, but, as it occurs in a literary and theoretical work, is probably more considered. In any case there is no substantial difference. We have seen that the current quotation does not accurately represent either. But we must not be tempted farther towards putting a juristic sickle into the harvest of Ciceronian scholarship.

II

Horace has been even more scurvily treated than Cicero. In his Epistles [1] he gives about fifty lines to warning a friend how foolish it is to be moved by the praise or blame of the ignorant, and especially to court their praise. The passage being too long to quote in full, I must give in short so much of the sense as needful. Whom do we deem a righteous man? Horace asks. An answer follows, not Horace's own,

[1] I. xvi.

but that of an ordinary, rather careless person; Munro judiciously printed it within quotation marks. "Why, such an one as observes the laws, arbitrates in heavy cases, is good for security and witness." Indeed! replies Horace, a man may be all this while his family and neighbours know him for a rogue that keeps on the windy side of the law, no better than a slave who eschews theft and murder for fear of the whip and the gallows; a fellow whose real prayer is whispered to his dear Laverna, patroness of crooks, while his audible voice is worshipping Janus or Apollo. Such is Horace's own mind. The moral is plain enough and to spare; Horace points it elsewhere when he says that enactments without good customs avail nothing to curb the reckless pursuit of gain:

> Quid leges sine moribus
> vanae proficiunt . . . ?[1]

It seems hardly credible that the words

> . . . vir bonus est quis ?
> qui consulta patrum, qui leges iuraque servat,

should have been cut out of their satirical context to pass as a platitude which moreover is a false one by Horace's careful showing. Yet it has happened. The fragment may be seen figuring in this lamentable plight on the title-pages of eighteenth-century law books, two or three of them if I mistake not; and any layman who notes the blunder may think, if he is a scholar, that such is lawyers' scholarship, and,

[1] *C.* iii. 24.

whether he is a scholar or not, that our profession recognises no morality beyond legality. To assert this as the general habit of lawyers or anything like it would be defamation, but I fear excusable, or at least giving little hope of substantial damages, by reason of the literary stupidity which invited misunderstanding.

It must be confessed, unfortunately, that a particular kind of uncritical slovenliness in matters outside professional skill and practice is so frequent among inferior lawyers as to be the common badge of their quality. Not that even successful ones who rose to high places have always been exempt from it. Lord Campbell's lively but wholly untrustworthy biographies are a notorious example. "The lawyer brings to historical research a sense of evidence and a power of testing it"; so said the Master of Balliol ten years ago, when he was just Mr. A. L. Smith, a well-known Oxford tutor. Of Maitland, his immediate subject, this and much more was true, but as a general compliment to the profession it is, with all respect for the Master of Balliol, a hoary fallacy. Some of the worst nonsense I have met with about historical evidence was written by respectable lawyers from Coke downwards.

More than this, it is not enough to say that a body of law is not a complete system of precepts for the conduct of life. So far as its field coincides with that of ethics, its contents must be conformable to the received precepts of social morality, but it is not itself a system of precepts at all. Its business is not to give lessons in conduct, but to keep the peace and settle or prevent disputes; and not the less so because the amount of ethical rule embodied in positive law has increased largely in modern times and is still increasing.[1] The moral sense of the community, including therein, of course, that of lawyers, but not as anything different from that of other reasonable citizens, tells us what reasonable men expect of each other in the business of life. Courts and legislatures tell us how much of those expectations will be reinforced by public authority. They also prescribe the various ways and forms in which this shall be done; and that part of their task, as lawyers know, presents infinite difficulties and complexity, together with most dangerous possibilities of doing more harm than good with the best intentions; but of such things very few laymen have anything like an adequate conception.

III

Another thing overlooked by most laymen is the vast bulk of modern law dealing with matters of public order for which a rule of some kind is wanted, but, until the rule is made by competent authority, it is indifferent from an ethical point of view what it shall be. There is no cause for surprise if different or opposite rules are laid down for such matters in different jurisdictions, though in some cases it might be convenient to procure general uniformity by

[1] See Ames' essay on "Law and Morals" in *Lectures on Legal History.*

international agreement. In private law, too, there are many points of detail evidently calling for a settled rule, but such that no one solution can easily be said to be in itself more just or convenient than another. The assumption that there must be one and only one intrinsically right way of dealing with any practical question is often tacitly made, to the hindrance of rational agreement. Its fallacy is evident to any one who has learned the distinction between natural and conventional justice; but that distinction itself, so far from being familiar to laymen, has been ignored and even despised by learned persons who should have known better. Certainly no man is like to become wise by presuming that Aristotle was a fool—but some teachers who enjoyed high repute in the nineteenth century talked as if that was their expectation. Lay people suppose that every legal problem is like a simple equation; whereas the problems of the political sciences, not excluding law, not seldom are more like equations of higher degrees in being capable of two or more solutions.

Yet it must be allowed that the lay people are not without excuse in confounding the judge's office with the moralist's. For the law of the courts, though it cannot embrace the whole of morality, can exercise appreciable influence on moral standards within certain limits and under certain conditions; and those conditions are nowadays to be found in many jurisdictions, and perhaps are wholly wanting in few or none that need be considered. In a jurisdiction of moderate extent and homogeneous population, whose laws have never been affected by foreign conquest, it is generally true that positive law will only reflect current moral opinion. In such a commonwealth the embodiment of such opinion and practice in formulated law can only furnish a conservative element at times when there is danger of relaxation. Even so, the moral standard assumed by judges and legislators will probably be the standard of the better sort of men and somewhat, though not very much, above the average level of common practice. But in modern societies the case is not often so simple. Ethical feeling and judgement are not uniform throughout a complex and specialised community, but vary accordingly to the education, surroundings, and pursuits of different social groups as soon as one passes from the rudimentary principles to their application. A Quaker's rules are or were stricter in some ways than an Anglican's; but if an Anglican divine is a Quaker merchant's customer he may (or in Charles Lamb's time might) find that the Quaker's morality in the things of his trade is of a mercantile quality which his own views of strict good faith will not pass as reaching the mark of the highest Christian ethics; and there was a time when John Bright, a member of the Society of Friends and full of philanthropic zeal, was obtuse in the matter of the Factory Acts.

Now the law, standing detached from mercantile and other class interests, will probably maintain in such cases a standard of requirement in matters of good faith and the like, at least as high as that of right-minded citizens outside the interest for the time being in question, and therefore higher than the standard accepted by most persons within it. Notoriously this is so as regards various usages of trade which the law disapproves and the traders with few exceptions declare to be not only harmless, but necessary for the conduct of their business. How far the traders may be right in particular cases is not a question material here. In some cases it is certain that the zeal of the court for perfect justice carried it so far as to make impracticable demands on plain men's knowledge and diligence, though not in matters of commerce. Old English practitioners can remember the time when the Court of Chancery judged trustees, who are usually no wiser, save as years may bring wisdom, than their cestuis que trust, by a standard of infallible omniscience and impeccable vigilance which probably no Chancellor or Master of the Rolls ever attained in his own person. The result was not that trustees became infallible, but that Parliament intervened to make it possible for a man of ordinary prudence to accept a trust. But on the whole the guardianship of class morality and custom by a central power representing the best mind of the Commonwealth has been effectual and profitable. The lawyers alone would never have made a law merchant at all, but lawyers and merchants together have made a far better one than merchants without lawyers would have made. Consider for example what our law of agency is, and what it would have been if divers arguments for laxer construction of an agent's duties, maintained in quite good faith for all that appears, had prevailed. At this day there is no difficulty in finding among the decisions reported from month to month ample proof of practices being approved or tolerated among traders which will not pass uncensured in a court of justice.

The layman—if a layman should overhear us—may well ask upon this: If the law keeps commercial morality in order, who looks after the professional morality of lawyers themselves? A question certainly deserving answer, but not likely to receive a short one, for the answer is spread over the whole history of the profession. No sooner were courts and judicature established, whether at Rome or at Westminster, and advocacy recognised as a profession, than it was also recognised that the profession of assisting men to seek or defend their just rights was legitimate only on condition of not becoming a mere trade. The practitioners of the Roman and of the Common Law guarded themselves and their successors by traditional and extremely stringent rules, different in details but aiming at the same objects by fundamentally similar means. If these rules do not, like some of those which the medical profession has imposed on itself, go back to Hippocrates, their severity at least has nothing to lose by the comparison. Not that lawyers are by nature much more virtuous and self-restraining than other men; but they have known well from the first that a strict and even austere professional discipline is the price of public confidence.

There are special conditions, moreover, and they are becoming more frequent in recent times, under which contact with a foreign system of law may have material effects on some parts of social conduct, and thereby, in the long run, on moral standards.

The greatest example of this process may be seen in India, where before the days of British rule there were divers and many customs of religions, castes, and even families, and each religion had its own schools of learned commentators, but there was not much general law of any kind and practically no commercial law. Within living memory, systematic legislation has introduced codified and more or less simplified versions of English law in several of its branches. These codes, or some of them, have also been adopted in some Indian protected states and in several colonies and protectorates beyond India. In this way not only the rules of the Common Law, but the standards of conduct implied therein, come to Asiatic and African people (for they have gone as far as the Sudan) speaking with authority, and the Anglo-Indian codes exercise a distinct ethical influence whose results are only beginning to appear. I have no doubt that French law is doing the same in the north of Africa. The process is of great interest to the student of social development and of what the philologists call, in no vituperative sense, "contamination." But such facts are a long way from justifying any expectation that even when it goes on a missionary journey, much less in its native air, any system of law should do the work of a complete moral schoolmaster.

Peradventure it is better for us if the lay people expect too much edification at our hands than if they regard the law of the land as a mere collection of arbitrary commands and prohibitions unrelated to any rational or ethical principle, which, it is to be feared, some of them do. This last delusion was rather fostered by the dogmatic (but by no means accurate) school of legal philosophy which prevailed in England in my youth. A similar doctrine has apparently made some way among German publicists of late years ; it is of a piece with the Prussian theory of the infallible state whose iron has entered deep into the German soul, to be purged away only at the cost of blood and iron untold. Hereupon we might ride off on vigorous denunciation of the German heresy, and so escape from examining our own conscience ; but I do not propose to take that course. I conceive this is a case where practising lawyers, being familiar with the necessity of certain distinctions, assume and act upon them without making them explicit ; and the result is to lay a trap for studious amateurs. We declare that law, whatever it is, must at least not be arbitrary, which is true, first, in the sense that justice must be administered without capricious preferences, truly and indifferently as the old form of oath goes ; and next, that the substance of the law must hang together somehow and not be a mere heap of isolated rules. Many persons might, perhaps, suppose that denying law to be arbitrary is the same thing as affirming it to be made or controlled by some kind of popular government. But this is matter of politics, not of law. There was no popular voice in Justinian's consolidation of the Roman law, nor in the making of the Napoleonic codes; none in that of the Anglo-Indian Codes, except that the Government of India made them in the exercise of powers conferred by the Parliament of the United Kingdom; not much in that of the German Codes, of which the Civil Code is the latest, although they were passed by the Reichstag. Yet nobody would affirm that any of these codifications was other than an honest endeavour to lay down just and impartial rules; and few competent persons would deny that, although none of them is free from shortcomings, on the whole they have all achieved good results. Even an amateur politician can see this; but when it comes to detail, he is apt to demand a scientific reason for every jot and tittle of the law, and talk of arbitrary technicality whenever lawyers fail to produce a reason obvious to his own understanding.

Now, just because civilised law must aim at consistency, and must be a work of art, there may often be a good reason which only lawyers can appreciate. Few laymen look beyond the first impression of the particular case. Then, as has already been observed, there are the cases in which it is easy to show that some rule is needful, but impossible or very difficult to prove that the rule actually preferred is better than any other. Here again there may be reasons of harmony with other parts of the law and settled rules (though such harmonies are too often neglected in current legislation), which an untrained mind is not capable of apprehending. But there are also many cases in which it really matters very little what the rule is, if only it is certain and not unreasonable. If lawyers would oftener have the courage to say so, the lay people might be the better for it. Sticking at such details obscures the general view. The fact remains that law, on the whole, expresses the common conscience of those who are subject to it. If it did not, it would not be obeyed, at least in a free country. Not that it can exactly keep pace with public opinion; sometimes it lags behind, sometimes it is in advance. When an enlightened minority complains, as often it does with justice, of matters requiring amendment that have too long been left unamended, it will almost invariably be found that the public do not really care. Either prejudice or pure ignorance may account for this.

The false conception of law merely under the form of prohibition is largely due to the exaggerated prominence of criminal law in the public eye. To nine lay folk out of ten the word "court" suggests a police-court first, and to some of them nothing else at any time. Merchants and special jurymen know better, but they are a minority. Now the criminalist point of view is wholly inadequate. "Thou shalt not" is well enough to clear the ground, but "Ita ius esto" must be the builder. The present is in some ways a good time for making people see that law does really build, even if part of the demonstration is painful—I mean the sight of the ruin left by the tread of the Prussian hoof wherever it has passed.

IV

Perhaps the greatest of all the fallacies entertained by lay people about the law is one which, though seldom expressed in terms, an observant lawyer may quite commonly find lurking not far below the surface. This is that the business of a court of justice is to discover the truth. Its real business is to pronounce upon the justice of particular claims, and incidentally to test the truth of the assertions of fact made in support of the claim in law, provided that those assertions are relevant in law to the establishment of the desired conclusion; and this is by no means the same thing. The difference holds good, in our system, even in criminal procedure. John Doe is found dead in suspicious circumstances. It is not for any ordinary court of justice, but for the police, or for a coroner's inquest, which has no power to render any definitive judgement at all, to find out whether John Doe was killed, and to whom suspicion points. On the information of the executive, the state's attorney prosecutes Richard Roe for the murder of John Doe. The Commonwealth is in the position of a plaintiff, and must prove its case as much as any other plaintiff; indeed a little more, the addition to the proof required in a civil court being expressed in the current formula "beyond reasonable doubt." And if the jury is not satisfied that Richard Roe killed John Doe, the court will not, indeed, may not, conjecture in public who then did kill him.

If a contradictor is minded to search for a more plausible appearance of inquisitorial procedure, as we now commonly say, in our courts, he may find it in the quarter most remote from criminal law, namely the administrative operations of a court of equity. Here the court seems to take the superintendence of deceased persons' estates into its own hand in masterful, or at any rate paternal fashion, putting things to rights all round, ascertaining what are the claims of a score or more, it may be, of different persons, and the means of satisfying them, and finally allotting to every claimant his rightful share or so much of it as the estate will satisfy in a due proportion. Certainly this is not much like the plain and single-acting function of justice in an action for goods sold and delivered. But the essential feature of litigation is there. The court is moved to action only by the claim of a definite person or group of persons in the same interest, a claim which cannot be justly satisfied without dealing with other claims also ; nor does the court, even here, profess to assist those who do not assert their rights.[1] However, the English Court of Chancery had a tender conscience in the matter of being quite sure that all proper parties were before it, and therefore directed elaborate inquiries with intentions almost too good for this world. What with meticulous procedure, and (it must be said) Lord Eldon's proneness to hesitation and delay which dominated the court for many

[1] See Langdell's *Brief Survey of Equity Jurisdiction*, Art. vii.

years, a Chancery suit became the synonym of hope deferred without limit, and such legends arose as the lay people read, and probably believe, in *Bleak House*. Contrariwise the catastrophe of that story, as framed by Dickens, makes an enormous demand on lay readers' credulity by ascribing miraculous powers of summary decision to this very court. A missing will is discovered, and the discovery puts an end to the suit with a swiftness that certainly seems to throw us back to patriarchal justice. Every tiro in equity practice knows that the only immediate effect must have been to add one or more parties to the suit. In fairness to Dickens, however, it must be observed that the scene in court is judiciously not described; we are told only so much as was picked up by a quite unlearned young person outside. "Esther's narrative" may be compatible, on strict examination, with *Jarndyce* v. *Jarndyce* having been adjourned and then settled among the parties, a process which would be hastened by the discovery that the estate had vanished in costs. If so, Dickens might plausibly maintain that he did not exceed the usual licence of novelists in compressing minor incidents and omitting details that are necessary in fact, but only tedious in a story.

Our tiro, being flushed with new learning, and not having digested the precept to suffer fools gladly, would probably reject any such compromise and protest that the legal credulity of laymen is even more omnivorous than the historical credulity of Sir Edward Coke, and it is impossible to explain anything to them. But he would be wrong. The unlucky truth is that most lay people, for one bad reason or another, believe all law to be so absurd that no statement whatever about it is too absurd to be credible ; and they know no better because lawyers have taken so little pains to enlighten them. Our art, like all arts and sciences, must have its proper terms, which can be understood only by training and rightly used only with trained experience. But there is no reason why its broad principles and even much of its particular application should not be set forth in language intelligible to all educated men ; and so far as we lawyers fail to do this in a democratic age, we shall have ourselves to thank for any ill consequences.

XII

REFORMATION AND MODERN DOCTRINE OF DIVORCE[1]

English Church Law and Divorce. Part I. Notes on the Reformatio Legum Ecclesiasticarum. By Sir LEWIS DIBDIN. Part II. Notes on the Divorce and Remarriage of Sir John Stawell. By Sir CHARLES E. H. CHADWYCK HEALEY. London: John Murray. 1912.

A History of Divorce. By S. B. KITCHIN. London: Chapman & Hall, Lim. 1912.

Report of the Royal Commission on Divorce and Matrimonial Causes. [Cd. 6478.] London: Stationery Office. 1912.

The Divorce Commission: the Majority and Minority Reports summarised. By the Secretaries to the Commission [H. GORELL BARNES and J. E. G. DE MONTMORENCY], with prefaces by [Lord GUTHRIE and Sir LEWIS DIBDIN]. Westminster: P. S. King & Son.

Minutes of Evidence [of same Commission]. 3 vols. (Cd. 6479–6481.)

Appendices to Minutes of Evidence and Report. (Cd. 6482.)

ANY one who wishes to follow either the history or the contemporary polemics of marriage and divorce without falling into confusion must fix it well in his mind that he is dealing with ambiguous terms and must constantly look out for ambiguities and misunderstandings. A positively valid marriage is one thing;

[1] Review reprinted from *L.Q.R.* xxix. 85 (1913), with one correction.

the reputation of marriage (or as it is sometimes called *de facto* marriage) is another; a promise to marry is another. But all these may be and have been mixed up at different times with bewildering results. Then Latin "divortium," or English or French "divorce," may in different contexts mean, first, a declaration of nullity, in other words that there has not been any marriage, or any valid marriage; or, secondly, a decree of separation which does not dissolve the marriage of the parties or authorise the re-marriage of either (divorce or separation *a mensa et toro*); or, thirdly, a decree which does dissolve the marriage and authorise the parties or at any rate the innocent party to marry again (divorce *a vinculo*). These distinctions are elementary, but need much repetition.

Sir Lewis Dibdin's and Sir Charles Chadwyck Healey's composite volume is a permanent contribution to historical scholarship. Sir Lewis discusses the "Reformatio Legum," a long-incubated project for the establishment of a new English canon law, which seemed more than once on the point of being formally enacted, but never was. Amateurs of renaissance MS. will welcome some beautiful facsimiles. As arising out of this, the opinions and practice of the early Reformation period in the matter of divorce are considered. It seems plain to the modern legal mind that the rejection of obedience to Rome could not *ipso facto* confer on ecclesiastical courts a new substantive jurisdiction which they had never claimed or exercised. But we doubt whether any one would have put it in that way at the time. Certainly many of the reformers appear to have thought, in effect, that the Church (not the State) had an inherent jurisdiction, whether by natural or by divine law, or both, which had been suspended by an usurped and abusive Roman discipline; and, although no case has been found of an ecclesiastical court purporting in terms to grant a divorce *a vinculo*, nor do the canons of 1603–4 recognise any such jurisdiction, many persons acted on the view that the familiar divorce *a mensa et toro* had acquired the same operation.

Ultimately a compromise of a peculiarly English kind was arrived at, which still exists in Ireland, and has been transplanted to Canada. The House of Lords undertook to grant divorces *a vinculo* by a process which took the form of a *privilegium*, an exercise of the whole Parliament's legislative sovereignty, but in substance was judicial; and they met scruples half-way, more or less, by making the process as cumbrous and expensive as possible.

The Stawell case, with which Sir Charles Chadwyck Healey's essay is concerned, is particularly instructive. The learned author has completed the ascertainment of the facts, which were unpublished till 1910. Sir John Stawell's suit for divorce was heard by a special commission of delegates in 1565. The decree was for separation *a mensa et toro* in approximately the common form, but without security against re-marriage. In 1572 Sir John, being minded to marry again, applied to the Bishop of Bath and Wells. A mediæval or modern bishop would have said at once that in the first wife's lifetime such a thing was impossible. Gilbert Berkeley passed on the question to Archbishop Parker as being beyond his competence, but evidently with the desire of a favourable answer. Then the Archbishop actually did issue a marriage licence, a dispensation from banns in the ordinary form, without mention of the first marriage or the divorce, but with a special reservation apparently intended to save all possible grounds of objection to all possible persons, including Stawell's former wife (*quasi diceret* "Take a licence at your own risk"). The marriage took place, and the first wife brought her suit for restitution, which was compromised before hearing. Sir John made a settlement carefully framed to guard against the risk of children of the second marriage being held illegitimate. After his death the first wife claimed and ultimately obtained her dower. These facts make it clear enough that there was a conflict of opinion, so grave a conflict as to make it impossible for any prudent man to think his own opinion quite safe.

Mr. Kitchin's history seems acceptable as a general popular account. It may be open to criticism in places, but the marriage problem in Europe resembles the agrarian problem in Ireland, as once reported to the present writer by a shrewd observer: there is no doubt as to the material facts, but endless divergence as to the inferences. It is certain that the earliest authorities are ambiguous, and conflicting opinions were held in high places down to the thirteenth century. Gratian and Vacarius both proposed to define the essentials of marriage in ways very different from that which prevailed. See Maitland in *L.Q.R.* xiii. 133, preferring Vacarius. It is also certain that in England opinion and practice were largely unsettled for a full century after the rejection of Papal authority, as we have just seen.

Agreeing with great part of the learned author's conclusions, and regarding many of his particular reasons as sound, we feel the more called on to state our dissent from one of his general propositions, namely, that "the burden of proof is on those who say that marriage is not dissoluble by the parties like any other contract." Marriage is not like any other contract. The contract *de praesenti*, when complete, creates a standing relation whose duration and incidents are determined not by the parties but by the law. Were it otherwise, parties marrying under a law which allows divorce could contract that neither of them should sue for a divorce at all, or not until after some fixed lapse of time such as ten years: which Mr. Kitchin would hardly approve. On what terms marriage shall be dissoluble is a question of public policy, and it has been so dealt with by every law in the world—even the Canon Law, however disastrous we think the failure of the canonical system. Neither are promises to marry *de futuro* treated exactly like other promises. In many systems of law they are not actionable. In the Common Law they are allowed, as mutual promises, to be good consideration for one another, and actionable accordingly. Nevertheless the contract has anomalous incidents as to measure of damages and otherwise.

We are sorry to have to observe that many entries in the list of authorities at the end are inaccurate or defective in dates and other particulars. An uninstructed reader would suppose that Lecky lived to publish or at least re-edit his books in the twentieth century. The present writer cannot tell at sight, for want of any date at all, whether the Fockema Andreae who wrote *Annotationes ad Grotium* is the living scholar of that name or some one of an earlier generation. On the other hand, references to Dante give a pleasant scholarly flavour to a book dealing with mediæval matters. Mr. Kitchin cannot suppose, as an unwary reader might think in one place, that passing a few centuries in Purgatory is a severe blot on the character of a Pope, or any one; Dante met many excellent persons there. Only saints, heroes, and martyrs go straight to Paradise, and Dante not only expected a share of Purgatory for himself but had a shrewd guess as to the appropriate circles.

On principle there is much to be said for a combination of wide legal freedom with a moral public opinion strong enough to check frivolous or capricious exercise of lawful discretion. But this cannot be realised except in a homogeneous and rather small community. For a time it was so under the Roman republic, but the moral equilibrium broke down when Rome became cosmopolitan. In modern times, moreover, a decided public opinion is apt to demand the sanction of positive law to its full extent; and it is hard to convince the modern citizen—especially the half-educated man who has dabbled in political theory and seen little of public affairs—that the demand may be unwise. We cannot restore Roman republican conditions, and it does not seem that it would be a hopeful experiment to restore Roman republican law.

Mr. E. S. P. Haynes, a witness before the Royal Commission, has collected in a small volume (*Divorce Problems of To-day:* Cambridge, W. Heffer & Sons) articles of various dates on lines generally resembling Mr. Kitchin's. As they are addressed to the lay public, there is no need to comment on them here; but the collection, though not systematic, is a handy and vigorous exposition of the writer's point of view.

As to the *Report of the Royal Commission*, those of our readers who are interested have already had it in their hands for about two months, and it would not be useful to give any account of its contents here. We may note, however, that in jurisdictions where divorce is allowed at all there is a very strong consensus for allowing desertion as a sufficient cause. England and Canada seem to stand alone in excluding it. The summary of the two reports prepared by the secretaries to the Commission will be of great convenience to the reader who has neither time to read through the full text nor the art of skimming blue-books. Its correctness is certified in general terms by Lord Guthrie, and explicitly as to the minority report by Sir Lewis Dibdin. Lord Guthrie's observations on the extent to which the two reports agree deserve special attention. "The sacredness of the marriage tie, and its normal indissolubility, are maintained in both, while neither proposes to repeal the Act of 1857. On the questions of equality between the sexes, and restraint of publication of offensive details, the two reports are at one. On the right of the poor to equal treatment with the rich there is no difference in principle, although there is divergence of view on certain details. It is only on the question of extension of grounds that there is radical difference of opinion." Accordingly those who would go farther than the majority get no encouragement; and the section of Anglicans who would like to abolish divorce *a vinculo* without restoring the older and wider canonical doctrine of nullity, and thereby to establish a harder rule than has ever existed in any considerable jurisdiction, is even more summarily ruled out.

It is a remarkable fact, though ignored by at least one Catholic controversialist, that the Church of Rome, confiding in the strength of her spiritual discipline over her own flock, acquiesced in the divorce provisions of the German Civil Code, which have been in force since 1900. The same ingenious writer, with exquisite impertinence, lectured the majority of the Commission for talking of things of which they had no practical experience and no sufficient imagination; as if Sir Frederick Treves were a mere laboratory physiologist, Mr. Spender an obscure journalist unversed in public affairs, and Lord Gorell an amateur jurist who had never been inside the Divorce Court. It is now known that Lord Hannen's conclusions from long special experience were like those of the majority report.

XIII

ARABINIANA[1]

Duncan. What bloody man is that ?
Malcolm. This is the serjeant.—*Macbeth*, Act I. sc. 1.

ONLY two published notices of this book have come to the present writer's knowledge. One is in Lady Holland's *Life of Sydney Smith*, as noted by the reporter himself in a copy of the book now in my possession ; this shall be set out in due course. The other is in an old article from the *Pall Mall Gazette* pasted into the same copy. Neither of them can be said to add much to our information. The anonymous article, published in 1867, contains at least one mistake ; for it calls Arabin Common Serjeant, an office he never held : and I do not think the author was a practising lawyer. His judgement was not amiss, however, whether derived only from the book itself or from some private tradition, when he described Serjeant Arabin as " an original, absent, eccentric man, not wanting in mother wit, but very much so in the faculty of expressing himself rationally." This William St. Julien Arabin, Serjeant-at-

[1] *Cornhill Magazine*, Jan. 1911, with some corrections from later information.

Law, one of the Commissioners of the Central Criminal Court, and Judge of the Sheriff's Court in London, administered justice from 1827 till his death in 1841, besides acting as Judge Advocate-General for a short time; and I have found no record of any public dissatisfaction with his performance. Indeed there is but scanty record of any kind. A short and not too careful obituary notice in the *Annual Register* tells us that the Serjeant was the only son of a general, succeeded to extensive estates in Middlesex and Essex, and died at the age of sixty-six at his residence, High Beech, Essex. It leaves the reader to suppose that Arabin was a bachelor, whereas in fact he was married and left issue (see Debrett, *s.v.* Meux). Father and son are alike unknown to the *Dictionary of National Biography*, neither has anything been found in legal periodicals. The seat at High Beech, Essex,[1] and the property in Middlesex, explain an intimate knowledge of the Uxbridge neighbourhood, and brickmakers' manners therein, of which a sample will be given. It may be difficult to laymen who have no experience of reporting to believe that a judge could be efficient who addressed a convicted prisoner in these terms: "I have no doubt of your guilt; you go into a public-house and break bulk, and drink beer; and that's what in law is called embezzlement."

Stronger judges have taken liberty, now and then,

[1] Occupied by the Tennyson family, 1837–1840, see *Tennyson: a Memoir*, i. 150. "The house and park were pleasant enough." Apparently the owners were somewhere near; Tennyson knew and liked Mrs. Arabin, see his letter from High Beech in *Tennyson and his Friends*, p. 27.

to be concise and masterful; there is a legendary summing-up of Baron Martin's in these words: "Gentlemen of the jury—the man stole the boots. Consider your verdict." Baron Martin's law, however, was beyond suspicion; he knew better than to confuse the lay people in court with the highly technical definition of larceny, but if he had given it at all he would have given it correctly.

Reporters and editors are more charitable than the lay people. They know very well that competent, learned, and even wise persons do say many things which would look passing strange if they were printed exactly as they were said and without the context and circumstances; and on the whole we are free to believe that Serjeant Arabin's charges were more likely to let a humorous rogue escape (as indeed the book shows they sometimes did) than to cause London juries to go astray to any serious extent. It would be too much to maintain that Arabin was learned or wise, but it may be a pious or at least a "probable" opinion that he was competent in his own eccentric fashion. If any person be living who could be offended by the present publication, which at this date is not likely, these considerations may suffice to show that there was never real cause of offence in the innocent mirth which *Arabiniana* has added for the last two generations to the professional diversions of the Common Law Bar. The reporter himself did not think it needful to conceal his identity, for he signed the preface—a piece of solemn burlesque too technical to be quoted here—

with his true initials "H. B. C." There is no reason for not giving his name in full except that it is good to reserve a few traditions for the faithful, and that the disclosure would signify very little to the world at large. He was assisted, moreover, by quite half-a-dozen learned friends, to whose communications several of the Serjeant's *dicta*, and some of the best, are due. These are acknowledged in the regular professional form as being *ex relatione* C. P., or as the case may be. No variation in style can be discovered between the sayings preserved by H. B. C. and his several companions, and this is pretty good warrant that the reporting was correct.

Here is a group of judicial remarks on the morals of the home counties. In the original the cases are duly identified by name and date, and one indication is peculiar to this volume of reports. "The student will observe," says the Preface, "that A.P. signifies *Ante Prandium*; and P.P., *Post Prandium.*" From this we may learn that in the reign of King William IV. the Court still sat after dinner (the luncheon interval not having been at that time introduced); but at least one student has diligently perused *Arabiniana* without finding any manner of difference between the ante-prandial and the post-prandial utterances of the Court. Any reader who thinks his research may be more successful is therefore referred to the book at large. If he is a member of Lincoln's Inn, he will find it in that honourable Society's library, rather ignominiously sandwiched in a volume of commonplace pamphlets.

Of bad neighbourhoods, brickmakers, and young women with children in their arms.

THE COURT. I know *High Wycombe*; it is the worst neighbourhood on the face of the earth. The whole country is covered with brickmakers. They come from all parts of the world. I know all about them.

. . . .

Indictment for stealing pigs.

Barry, for prisoner, called *Mary Hall.* On her entering the box, the Court addressed her in these words: "Now, young woman, for you are a young woman, and have a child in your arms, if I catch you tripping, I will put you where the prisoner is. I have given you warning kindly: you had better say you know nothing about it."

The prisoner received a good character from three witnesses.

THE COURT, *in charge.* He was a brickmaker. Now, we all know what a brickmaker's character is; at least, I do. Gentlemen, I know the prosecutor, *Mr. Austin*, well, and there is not a kinder-hearted man in the whole county of *Essex* [*the prosecutor lived at Uxbridge*], and I am quite sure he can have none but a proper feeling in this case.

Not guilty.

[The prisoner, in his brief, stated that his premises were searched, and no living animal was found in his possession except his own person, and suggested that the pigs had strayed for a little recreation.]

. . . .

THE COURT, *in charge.* This is a case from *Uxbridge.* I won't say a word, as can any one doubt the prisoner's guilt?

. . . .

THE COURT, *to constable.* Is Barnet a very honest place ?
Constable. No, my lord.
THE COURT. No. To my certain knowledge there ought to be fifty constables there.

Brickmakers were not Serjeant Arabin's only special aversion. Sincerity calls for the painful admission that although he was the father of a family he was an anti-feminist.

R. *v.* MARY ANN KELLY, May 18, 1833.

Verdict, *Guilty.*

THE COURT, *to prisoner.* You must go out of the country ; you have disgraced even your sex.

. . . .

A female witness did not speak out.

THE COURT, *to witness.* You come here with your heads in false wigs. If you can't speak out, I'll take off your bonnet ; if that won't do, you shall take your cap off ; and if you don't speak out then, I'll take your hair off.

[But on a recent occasion in a County Court a female witness, when the judge complained that he could not see her face, offered to take off her hat, which His Honour disallowed with some indignation.]

. . . .

Indictment for stealing a pail of milk.

Jane Watson examined by the Court.
THE COURT. What is your husband's name ?
Witness. I am not married.
THE COURT. I mean he who is *Ruth Watson.*
Thomas Watson examined by the Court.
THE COURT. Is that your pail ?
Witness. Yes.

THE COURT. Well, although you are married, I suppose you are man enough to swear to a pail of milk.

Nevertheless there are notes of a more chivalrous mood.

THE COURT. One woman is worth twenty men for a witness any day.

. . . .

Witness, a shoemaker, did not speak out, and said he had a cold.

THE COURT. A man with a cold is not fit to try a lady's shoes on.

It would even seem that women, or at any rate tall women, are presumed to be wise.

THE COURT, *to witness*. Woman, how can you be so stupid? You are tall enough to be wise enough.

What was the standard of intelligence applied by Serjeant Arabin to the mere man?—the "external standard" of reasonable competence which Mr. Justice Holmes of the American Supreme Court has shown to be a fundamental conception in our modern law? The report is rather meagre on this point.

Per curiam. No man is fit to be a cheesemonger who cannot guess the length of a street.

The credibility of Irish witnesses was a doubtful question for the learned Serjeant. Like many great men, he had prejudices, but did not fetter himself by rigid consistency.

April 9, 1832. A.P.

An Irish witness admitted that he had told some lies about the case; but insisted that all which he swore was true.

THE COURT, *in charge*. The witness is an Irishman, and

people from that country, very generally, do not speak the truth when they are not on oath; but they may be believed when they are.

July, 1832.

THE COURT, *in charge.* These Irish witnesses are a good-humoured set of people, and don't much mind what they swear.

Phillips, amicus curiae. Why, my lord, your father was an Irishman.

THE COURT. I know; I only mean that they have a very pleasant roundabout way of expressing themselves; they are all eloquent.

Ex relatione C. P.

Probably this Phillips was the same person as the learned friend C. P., for the Law List of 1832 shows a Charles Phillips practising on the Oxford Circuit, which was also H. B. C.'s, and at the London, Middlesex, and Westminster Sessions.

Londoners, it seems, were credited with being men of prompt action. "It don't take a man long to change his breeches in London"; to which H. B. C., after the custom of the early reporters, adds a note of his own: "*Semble e contrà* in the country." Sometimes we get ethical generalities on which the student must exercise his faith, hoping (as my Lord Coke saith) that in some other place, at some other time, the meaning will become clear to him. "Now, what honest man could have any object in turning a horse's head round the corner of a street? I have no opinion on the subject." Once or twice a considerable body of miscellaneous observation is collected.

Of fat pigs, horses, constables, and the justice of the case.

R. *v.* EDWARDS. February 22, 1834. A.P.

THE COURT, *in charge*. I know all about these things; the pigs were fat, if they were worth £4 each. And so a man drove the cart, and another went behind to keep the pigs between him and the cart; and you see, gentlemen, that it is a great happiness in our courts, that we can see the witnesses examined, and know exactly whether they tell the truth or not. And this witness said, "I know the coat, and I am sure of it, for it was blue or black," and he cannot be mistaken. The constable is a shrewd man, as most men in the country are, who know the habits of horses, and he lets the horse go, and he finds his way to a row of houses. It was not necessary that he should go to the very house; he goes to one, which is enough to satisfy the justice of the case, and nothing can be clearer.

The words last quoted lead the memory to another *dictum* which stands alone in its curious verbal infelicity: "If ever there was a case of clearer evidence than this of persons acting together, this case is that case." As a contrast we may take one really pointed remark, "a little out of fashion," but sensible enough.

How many Wives and Children a man may have.

R. *v.* FAULKNER. January 3, 1834. A.P.

Prisoner said he had a wife and four children.

THE COURT. Never mind. You may have twenty wives and twenty children, but you must not abuse the public.

Ex relatione F. P. W.

So did the learned Serjeant vindicate the law's impartiality. Regard for its majesty sometimes led him into excess of zeal.

Of the wishes of all good men.

R. *v.* WALKER. January 1833. P.P.

Indictment for uttering counterfeit coin.

THE COURT, *to jury.* Gentlemen, the lowest punishment is imprisonment for one year.

Ellis, for prosecution. The words of the Act are, "not exceeding one year."

THE COURT. Yes. But every good man would wish—Gentlemen, consider your verdict.

Arabin, we fear, was not free from anti-Semite bias.

Of Apollo.

A Jew had given the prisoner a good character.

THE COURT, *in charge.* Now, gentlemen, you have heard the case; and the Jew says, that the prisoner has borne a good character; and that he, the Jew, never heard anything against him. All I shall say to that is, *Credat Judaeus Apollo.* If he does, I don't, and dare say you won't, gentlemen.

A rather puzzling question arises from the perusal and meditation of *Arabiniana.* Not only H. B. C., but several other learned friends, were watching and collecting Arabin's *dicta.* They must have been talked over and must have circulated among the Bar. In such circumstances one might expect a cycle of oral tradition to grow up, which would be preserved in more than one version, and exhibit the usual features of agreement, amplification, and variance. Now such a cycle has been preserved in our own time among those members of the Western Circuit who had the happiness of being acquainted with Mr. Hicks of Bodmin, a great collector and teller of dialect stories. Incidentally the Hicks tales have shown that exact oral tradition is quite possible even in an age of print and writing. My friend W. F. Collier of

Plymouth wrote down, and in time published, a collection of Hicksian stories as he remembered them; the late Mr. Furneaux of Corpus Christi College, Oxford, who dwelt still nearer to Hicks, used to repeat them from his own memory; and their text of the longest and best-known story, concerning the deliberations of a Cornish jury, was the same almost word for word. There exists, however, another version which goes back to an excellent authority in West Country matters, the late Lord Iddesleigh; this is much shorter. I do not know that it has ever been printed. Nothing of this kind has happened with Arabin's sayings; I never heard of any record or distinct remembrance of them outside the thin but now precious volume of H. B. C.'s making. Again, one would expect that Arabin's notoriety would provide shelter for some of the masterless professional anecdotes which float down from generation to generation, and are retold sometimes without a name, sometimes with a name taken at random. This also, so far as I know, did not happen. It is true that my grandfather, sometime Chief Baron of the Exchequer, attributed to Arabin, as I am assured by good authority, a saying which is still current enough in such words as these: "Prisoner, God has given you good abilities, instead of which you go about the country stealing ducks." On its face the attribution seems plausible; compare the reported *dictum*, "If you are in distress, you must apply to the proper authorities, and not take the law into your own hands and steal." But in fact we have good and clear witness that the true author was the Rev. Mr. Alderson, a cousin of Baron Alderson's who was chairman of Quarter Sessions at Sheffield.[1] It seems then, on the whole, that there was never an independent Arabinian tradition. Perhaps H. B. C.'s report was accepted among his companions as being authentic and sufficient, and leaving them no occasion to tax their memories. If this be not a convincing explanation, I can offer none better.

The fame of *Arabiniana* reached America pretty soon, as witnessed by a note in H. B. C.'s own writing, and initialled by him, which is pasted into the fly-leaves of a copy in my possession:

> *Arabiniana* was reprinted at Philadelphia in 1846. The edition was of twelve copies only, one of which was sent to Lord Macaulay, and given by him to me. The only addition is:
>
> "Mr. Justice Story,
> from Edward Everett."
>
> I am told that these anecdotes, incredible as they seem, are true.
>
> Manuscript note in the English copy in Harvard College Library.

That copy could not be found when I made inquiry some years ago, neither have I met any learned friend in America who has seen the Philadelphia reprint. Here is a little hunt, not without reward if it succeeds, to be taken up by some diligent American bibliographer.

On the same leaf is an extract from a letter of

[1] Sir Francis Doyle, *Reminiscences and Opinions*, London, 1886, p. 243.

Sydney Smith's to Lord Murray: "Tell William Murray, with my kindest regards, to get for you, when he comes to town, a book called *Arabiniana, or Remains of Mr. Serjeant Arabin* [the title is amplified without warrant],—very witty and humorous. It is given away—not sold, but I have in vain endeavoured to get a copy." The reference is to Lady Holland's *Life of Sydney Smith*, vol. ii. p. 506 [should be 505]; the date is December 4, 1843. H. B. C. adds: "I sent him a copy by Barham (Thomas Ingoldsby)." What became of that copy?

The anonymous writer in the *Pall Mall Gazette* (April 27, 1867), whose judgement on Arabin has been already mentioned, drew a parallel between *Arabiniana* and a collection, also privately printed, of sayings delivered by a learned professor of geography at Gotha, named Galletti, about the beginning of the nineteenth century. He found specimens of these in Petermann's *Geographical Miscellany* (*qu.* Mittheilungen?). With great respect, we conceive that the Gallettiana were not strictly in the same line, but rather of the Malaprop genus.

The earth has, like all bodies, parallel circles, which intersect each other. That is mathematical geography.

. . . .

Which is the right and which the left bank of a river can only be determined at its source.

. . . .

If Persia was a three-sided square like America, it would be easy to measure it.

. . . .

The Cimbri and Teutones were in fact descended from each other.

. . . .

Some years ago a giant was here, who was three feet and a half high, leaving out his head. A student: That was not very high. Professor: Yes; but he was also a dwarf.

Merit cannot be denied to these derangements; but the likeness is superficial, and Galletti cannot be set up as a rival to Arabin. As a book of reports, at all events—a book that rigorously fulfils the condition of being warranted throughout by members of the Bar present in Court—*Arabiniana* must remain unique.

The book being privately printed and scarce, I transcribe the title-page in due form:

Arabiniana [motto as given at the head of this article.] For private distribution only. London MDCCCXLIII. Not published.

INDEX

Amari, Emerico, 3, 22
America, former repugnance to courts of equity in, 194
Annuity, life, mediæval equivalent of, 189
Aquinas, St. Thomas, 33, 36, 42, 51
Arabin, Serjeant, his office, 287
 the Tennysons his tenants, 288
 his justice, 289
Arabiniana, reporters of, identifiable, 291
 no other tradition of Serjeant Arabin's sayings, 297
 a singular but formally regular book of reports, 300
Aristotle, natural justice in his school, 33
 his authority in Middle Ages, 39
Austin, John, 158 *n.*

Blackstone, Sir William, on corporations, 160
Boards, departmental, 123
Bracton, rules as to gifts and delivery in, 145

Cabinet, 124, 129
Chancery, Court of, 187, 191
 Puritan dislike of, 194
 not now a court of conscience, 195
 pleadings in, 226, 234
 whether court of record, 229
 its administrative functions, 276
Chattels, gifts of, 141 *sqq.*
 recaption, 148
Cicero, Marcus Tullius, on the nature of law, misunderstood, 260
 on natural law, 39
Coke, Sir Edward, on corporations, 164
Committees, varieties of, 113
 of the King's Council, 117, 121
 the Judicial Committee, 117, 120
 of Parliament, 130
Common Law, moral authority of, in India, 271
Composition, for feuds in early Greek custom, 186
Contract, in early Roman and English law, 8
 the social, 92, 102
Corporations, doctrine of, in the Common Law, 151 *sqq.*

Davies, Sir John, 171
Deed, originally conclusive, 208
Defence, Committee of Imperial, 126
Delivery, constructive, in case of gift, 147
Dibdin, Sir Lewis, on the *Reformatio Legum*, 280
Dickens, Charles, query as to the end of *Jarndyce* v. *Jarndyce* as related by, 277
Divorce, various meanings of, 280
 Elizabethan conflicts of opinion, 281
 Mr. Kitchin's history of, 282
 Mr. Haynes on, 285
 Royal Commission's report, 285

Equity, general notion of, 181
 originally a dispensing power, 182
 St. German on, 192
Ethics, relation of, to law, 265, 269
 professional, 270
Evidence, no degrees of, in archaic law, 204
Eyre, bills in, 187

Fiction theory of corporations, not involved in modern English authorities, 155
nor in Blackstone, 160
Filmer, Sir Robert, 79-84
Fortescue, Sir John, 16, 53
Frauds, the Statute of, 217
Fulbecke, William, 18

Gentili, Alberico, 64
German Civil Code, as to divorce, 286
Gift, of chattels by parol, 141 *sqq.*
at donee's election, 144
where thing in donee's or third person's control, 146
Gratian, the Decretum of, 40

Haynes, E. S. P., on divorce, 285
Healey, Sir Charles Chadwyck, on Sir John Stawell's case, 281
High Wycombe, Serjeant Arabin's knowledge of, 291
Hobbes, Thomas, on natural law, 59, 86
why not criticised by name in Locke on Civil Government, 82
on the Social Contract, 105
Horace, misquoted in unscholarly law books, 264

India, British, application of natural justice in, 74
Indian Appeals, reports of, 248
Inns of Court, government of, 134
International Law, foundations of, 63
Ius gentium, 13, 34
naturale, 35, 37

Jurisprudence, comparative nomenclature, 2
methods, 6
history, 10 *sqq.*
modern position, 25
Jury, history of the grand, 210
the petty, 215
Justice, natural and conventional, 33
natural, in English law, 70
See Nature, law of
Justinian, his Institutes on natural law, 36

Kitchin, S. B., on history of divorce, 282

Latin, necessary for study of English law, 237
Law Merchant, 55, 68
Law Reporting, Council of, 137
Law Reports, the, 241 *sqq.*
not official, 243
constitution of, 245
discretion of reporters, 250
preparation of reports, 254
Laymen, their erroneous assumptions about law, 259
Leibniz, 18
Lindley, Nathaniel, Lord, 152, 159
Locke, John, his theory of the State, 80 *sqq.*

Maine, Sir Henry, 3, 11, 25, 27
Mansfield, William, Lord, 64
Marriage, antiquity of Anglican form, 200
of divorced persons, Reformation controversies as to, 281
not an ordinary contract, 283
Montesquieu, Charles de Secondat, Baron de, 19

Nature, law of, 30 *sqq.*
" secondary " rules in, 51
relation of, to English law, 53 *sqq.*
in British India, 74
Nature, state of, 87

Oath of grand jurors, 212
Ockham, William of, 37, 44, 46

Parliament, committees of, in Civil War period, 131
Penang, under no positive law till 1807, 77
Persons, fictitious and artificial, 153
Philadelphia, *Arabiniana* reprinted at, 298
Philip the Fair, king of France, his enfranchisement of bondmen, 47
Pleading, mediæval and later, 224
Portia, Shakespeare's, not an advocate, 198
Possession, relativity of, 152
in Germanic law, 220
Procedure and substantive law, 235
judicial and inquisitorial, 275
Proof, archaic methods of, in Germanic law, 206

Property, Locke's theory of, 94
 formerly synonymous with right to possess, 143
Purgatory, 284

" Reason " in the Common Law, 57
Record, what is a court of, 229
Records, judicial, their custody, 222
 use of, to check reports, 231
 guides to, 239
Reformatio Legum, Dibdin and Chadwyck Healey on, 280
Reformation, controversies as to natural law produced by, 50
 the like as to divorce, 281
Reporting. See *Law Reports*
Reports, law, relation of, to records, 233
Rousseau, Jean Jacques, 102, 108
Russell of Killowen, Charles, Lord, 64

St. German, Christopher, 16
 on Reason in the Common Law, 57
 on Equity, 192
Saints, popular petitions to, 184
Sale of goods, 218
Shakespeare, William, his law in *The Merchant of Venice*, 196
Smith, Sydney, on *Arabiniana*, 299
Smith, Sir Thomas, 96
Sovereign, commands of, in conflict with natural law, 51
Stowell, Lord, on weight of opinions in the law of nations, 66

Tennyson, Alfred, acquainted with Serjeant Arabin's family, 288
Trespass, why corporation cannot commit, 177
Twelve Tables, 13

Ultra vires, 157
Uxbridge, reputation of, *temp.* Will. IV., 291

Vico, Giambattista, 21
Vinogradoff, Sir Paul, 180, 229

Witchcraft, complaints of, in Chancery, 191

Year Books, cases on corporate capacity in, 175

THE END